# Digital Currency Embedded In Identities of All Society Members

# I

## Guoping Jie

**Digital Currency Embedded In Identities Of All Society Members  I**

**First Edition**

ISBN-10: 0995820325

ISBN-13: 978-0-9958203-2-6 (Guoping Jie)

www.mathaccounting.com

# Acknowledgements

I wish to take this opportunity to sincerely thank OSAP system (Canada) which gave me a chance to study.

# Guoping Jie

Graduated from the Beijing University of Aeronautics and Astronautics, I immediately went to The National University of Defense Technology in Changsha, China. Three years later, I got my master degree and went to Shanghai XinLi Machinery Factory where I design and develop motors as an engineer. In 2005, I immigrated to Canada after having worked for many years. In 2007, I entered the Centennial College in Toronto, Canada to study accounting. During two years, I had had some thoughts about mathematical accounting and its software. I went to the York University in Toronto, Canada in 2009 and graduated with the Honors BAS four years later. After having taken many years to research and develop mathematical accounting model and its MathAccounting software, I opened the Foreverr MathAccounting Software Company Ltd. in February, 2015 (www.mathaccounting.com).

For relaxation, I enjoy reading, driving, and travelling.

# ABSTRACT

The digital currency may have other definition. However, I give the digital currency a new definition in this book. Based on the MathAccounting software, the digital currency is the electric extension of the traditional money. The most advantage of the MathAccounting software is that it can embed an identity ID into every dollar in the process of money circulation regardless of the cash receipts and the cash payments. Because all members of the society in the world will touch money, all identity IDs of society members can be embedded in the money. Embedding an identity ID into the money can be achieved by adding the three-level subaccount to existing multi-subaccount name of the parent account cash. Namely, the multi-subaccount name form of the cash account is the "Identity ID < Cash receipts from xxx or Cash payments for (to) xxx < Financial activities or Investment activities or Operating activities" in the MathAccounting software. I have developed two models of the simple digital currency and the mixed digital currency. The MathAccounting software is the technical support and security of the two models. The Simple digital currency means that there is not any paper money in the process of money circulation. Obviously, it is an ideal society and the MathAccounting software will be a perfect solution of the digital currency. The most advantage of digital currency is that the Tax Bureau can get the cash flows statement of an organization or company by using of data which is provided by other related organizations or companies. In this situation, drawing up false accounts, tax evasion, and money laundering will be impossible to occur. The mixed digital currency means that there is some paper money in the process of money circulation. In this situation, the MathAccounting software is also a good solution and the possibility of drawing up false accounts, tax evasion, and money laundering is very small. Moreover, taking some measures and doing analysis can prevent them to occur.

Keywords: digital currency, MathAccounting software, multi-subaccount name, simple digital currency model, and mixed digital currency model

X

# Contents

# Chapter 1

# Digital Currency Summary

## 1.1 Digital Currency Definition

The digital currency may have other definition. However, I give the digital currency a new definition in this book. Based on the MathAccounting software, the digital currency is the electric extension of the traditional money and has an important character which is that every dollar in circulating process is embedded an identity ID. The identity IDs of all members of a society will be embedded in the circulating money because all members of a society will touch money. The most advantage of digital currency is that the Tax Bureau can get the cash flows statement of an organization or company by using of data which is provided by other related organizations or companies. In this situation, drawing up false accounts, tax evasion, and money laundering will be impossible to occur.

For recording the detail information of all circulating money (data), I design a table, seeing the Figure 1.1-1 on the next page. The table will record cash (received cash and paid cash) by all social members (all organizations and all individuals) through the MathAccounting software. The detail information of a social member (an organization or an individual) in this table is recorded by other different organizations, so the data is fair, reliable, and correct. In other words, an organization can build itself cash flows statement by using of itself data while the administrators of the Tax Bureau can build this organization's cash flows statement by using of other organizations' data recorded in a table. Of course, this table is in a public database dcj100 of the Tax Bureau.

| ID | Amount | Symbol | MultiSubaccount Names | Transaction Date | Recorder |
|---|---|---|---|---|---|
|  |  |  |  |  |  |
|  |  |  |  |  |  |

Figure 1.1-1   Cash received and paid by all social members table

In addition, every organization has four tables to record detail information of cash received and paid by other organizations or by individuals because the cash receipts and cash payments are in different function departments. The Figure 1.1-2 shows two sample tables which records cash received or paid by all organizations respectively. The Figure 1.1-3 shows another two sample tables which records cash received or paid by all individuals respectively.

| Business No. (Receipts) | Amount | Symbol | Transaction Date |
|---|---|---|---|
|  |  |  |  |
|  |  |  |  |

| Business No. (Payments) | Amount | Symbol | Transaction Date |
|---|---|---|---|
|  |  |  |  |
|  |  |  |  |

Figure 1.1-2   Cash Received or Paid by all Organizations Table

| ID (Receipts) | Amount | Symbol | Transaction Date |
|---|---|---|---|
|  |  |  |  |
|  |  |  |  |

| ID (Payments) | Amount | Symbol | Transaction Date |
|---|---|---|---|
|  |  |  |  |
|  |  |  |  |

Figure 1.1-3   Cash Received or Paid by all Individuals Table

Cash can be divided into two classes of cash receipts and cash payments and can be distinguished by the symbols of the "+" and "-". For every social member, the sum of cash receipts and cash payments is his or her balance of cash he or she holds. The cash receipts can be divided into three classes of taxable receipts, no taxable receipts, and deposits. The cash payments can also be divided into three classes of investment, consumption, and deposits. The two deposits of cash can be merged and have same the two-level subaccount and one-level subaccount names (Cash receipts from customers deposits < Operating activities). Therefore, the balance of cash held by a member is different from the balance of asset owned by the same member. For getting the cash or asset detail information of every member, I design a table to explain the meanings of the symbols used in the Figure 1.1-2 and the Figure 1.1-3 on the page 4, seeing the following Figure 1.1-4.

| Cash (**Symbol**) | Symbols | Meanings | Examples |
|---|---|---|---|
| Receipts ( + ) | -t | Taxable income | Salary, Dividend, Investment income, and Sales |
| Receipts ( + ) | -n | No taxable income | Transfer between friends, OSAP, and Other |
| Receipts ( + ) | -d | Deposit | Deposits in business bank |
| Payments ( - ) | -i | Investment | Open company, buy shares, and buy bonds |
| Payments ( - ) | -c | Consumption | Buy machinery or Operating expenses. Reference of MultiSubaccount Names in Figure 1.1-1 |
| Payments ( - ) | -m | Not deductible expenses | Fine fees |
| Payments ( - ) | -d | Deposit | Deposits in business bank |

Figure 1.1-4   Meanings of Symbols Table

The conceptual framework of all society members is consisted of the four ranks. They are the Central Bank, the governments at all levels, the organizations or the companies (including the proprietorships), and the individuals. The Figure 1.1-5 on the next page shows a pyramid pattern of the conceptual framework of society members. From the Figure 1.1-5, the Central Bank is at the top of the pyramid pattern. It is source of the money because it issues money. The Governments at all levels are at the second rank. They receive the planned national budgets from the Central Bank (hypothesis in this book) and their tax rate is zero. The Organizations or the Companies are at the third rank. They produce and sell their products each other. They have different tax rates. Individuals is at the button of the pyramid pattern. The number of the individuals is maximum. Moreover, the environment and the process of money circulation between the individuals and the organizations or the companies (including the proprietorships) are the most complex if there is some paper money in the money circulation.

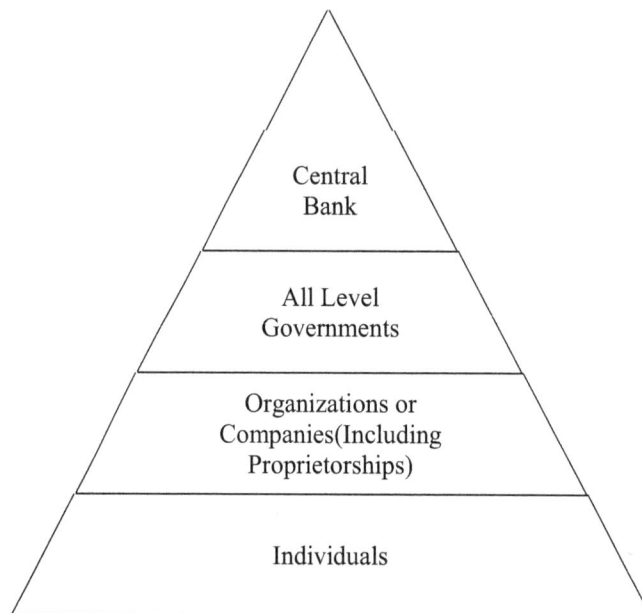

Figure 1.1-5　Conceptual Framework of Pyramid Pattern

I once said that the centered management of accounting is an inexorable trend in the great data time and every business company can login in a government's centered database by using of its business number in the book of the "A Mathematical Accounting Model and its MathAccounting software". Here, the concept of the business companies has been extended, and it includes the Central Bank, the governments at all levels, and the organizations. When a company login in a government's centered database, it has itself database and entering interface. However, when the money embedded in identity ID is recorded in the table in the Figure 1.1-1 on the page 4, this table is a public table for all companies and is recorded in another database. Obviously, this database is different from the companies' databases and the companies cannot show the table by the reports function model or SQL Server's query searching. Of course, every company can show itself data by clicking the "EachSubaccount" box and entering the three-level subaccount of the Cash account. The administrators of the

Tax Bureau manages the table and can show it.

## 1.2 Technical Support and Security of Digital Currency

The most advantage of the MathAccounting software is that it can embed an identity ID into every dollar in the process of money circulation regardless of the cash receipts and the cash payments. Therefore, the MathAccounting software is the strong technical support and security of the digital currency. All members of the society in the world will touch money and the digital currency is the electric extend of the traditional money, so all identity IDs of society members can be embedded in the money.

The identity IDs of all members of a society can be divided to two class of the individuals (social insurance number) and other social members (business number). For computer distinguishing the social insurance number from the business number, I assume that the social insurance number is only consisted of the nature numbers and the business number is consisted of the nature number and a hyphen symbol "-".

Based on the MathAccounting software, to embed an identity into every dollar will be achieved by adding the three-level subaccounts of the "Identity ID-symbol" to the parent account Cash. Its entering form in the "MultiSubaccount Name" box is the "Identity-symbol < Cash receipts from XXXX or Cash payments for (to) XXXX < Financial activities or Investment activities or Operating activities". Please pay attention here. The "Identity ID" is opposite social member's ID in a transaction. There is an exception for the symbol "d" and the "Identity ID" is social member's ID itself in a transaction. In addition, there is not any space between the one-level (two-level or three-level) subaccount name and the symbol "<" during entering any multi-subaccount name into the database in the MathAccounting software. Of cause, the "Identity ID" is the all possible social members' IDs which may include the customers' IDs (suppliers' IDs) and the individuals' IDs mainly. When a company records a cash receipt from a customer, this customer will be recorded a cash payment and the customer's cash will decrease; when a company records a cash payments to suppliers, this supplier will be recorded a cash receipt and the supplier's cash will increase.

Because a social member may occur many different cash transactions in an organization, a suffix of the "-xxxx" must be added into the "Identity ID" to distinguish them. The entering form in the "MultiSubaccount Name" box should be the "Identity ID-symbol-xxxx < Cash receipts from XXXX or Cash payments for (to) XXXX < Financial activities or Investment activities or Operating activities".

You may ask that this will increase workload of the accounting department. However, my answer is the "No" by the experience of designing and developing the MathAccounting software in a few of years, and it even will decrease the workload of the accounting department.

When I enter a new account every time or do creation and initialization of the possible accounts at the beginning of using the MathAccounting software, I increase the workload of entering the three-level subaccount "Identity ID-symbol-xxxx <" of the Cash account into the database. Business number (BN) of an organizations is 9 nature number and social insurance number of the individuals (SIN) is also 9 nature number, so the increasing workload is to enter about 20 characters into database. However, after doing that, I will decrease entering workload in the "MultiSubaccount name" box while entering the Cash account into the database again.

I must emphasize such a fact that the lowest-level subaccount for any parent account is sole again. Then, computer can help me do more work during the process of entering a transaction.

The Figure 1.2-1 on the next page shows possible multi-subaccounts of the Cash parent account in this book. The two-level subaccounts are the lowest-level subaccount of the Cash account, and they are also sole. Please pay attention. If I add a three-level subaccount of the "Identity ID-symbol-xxxx" to the "MultiSubaccount Name" of the Cash account, then the two-level subaccount will not be sole again. Obviously, an employee can repeatedly occur the "Salary expenses" fees.

| Order | Cash receipts | Cash payments |
|---|---|---|
| 1 | Cash receipts from banks < Financial activities | Cash payments for investments < Investing activities |
| 2 | Cash receipts from customers < Operating activities | Cash payments for machinery < Operating activities |
| 3 | Cash receipts from investments < Investing activities | Cash payments for operating expenses < Operating activities |
| 4 | Cash receipts from owners < Financial activities | Cash payments to suppliers < Operating activities |
| 5 | Cash receipts from customers deposits < Operating activities | Cash payments to owners < Financial activities |
| 6 | Cash receipts from issued bonds < Financial activities | Cash payments to note lenders < Operating activities |
| 7 | Cash receipts from note accrued interest (customers) < Operating activities | Cash payments to bond holders < Operating activities |
| 8 | Cash receipts from central bank budgets < Financial activities | - |

Figure 1.2-1   Two-Level Subaccount Names of Cash

For cash receipts, when I enter the "cash r" into the "MultiSubaccount Name" box, the box appears a drop-down menu. Then I can make a choice by clicking the correct item in the drop-down menu. I do not like to do that because doing a choice may takes more time. I continually enter the two-level subaccount into the box until the "cash receipts from b" or the "cash receipts from c" into the box, the drop-down menu has only one item of the "Cash receipts from banks < Financial activities" or the "Cash receipts from customers < Operating activities" and this item is also in the "MultiSubaccount Name" box. I just press the "tab" key to complete the entry of the "MultiSubaccount Name" box. The Figure 1.2-2 on the next page shows the entering process of the "Cash receipts from banks < Financial activities".

Figure 1.2-2   Entering Process of Multi-Subaccount Name

For completing the cash receipts' entry in the "MultiSubaccount Name" box, I must enter 15 characters (including the blank) into this box.

The cash payments is similar as the cash receipts. For completing the cash payments' entry in the "MultiSubaccount Name" box, I must enter 13-17 characters (including the blank) into this box.

If the Cash account has a three-level subaccount, then I normally need to enter 13 characters (9 characters of the Identity ID plus 4 characters of the symbol "-c" and the suffix "-x") into the "MultiSubaccount Name" box to complete the cash receipts' entry or the cash payments' entry in the "MultiSubaccount Name" box. Obviously, it will decreases the entering workload of the accounting department for massive data.

In addition, for the large repeated transactions of the individuals, the MathAccounting software can be designed to automatically get the Identity ID and the symbols and enter them while the individuals (members) use their various smart cards with identity ID.

Just as said before, the digital currency is the electric extend of the traditional money, so the digital currency may be divided to the simple digital currency (ideal condition) and the mixed digital currency.

# Chapter 2

# Simple (Pure) Digital Currency Model

Simple digital currency means that there is not any paper money in the process of money circulation. Obviously, it is an ideal society and the MathAccounting software will be a perfect solution of the digital currency. In this situation, drawing up false accounts, tax evasion, and money laundering will be impossible to occur.

When all members (except of individuals) of a society use the MathAccounting software to record their business transactions, the Tax Bureau will get information of the received cash and the paid cash of every member (including individuals). From the conceptual framework of pyramid pattern (seeing the Figure 1.1-5), all society members are divided to four ranks of social members. Below, I will discuss the detail process of money circulation in the four ranks of social members respectively by using of a sample of a small society.

## 2.1 Sample of a Small Society Model

If there is a small society with the 10 organizations and the 30 persons, its conceptual framework of all society members is showed in the Figure 2.1-1 on the next page.

The Figure 2.1-2 on the next page shows some basic information of the 10 organizations on December 31, 2015. Because the 10 organizations will convert to the MathAccounting software on December 31, 2015, the detail information of the dynamic accounting equation for every organization will be introduced later by constructing 10 reference tables for the 10 organizations respectively. In addition, some multi-subaccounts of the Cash account have not any three-level subaccount, so I do not enter any twin transaction (Cash (1): xxx = Deposits payable (2): xxx) of the Cash account during the conversion.

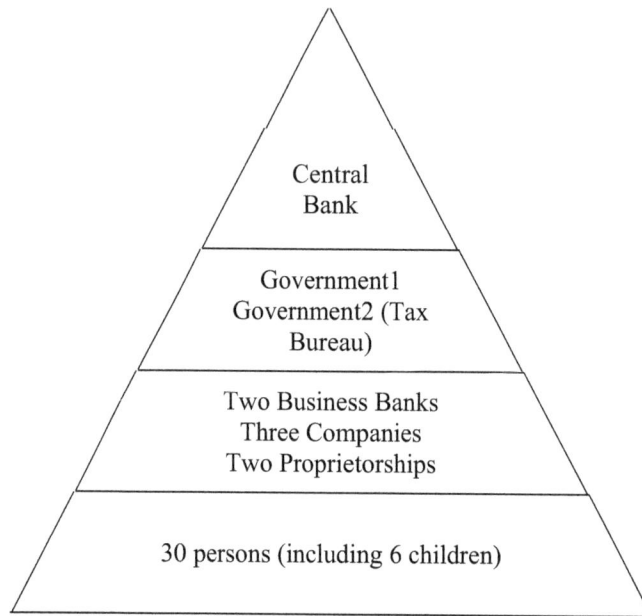

Figure 2.1-1   Pyramid Pattern of Small Society

| Order | Business No. | Name | Phone number | Tax rate | Business Bank1 | Business Bank2 | Balance | Primary Account |
|---|---|---|---|---|---|---|---|---|
| 1 | 88-654300 | Cash Management Center | 123456700 | 0 | 1058058.20 | 0 | 1058058.20 | Business Bank1 |
| 2 | 88-654301 | Central Bank | 123456789 | 0 | 0 | 4090.65 | 4090.65 | Business Bank2 |
| 3 | 88-654302 | Government1 | 123456788 | 0 | 1289.11 | 610.08 | 1899.19 | Business Bank1 |
| 4 | 88-654303 | Tax Bureau | 123456787 | 0 | 1003.72 | 1117.96 | 2121.68 | Business Bank1 |
| 5 | 88-654304 | Business Bank1 | 123456786 | 0.3 | - | 0 | 0 | Business Bank1 |
| 6 | 88-654305 | Business Bank2 | 123456785 | 0.3 | 0 | - | 0 | Business Bank2 |
| 7 | 88-654306 | Company1 | 123456784 | 0.3 | 67873.98 | 0 | 67873.98 | Business Bank1 |
| 8 | 88-654307 | Company2 | 123456783 | 0.3 | 0 | 47393.19 | 47393.19 | Business Bank2 |
| 9 | 88-654308 | Company3 | 123456782 | 0.3 | 3906.47 | 6753.89 | 10660.36 | Business Bank2 |
| 10 | 88-654309 | Proprietorship1 | 123456781 | 0.2 | 18783.78 | 0 | 18783.78 | Business Bank1 |
| 11 | 88-654310 | Proprietorship2 | 123456780 | 0.2 | 0 | 8768.69 | 8768.69 | Business Bank2 |
| **12** | **Total** | - | - | - | **1150915.26** | **68734.46** | **1219649.72** | - |

Figure 2.1-2   Organizations Information Table

The following Figure 2.1-3 shows the detail information of the 30 persons (including five children) on December 31, 2015.

| Order | SIN | Name | Employer Name | Business Bank1 | Business Bank2 | Balance | Primary Account |
|---|---|---|---|---|---|---|---|
| 1 | 909876501 | A1 | Central Bank | 15900.10 | 12000.15 | 27900.25 | Business Bank1 |
| 2 | 909876502 | A2 | Central Bank | 12200.11 | 16500.55 | 28700.66 | Business Bank1 |
| 3 | 909876503 | A3 | Government1 | 11800.23 | 16260.10 | 28060.33 | Business Bank1 |
| 4 | 909876504 | A4 | Government1 | 17230.03 | 11400.61 | 28630.64 | Business Bank1 |
| 5 | 909876505 | A5 | Tax Bureau | 15960.96 | 11970.23 | 27931.19 | Business Bank1 |
| 6 | 909876506 | A6 | Tax Bureau | 17200.52 | 11100.54 | 28301.06 | Business Bank1 |
| 7 | 909876507 | A7 | Business Bank1 | 28500.03 | 0 | 28500.03 | Business Bank1 |
| 8 | 909876508 | A8 | Business Bank1 | 15620.65 | 11000.11 | 26620.76 | Business Bank1 |
| 9 | 909876509 | A9 | Business Bank1 | 27700.11 | 0 | 27700.11 | Business Bank1 |
| 10 | 909876510 | A10 | Business Bank2 | 0 | 28600.21 | 28600.21 | Business Bank2 |
| 11 | 909876511 | A11 | Business Bank2 | 11710.41 | 14520.56 | 26230.97 | Business Bank2 |
| 12 | 909876512 | A12 | Business Bank2 | 15720.23 | 11680.34 | 27400.57 | Business Bank2 |
| 13 | 909876513 | A13 | Company1 | 16510.35 | 11810.18 | 28320.53 | Business Bank1 |
| 14 | 909876514 | A14 | Company1 | 17980.41 | 12200.45 | 30180.86 | Business Bank1 |
| 15 | 909876515 | A15 | Company1 | 26250.27 | 0 | 26250.27 | Business Bank1 |
| 16 | 909876516 | A16 | Company2 | 18790.58 | 11300.74 | 30091.32 | Business Bank1 |
| 17 | 909876517 | A17 | Company2 | 0 | 26150.88 | 26150.88 | Business Bank2 |
| 18 | 909876518 | A18 | Company2 | 18260.63 | 10510.99 | 28771.62 | Business Bank1 |
| 19 | 909876519 | A19 | Company3 | 11230.11 | 16910.92 | 28141.03 | Business Bank2 |
| 20 | 909876520 | A20 | Company3 | 11082.23 | 15900.51 | 26982.74 | Business Bank2 |
| 21 | 909876521 | A21 | Company3 | 0 | 26210.18 | 26210.18 | Business Bank2 |
| 22 | 909876522 | A22 | Proprietorship1 | 16510.03 | 11720.14 | 28230.17 | Business Bank2 |
| 23 | 909876523 | A23 | Proprietorship1 | 11960.84 | 15150.21 | 27111.05 | Business Bank2 |
| 24 | 909876524 | A24 | Proprietorship2 | 28100.25 | 0 | 28100.25 | Business Bank1 |
| 25 | 909876525 | A25 | Proprietorship2 | 11230.32 | 16150.25 | 27380.57 | Business Bank1 |
| 26 | 909876526 | A1A8 | Child of A1 and A8 | 0 | 0 | 0 | A1: Business Bank2 |
| 27 | 909876527 | A1A8 | Child of A1 and A8 | 0 | 0 | 0 | A8: - |
| 28 | 909876528 | A12A20 | Child of A12 and A20 | 0 | 0 | 0 | A12: Business Bank1 |
| 29 | 909876529 | A13A25 | Child of A13 and A25 | 0 | 0 | 0 | A13: - |
| 30 | 909876530 | A16A23 | Child of A16 and A23 | 0 | 0 | 0 | A16: - |
| 31 | Total | | | 377449.40 | 319048.85 | 696498.25 | - |

Figure 2.1-3   Individuals Information Table

The following Figure 2.1-4 shows the cash detail information of the Business Bank1 and the Business Bank2.

| Order | Name | Balance | Self-Cash | Total Deposits | Companies Deposits | Individuals Deposits |
|---|---|---|---|---|---|---|
| 1 | Business Bank1 | 1609115.51 | 80750.85 | 1528364.66 | 1150915.26 | 377449.40 |
| 2 | Business Bank2 | 390884.49 | 3101.18 | 387783.31 | 68734.46 | 319048.85 |
| **3** | **Total** | **2000000.00** | **83852.03** | **1916147.97** | **1219649.72** | **696498.25** |

Figure 2.1-4   Two Business Banks Information Table

The balance of the Cash in the Business Bank1 and the balance of the Cash in the Business Bank2 are $1,609,115.51 and $390,884.49 respectively. Their sum is $2,000,000 which is also the issued money by the Central Bank.

For simplification, there is not the accounts of the Net payroll payable and the Salary tax payable for employee's salary expenses in this sample; there is also not the accounts of the Utility expenses, the Office rent expenses, and so on. In addition, I do not need to know the detail information of every individual's receipt and payment before December 31, 2015. I only need to know the balances of the 25 individuals on December 31, 2015. These balances are the deposits in the Business Bank1 and the Business Bank2. Therefore, if the multi-subaccount names of the Cash account has not any three-level subaccount in a transaction, the amounts of the Cash are related to the individuals.

## 2.2 Top Rank of Social Members

The Central Bank is at the top of pyramid pattern from the Figure 2.1-1 on the page 14. It have two financial statements. One is for an abstract Cash Management Center. It only issues money and manages the planned national budgets because it does not have any equipment and only have interest expenses. Therefore, the abstract Cash Management Center is also given a business number and telephone number which are 88-654300 and 123456700 respectively. Another is the Central Bank itself. Its function is as same as a government. The Central Bank issues money and is the source of all money in the society. Meanwhile, it also recycles the money from the other ranks in the society by issuing bonds or bills. It pays the money to governments at all levels according to the national budgets or national tax revenues (hypothesis). Of course, it also pays the money to itself. For simplification, it mainly has the following types of the transactions:

- The Central Bank issues money.

  It is a transaction of the financial activities. The Central Bank receives cash as the national capital. Then, the Central Bank puts the issued money to the public market. The Balance of the Cash decreases and the Balance of the National capital receivable increases.

  Please pay attention, the Cash account have not any three-level subaccount in the two transactions because I do not know the detail information of the issued money distribution. I only know the result which is how many dollars every social members hold on December 31, 2015. It is enough. Historic deposits interest income, dividend distributions, and tax receipts are as same as issued money.

- The Central Bank recycles the money from the business banks by raising bank reserve requirement ratio.

  It is a financial activities' transaction. The Central Bank receives cash and the Business bank reserves payable account increases.

  Because the Central bank will pay interest to the business banks, there is another transaction which must be recorded. If the interest will be paid at the ending of every fiscal year, the Central Bank records the interest expenses and the balance of the Accrued interest payable account increases during the fiscal year. Of course, at the ending of each fiscal year, the Central Bank pays cash to the business bank and the balance of the account Accrued interest payable decreases.

- The Central Bank issues bonds in the public market.

  It is an investing activities' transaction (for organizations or companies, it should be a financial activities). The Central Bank receives cash and the balance of the Bonds payable account increases. In addition, the Central Bank can lend the cash to the Business banks and get some interest income, which is an operating activities' transaction.

- The Central Bank receives the money from the government of the Tax Bureau as the basis of the planned national budgets.

  It is an operating activities' transaction. The Central Bank receives the cash and the balance of the Tax receipts payable account increases. The money will be deposit to a special account. Here, I presume that this account is opened in the Business Bank1.

  At beginning of each fiscal year, the balance of the Tax receipts payable account will transfer to the planned national budgets account. There are the following two situations.

  If the received money (tax receipts) is less than the amount of the planned national budgets, the Central Bank will issue some money to make them balance. It is a financial activities' transaction. The balances of the Cash account and the National capital account increase.

  If the received money (tax receipts) is greater than the amount of the planned national budgets, the difference between the received money and the amount of the planned national budgets will transfer to the "National capital" account at the beginning of each fiscal year.

- The Central Bank pays the money to governments at all levels (including itself) according to the planned national budgets.
  It is an operating activities' transaction. The Central Bank pays the cash and the balance of the Planned national budgets account decreases.

  Because the Central Bank receives itself budget, there is another transaction which must be recorded. In this transaction, the Central Bank receives the cash from itself, the balance of the Cash account increases and the balance of the Budgets capital account increases. Of course, the money will be deposit to another account in the Business Bank2. The amount of the net income will transfer to the Budgets capital account at the ending of each fiscal year. In other words, the balance of the Retained earnings is always zero.

- The Central Bank can buy some bonds by using of its spare money.
- The Central Bank pays all expenses of its employees and other expenses (including the offices and equipment).

The Central Bank pays the cash and the related accounts increases.

## 2.2.1 Sample of the Cash Management Center

### 2.2.1.1 Conversion of the Cash Management Center

The Cash Management Center (the Central Bank) issued money $2,000,000 a few years ago. Now, the Cash Management Center will convert to the MathAccounting software on January 1, 2016, so I design a converting reference table, seeing the following Figure 2.2-1, in order to enter its dynamic accounting equation on December 31, 2015 into the database dcj021.

| Order | Class | Account Name (**Subtotal Name**) | Balance | Row |
|-------|-------|----------------------------------|---------|-----|
| **1** | **1** | **(Current assets)** | - | **103** |
| 2 | 1 | Cash | 1058058.20 | 104 |
| 3 | 1 | Planned national budgets | 0 | 106 |
| **4** | **2** | **(Current liabilities)** | | **203** |
| 5 | 2 | Business bank reserves payable | 0 | 204 |
| 6 | 2 | Tax receipts payable | 272062.66 | 206 |
| 7 | 2 | Accrued interest payable | 0 | 208 |
| **8** | **2** | **(Long term liabilities)** | - | **251** |
| 9 | 2 | Bonds payable | 60000.00 | 252 |
| **10** | **3** | **(Owners' capital)** | - | **303** |
| 11 | 3 | National capital | 725995.54 | 304 |
| 12 | 3 | Retained earnings | 0 | 306 |
| **13** | **4** | **(Revenues)** | - | **403** |
| 14 | 4 | Sales | 0 | 404 |
| **15** | **5** | **(Cost)** | - | **431** |
| 16 | 5 | Cost of goods sold | 0 | 432 |
| **17** | **5** | **(Operating and administrative expenses)** | - | **453** |
| 18 | 5 | Interest expenses | 0 | 454 |
| 19 | 5 | Bank fee expenses | 0 | 456 |
| **20** | **4** | **(Other income)** | - | **475** |
| 21 | 4 | Investment incomes | - | 476 |

Figure 2.2-1　Cash Management Center Converting Reference Table

The cash of the Cash Management Center is put in the Business Bank1. Because the Business Bank cannot use the cash, it does not pay interest to the Cash Management Center. Instead, the Cash Management Center pays administrative fee (Bank fee expenses) $2,500 to the Business Bank1 at the ending of each year.

From the Figure 2.2-1, there are total 13 accounts among which the balances of the Sales account, the Cost of goods sold account, and the Interest expenses account are zero.

The Cash Management Center cannot buy any bond.

The Planned national budgets account has three one-level subaccounts of the "Central Bank-budgets", the "Government1-budgets", and the "Tax bureau-budgets". Their balances are zero prior to the conversion.

The Cash account has the three-level subaccounts which are the identities' of the opposite side, such as a customer's or supplier's ID.

The issued money was put into the public market, so the balance of the National capital receivable account increases and the balance of the Cash account decreases.

The National capital account has one one-level subaccounts of the "Nation".

The Cash Management Center issued one bond, so the Bonds payable account has one one-level subaccount of the "Bond01-payable" ($60,000, beginning on November 1, 2015, two years, and annual interest rate 4%), seeing the Figure 2.2-2 on this page and the next page, which shows the detail information of the issued bond. Its balance is $60,000. Accordingly, the Bonds payable account has also many two-level subaccounts and its balance is $60,000 too.

| Order | Bond | Amount | Term | Purchaser Name | Identity |
|---|---|---|---|---|---|
| 1 | Bond01 | 5000 | November 1, 2015, two years, 4% annually | A1 | 909876501 |
| 2 | Bond01 | 5000 | November 1, 2015, two years, 4% annually, pay at end of each year | A2 | 909876502 |
| 3 | Bond01 | 5000 | November 1, 2015, two years, 4% annually, pay at end of each year | A3 | 909876503 |
| 4 | Bond01 | 5000 | November 1, 2015, two years, 4% annually, pay at end of each year | A7 | 909876507 |
| 5 | Bond01 | 5000 | November 1, 2015, two years, 4% annually, pay at end of each year | A9 | 909876509 |
| 6 | Bond01 | 5000 | November 1, 2015, two years, 4% annually, pay at end of each year | A10 | 909876510 |
| 7 | Bond01 | 5000 | November 1, 2015, two years, 4% annually, pay at end of each year | A11 | 909876511 |

| 8 | Bond01 | 5000 | November 1, 2015, two years, 4% annually, pay at end of each year | A12 | 909876512 |
| 9 | Bond01 | 5000 | November 1, 2015, two years, 4% annually, pay at end of each year | A15 | 909876515 |
| 10 | Bond01 | 5000 | November 1, 2015, two years, 4% annually, pay at end of each year | A16 | 909876516 |
| 11 | Bond01 | 5000 | November 1, 2015, two years, 4% annually, pay at end of each year | A21 | 909876521 |
| 12 | Bond01 | 5000 | November 1, 2015, two years, 4% annually, pay at end of each year | A22 | 909876522 |
| 13 | **Total** | **60000** | | | |

Figure 2.2-2   Cash Management Center Issued Bond Information Table

The Accrued interest payable account has two one-level subaccounts of the "Bonds-interest payable" and the "Business bank reserves-interest payable". Of course, they may have their two-level subaccounts and the three-level subaccounts. Their balances are zero prior to the conversion. When cash for issued bond interest expenses were paid to the owners of the bond, the Cash account has only two-level subaccounts in the transaction because I must not know the detail information of the interest distribution prior to the conversion. Moreover, the company owners of the issued bond have record the investment income. Its "MultiSubaccount name" form of the Cash account is the "Cash payments to public markets < Operating activities" here. This transaction sub-equation is:

Cash (1): -400 = National capital (3): -400

The sum of the balance of the "Cash receipts from issued money < Financial activities" subaccount, the balance of the "Cash receipts from public markets < Operating activities" subaccount, and the "Cash payments to public markets < Operating activities" subaccount is equal to the balance of the National capital account.

The Business bank reserves payable account has two one-level subaccounts of the "Business bank1-reserves" and the "Business bank2-reserves". The Tax receipts payable account has not any subaccount.

Following above information, I can build a table of the multi-subaccount names, seeing the Figure 2.2-3 on the following pages.

| Order | Class | Multi-subaccount Name | Parent Name | Lowest Subaccount Balance |
|---|---|---|---|---|
| 1 | 1 | Cash receipts from issued money < Financial activities | Cash | 2000000.00 |
| 2 | 1 | 88-654302-i-reserve < Cash receipts from business bank reserves < Financial activities | Cash | 0 |
| 3 | 1 | 88-654303-i-reserve < Cash receipts from business bank reserves < Financial activities | Cash | 0 |
| 4 | 1 | Cash receipts from public markets < Operating activities | Cash | 726395.54 |
| 5 | 1 | 909876501-i-bond01 < Cash receipts from issued bonds < Financial activities | Cash | 5000.00 |
| 6 | 1 | 909876502-i-bond01 < Cash receipts from issued bonds < Financial activities | Cash | 5000.00 |
| 7 | 1 | 909876503-i-bond01 < Cash receipts from issued bonds < Financial activities | Cash | 5000.00 |
| 8 | 1 | 909876507-i-bond01 < Cash receipts from issued bonds < Financial activities | Cash | 5000.00 |
| 9 | 1 | 909876509-i-bond01 < Cash receipts from issued bonds < Financial activities | Cash | 5000.00 |
| 10 | 1 | 909876510-i-bond01 < Cash receipts from issued bonds < Financial activities | Cash | 5000.00 |
| 11 | 1 | 909876511-i-bond01 < Cash receipts from issued bonds < Financial activities | Cash | 5000.00 |
| 12 | 1 | 909876512-i-bond01 < Cash receipts from issued bonds < Financial activities | Cash | 5000.00 |
| 13 | 1 | 909876515-i-bond01 < Cash receipts from issued bonds < Financial activities | Cash | 5000.00 |
| 14 | 1 | 909876516-i-bond01 < Cash receipts from issued bonds < Financial activities | Cash | 5000.00 |
| 15 | 1 | 909876521-i-bond01 < Cash receipts from issued bonds < Financial activities | Cash | 5000.00 |
| 16 | 1 | 909876522-i-bond01 < Cash receipts from issued bonds < Financial activities | Cash | 5000.00 |
| 17 | 1 | 88-654303-c-tax < Cash receipts from public markets-tax < Financial activities | Cash | 34112.53 |
| 18 | 1 | 88-654303-c-tax < Cash receipts from public markets-tax < Financial activities | Cash | 31671.27 |
| 19 | 1 | 88-654303-c-tax < Cash receipts from public markets-tax < Financial activities | Cash | 52674.38 |
| 20 | 1 | 88-654303-c-tax < Cash receipts from public markets-tax < Financial activities | Cash | 71318.63 |
| 21 | 1 | 88-654303-c-tax < Cash receipts from public markets-tax < Financial activities | Cash | 51453.71 |
| 22 | 1 | 88-654303-c-tax < Cash receipts from public markets-tax < Financial activities | Cash | 20752.91 |
| 23 | 1 | 88-654303-c-tax < Cash receipts from public markets-tax < Financial activities | Cash | 10079.23 |
| 24 | 1 | Cash payments to public markets < Operating activities | Cash | -2000000.00 |
| 25 | 1 | Cash payments for operating expenses < Operating activities | Cash | -400.00 |
| 26 | 1 | Planned national budgets-central bank | Planned national budgets | 0 |
| 27 | 1 | Planned national budgets-government1 | Planned national budgets | 0 |
| 28 | 1 | Planned national budgets-tax bureau | Planned national budgets | 0 |
| 29 | 2 | Business bank reserves-bank1 | Business bank reserves payable | 0 |
| 30 | 2 | Business bank reserves-bank2 | Business bank reserves payable | 0 |
| 31 | 2 | n | Tax receipts payable | 272062.66 |
| 32 | 2 | Bond01-interest payable < Bonds-interest payable | Accrued interest payable | 0 |

| 33 | 2 | Business bank1 reserves-interest payable < Business bank reserves-interest payable | Accrued interest payable | 0 |
|----|---|---|---|---|
| 34 | 2 | Business bank2 reserves-interest payable < Business bank reserves-interest payable | Accrued interest payable | 0 |
| 35 | 2 | Bond01-909876501 < Bond01 | Bonds payable | 5000.00 |
| 36 | 2 | Bond01-909876502 < Bond01 | Bonds payable | 5000.00 |
| 37 | 2 | Bond01-909876503 < Bond01 | Bonds payable | 5000.00 |
| 38 | 2 | Bond01-909876507 < Bond01 | Bonds payable | 5000.00 |
| 39 | 2 | Bond01-88-654309 < Bond01 | Bonds payable | 5000.00 |
| 40 | 2 | Bond01-88-654310 < Bond01 | Bonds payable | 5000.00 |
| 41 | 2 | Bond01-909876511 < Bond01 | Bonds payable | 5000.00 |
| 42 | 2 | Bond01-909876512 < Bond01 | Bonds payable | 5000.00 |
| 43 | 2 | Bond01-909876515 < Bond01 | Bonds payable | 5000.00 |
| 44 | 2 | Bond01-909876516 < Bond01 | Bonds payable | 5000.00 |
| 45 | 2 | Bond01-909876521 < Bond01 | Bonds payable | 5000.00 |
| 46 | 2 | Bond01-909876522 < Bond01 | Bonds payable | 5000.00 |
| 47 | 3 | Nation | National capital | 725995.54 |
| 48 | 5 | Bond01- interest expenses < Bonds-interest expenses | Interest expenses | 0 |
| 49 | 5 | Business bank1 reserves-interest expenses < Business bank reserves-interest expenses | Interest expenses | 0 |
| 50 | 5 | Business bank2 reserves-interest expenses < Business bank reserves-interest expenses | Interest expenses | 0 |
| 51 | 5 | Business bank1 | Bank fee expenses | 0 |

Figure 2.2-3   Cash Management Center Converting Multi-Subaccount Names Table

From the Figure 2.2-1 and the Figure 2.2-3, the dynamic accounting equation on December 31, 2015 must be divided to the N transaction sub-equations because of the restriction of the MathAccounting software. Every sub-equation has maximum twelve items. For simplification of not changing the MathAccounting software here, I first enter two initialization sub-equations. All converting transaction sub-equations can be designed and written as the followings.

- The first and second transaction sub-equations are respectively two initialization sub-equations.

   Account receivable (1): 0 = Account payable (2): 0

   0 = Sales (4): 0 – Cost of goods sold (5): 0

- The transaction sub-equation includes the Cash account with the Order 5 to the Order

10 and the Bonds payable account with the Order 35 to the Order 40. The third transaction sub-equation is:

Cash (1): 5000 + Cash (1): 5000 + Cash (1): 5000 + Cash (1): 5000 + Cash (1): 5000 + Cash (1): 5000 = Bonds payable (2): 5000 + Bonds payable (2): 5000 + Bonds payable (2): 5000 + Bonds payable (2): 5000 + Bonds payable (2): 5000 + Bonds payable (2): 5000

- The transaction sub-equation includes the Cash account with the Order 11 to the Order 16 and the Bonds payable account with the Order 41 to the Order 46. The fourth transaction sub-equation is:

Cash (1): 5000 + Cash (1):5000 + Cash (1): 5000 + Cash (1): 5000 + Cash (1): 5000 + Cash (1): 5000 = Bonds payable (2): 5000 + Bonds payable (2): 5000 + Bonds payable (2): 5000 + Bonds payable (2): 5000 + Bonds payable (2): 5000 + Bonds payable (2): 5000

- The transaction sub-equation includes the Cash account with the Order 1, the Order 4, the Order 24, and the Order 25, and the National capital account with the Order 47. The fifth transaction sub-equation is:

Cash (1): 2000000 + Cash (1): 726395.54 + Cash (1): -2000000 + Cash (1): -400 = National capital (3): 725995.54

- The transaction sub-equation includes the Cash account with the Order 17 to the Order 22 and the Tax receipts payable account with the Order 31. The sixth transaction sub-equation is:

Cash (1): 34112.53 + Cash (1): 31671.27 + Cash (1): 52674.38 + Cash (1): 71318.63 + Cash (1): 51453.71 + Cash (1): 20752.91 + Cash (1): 10079.23 = Tax receipts payable (2): 272062.66

After completing this transaction, the dynamic accounting equation of the Cash Management Center on December 31, 2015 has entered into the database dcj021.

## 2.2.1.2 Brief Summary of the Cash Management Center

The following Figure 2.2-4 shows an entering interface of a shareholder profile. The Figure 2.2-5 on the next page shows the detail information of cash received or paid by other social members in the public database dcj100. The balance of the Cash account is -$1,058,058.20. The negative balance means that amounts paid by other social members are greater than amounts received by other social members.

| Shareholder | Class | Percentage | BusinessNumber | PhoneNumber | CompanyClass | Address | PostalCode | City | State | Country |
|---|---|---|---|---|---|---|---|---|---|---|
| entral Bank | 2 | 1 | 88-654300 | 123456700 | 1 | Cash1 | Cash2 | Cash3 | Cash4 | Cash5 |

Figure 2.2-4   Cash Management Center Shareholder Profile Interface

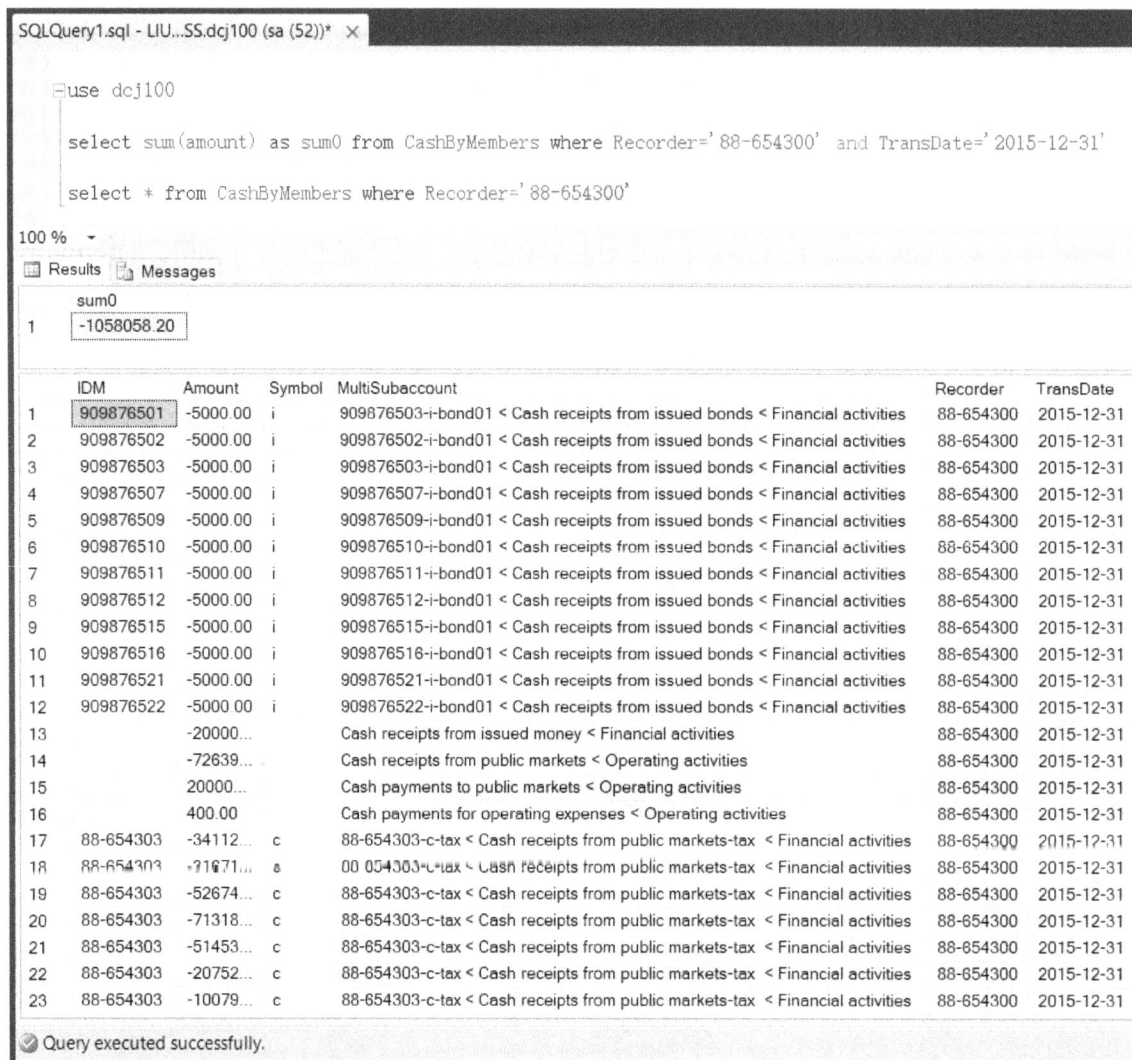

```
SQLQuery1.sql - LIU...SS.dcj100 (sa (52))*  ×

use dcj100

select sum(amount) as sum0 from CashByMembers where Recorder='88-654300' and TransDate='2015-12-31'

select * from CashByMembers where Recorder='88-654300'
```

100 %  ▾

Results  Messages

| | sum0 |
|---|---|
| 1 | -1058058.20 |

| | IDM | Amount | Symbol | MultiSubaccount | Recorder | TransDate |
|---|---|---|---|---|---|---|
| 1 | 909876501 | -5000.00 | i | 909876501-i-bond01 < Cash receipts from issued bonds < Financial activities | 88-654300 | 2015-12-31 |
| 2 | 909876502 | -5000.00 | i | 909876502-i-bond01 < Cash receipts from issued bonds < Financial activities | 88-654300 | 2015-12-31 |
| 3 | 909876503 | -5000.00 | i | 909876503-i-bond01 < Cash receipts from issued bonds < Financial activities | 88-654300 | 2015-12-31 |
| 4 | 909876507 | -5000.00 | i | 909876507-i-bond01 < Cash receipts from issued bonds < Financial activities | 88-654300 | 2015-12-31 |
| 5 | 909876509 | -5000.00 | i | 909876509-i-bond01 < Cash receipts from issued bonds < Financial activities | 88-654300 | 2015-12-31 |
| 6 | 909876510 | -5000.00 | i | 909876510-i-bond01 < Cash receipts from issued bonds < Financial activities | 88-654300 | 2015-12-31 |
| 7 | 909876511 | -5000.00 | i | 909876511-i-bond01 < Cash receipts from issued bonds < Financial activities | 88-654300 | 2015-12-31 |
| 8 | 909876512 | -5000.00 | i | 909876512-i-bond01 < Cash receipts from issued bonds < Financial activities | 88-654300 | 2015-12-31 |
| 9 | 909876515 | -5000.00 | i | 909876515-i-bond01 < Cash receipts from issued bonds < Financial activities | 88-654300 | 2015-12-31 |
| 10 | 909876516 | -5000.00 | i | 909876516-i-bond01 < Cash receipts from issued bonds < Financial activities | 88-654300 | 2015-12-31 |
| 11 | 909876521 | -5000.00 | i | 909876521-i-bond01 < Cash receipts from issued bonds < Financial activities | 88-654300 | 2015-12-31 |
| 12 | 909876522 | -5000.00 | i | 909876522-i-bond01 < Cash receipts from issued bonds < Financial activities | 88-654300 | 2015-12-31 |
| 13 | | -20000... | | Cash receipts from issued money < Financial activities | 88-654300 | 2015-12-31 |
| 14 | | -72639... | | Cash receipts from public markets < Operating activities | 88-654300 | 2015-12-31 |
| 15 | | 20000... | | Cash payments to public markets < Operating activities | 88-654300 | 2015-12-31 |
| 16 | | 400.00 | | Cash payments for operating expenses < Operating activities | 88-654300 | 2015-12-31 |
| 17 | 88-654303 | -34112... | c | 88-654303-c-tax < Cash receipts from public markets-tax < Financial activities | 88-654300 | 2015-12-31 |
| 18 | 88-654303 | -21971... | a | 00 654303-c-tax < Cash receipts from public markets-tax < Financial activities | 88-654300 | 2015-12-31 |
| 19 | 88-654303 | -52674... | c | 88-654303-c-tax < Cash receipts from public markets-tax < Financial activities | 88-654300 | 2015-12-31 |
| 20 | 88-654303 | -71318... | c | 88-654303-c-tax < Cash receipts from public markets-tax < Financial activities | 88-654300 | 2015-12-31 |
| 21 | 88-654303 | -51453... | c | 88-654303-c-tax < Cash receipts from public markets-tax < Financial activities | 88-654300 | 2015-12-31 |
| 22 | 88-654303 | -20752... | c | 88-654303-c-tax < Cash receipts from public markets-tax < Financial activities | 88-654300 | 2015-12-31 |
| 23 | 88-654303 | -10079... | c | 88-654303-c-tax < Cash receipts from public markets-tax < Financial activities | 88-654300 | 2015-12-31 |

Query executed successfully.

Figure 2.2-5    Cash Management Center Cash Received or Paid by Other Members

The Figure 2.2-6 on the next page shows cash flows statement of the Cash Management Center on December 31, 2015. Its balance is $1,058,058.20. Obviously, the balance should be equal to the absolute value of the balance in the Figure 2.2-4. It is true.

Cash Flow Statement

| Cash Flows Statement Year Ended 2015-12-31 | |
|---|---|
| **Operating activities** | |
| Cash payments for operating expenses | -$400.00 |
| Cash payments to public markets | -$2,000,000.00 |
| Cash receipts from public markets | $726,395.54 |
| Net cash provided by Operating activities | -$1,274,004.46 |
| | |
| Financial activities | |
| Cash receipts from issued bonds | $60,000.00 |
| Cash receipts from issued money | $2,000,000.00 |
| Cash receipts from public markets-tax | $272,062.66 |
| Net cash provided by Financial activities | $2,332,062.66 |
| | |
| Other activities | |
| Net cash provided by other activities | $0.00 |
| | |
| Net change in cash | $1,058,058.20 |
| Cash, Begining | $0.00 |
| Cash, Ending | $1,058,058.20 |

Figure 2.2-6   Cash Management Center Cash Flows Statement

The Figure 2.2-7 on the next page shows detail information of the Cash account. Its balance is also $1,058,058.20. The Figure 2.2-8 on the page 29 shows balance sheet of the Cash Management Center on December 31, 2015. Of course, the balance of the cash is $1,058,058.20 too.

Cash

| | ID | Multi-Name | Amount | Balance | General ID | Transaction Date |
|---|---|---|---|---|---|---|
| ▶ | 1 | 909876501-i-bond01 < Cash receipts from issued bonds < Financial activities | $5,000.00 | $5,000.00 | 3 | 2015-12-31 |
| | 2 | 909876502-i-bond01 < Cash receipts from issued bonds < Financial activities | $5,000.00 | $10,000.00 | 3 | 2015-12-31 |
| | 3 | 909876503-i-bond01 < Cash receipts from issued bonds < Financial activities | $5,000.00 | $15,000.00 | 3 | 2015-12-31 |
| | 4 | 909876507-i-bond01 < Cash receipts from issued bonds < Financial activities | $5,000.00 | $20,000.00 | 3 | 2015-12-31 |
| | 5 | 909876509-i-bond01 < Cash receipts from issued bonds < Financial activities | $5,000.00 | $25,000.00 | 3 | 2015-12-31 |
| | 6 | 909876510-i-bond01 < Cash receipts from issued bonds < Financial activities | $5,000.00 | $30,000.00 | 3 | 2015-12-31 |
| | 7 | 909876511-i-bond01 < Cash receipts from issued bonds < Financial activities | $5,000.00 | $35,000.00 | 4 | 2015-12-31 |
| | 8 | 909876512-i-bond01 < Cash receipts from issued bonds < Financial activities | $5,000.00 | $40,000.00 | 4 | 2015-12-31 |
| | 9 | 909876515-i-bond01 < Cash receipts from issued bonds < Financial activities | $5,000.00 | $45,000.00 | 4 | 2015-12-31 |
| | 10 | 909876516-i-bond01 < Cash receipts from issued bonds < Financial activities | $5,000.00 | $50,000.00 | 4 | 2015-12-31 |
| | 11 | 909876521-i-bond01 < Cash receipts from issued bonds < Financial activities | $5,000.00 | $55,000.00 | 4 | 2015-12-31 |
| | 12 | 909876522-i-bond01 < Cash receipts from issued bonds < Financial activities | $5,000.00 | $60,000.00 | 4 | 2015-12-31 |
| | 13 | Cash receipts from issued money < Financial activities | $2,000,000.00 | $2,060,000.00 | 5 | 2015-12-31 |
| | 14 | Cash receipts from public markets < Operating activities | $726,395.54 | $2,786,395.54 | 5 | 2015-12-31 |
| | 15 | Cash payments to public markets < Operating activities | -$2,000,000.00 | $786,395.54 | 5 | 2015-12-31 |
| | 16 | Cash payments for operating expenses < Operating activities | -$400.00 | $785,995.54 | 5 | 2015-12-31 |
| | 17 | 88-654303-c-tax < Cash receipts from public markets-tax < Financial activities | $34,112.53 | $820,108.07 | 6 | 2015-12-31 |
| | 18 | 88-654303-c-tax < Cash receipts from public markets-tax < Financial activities | $31,671.27 | $851,779.34 | 6 | 2015-12-31 |
| | 19 | 88-654303-c-tax < Cash receipts from public markets-tax < Financial activities | $52,674.38 | $904,453.72 | 6 | 2015-12-31 |
| | 20 | 88-654303-c-tax < Cash receipts from public markets-tax < Financial activities | $71,318.63 | $975,772.35 | 6 | 2015-12-31 |
| | 21 | 88-654303-c-tax < Cash receipts from public markets-tax < Financial activities | $51,453.71 | $1,027,226.06 | 6 | 2015-12-31 |
| | 22 | 88-654303-c-tax < Cash receipts from public markets-tax < Financial activities | $20,752.91 | $1,047,978.97 | 6 | 2015-12-31 |
| | 23 | 88-654303-c-tax < Cash receipts from public markets-tax < Financial activities | $10,079.23 | $1,058,058.20 | 6 | 2015-12-31 |

Figure 2.2-7　Cash Management Center Cash Account Table

| | As at 12/31/2015 |
|---|---|
| **ASSETS** | |
| Current assets | |
| Cash | $1,058,058.20 |
| Account receivable | $0.00 |
| | $1,058,058.20 |
| Equipment | |
| Vehicle | $0.00 |
| Accumulated amortization: Vehicle | $0.00 |
| | $0.00 |
| Total Assets | $1,058,058.20 |
| | |
| LIABILITIES | |
| Current liabilities | |
| Tax receipts payable | $272,062.66 |
| Account payable | $0.00 |
| | $272,062.66 |
| Long term liabilities | |
| Bonds payable | $60,000.00 |
| Total Liability | $332,062.66 |
| | |
| | |
| SHAREHOLDERS' EQUITY | |
| Owners capital | |
| National capital | $725,995.54 |
| Retined earnings | $0.00 |
| Accumulated other comprehensive income | $0.00 |
| Total Shareholders' Equity | $725,995.54 |
| | |
| Total Liabilities and Shareholders' Equity | $1,058,058.20 |

Figure 2.2-8    Cash Management Center Balance Sheet

## 2.2.2 Sample of the Central Bank

### 2.2.2.1 Conversion of the Central Bank

The Central Bank (Cash Management Center) issued money $2,000,000 a few years ago. Now, the Central Bank will convert to the MathAccounting software on January 1, 2016, so I design a converting reference table, seeing the Figure 2.2-9 on the next page, in order to enter its dynamic accounting equation on December 31, 2015 into the database dcj022.

| Order | Class | Account Name (**Subtotal Name**) | Balance | Row |
|---|---|---|---|---|
| **1** | **1** | **(Current assets)** | - | **103** |
| 2 | 1 | Cash | 4090.65 | 104 |
| 3 | 1 | Supplies | 171.53 | 106 |
| **4** | **1** | **(Long term investments)** | - | **141** |
| 5 | 1 | Bonds | 0 | 143 |
| **6** | **1** | **(Equipment)** | - | **171** |
| 7 | 1 | Vehicle | 85000.00 | 172 |
| 8 | 1 | Accumulated amortization: vehicle | -42500.00 | 173 |
| 9 | 1 | Computer | 5900.00 | 174 |
| 10 | 1 | Accumulated amortization: computer | -4916.66 | 175 |
| **11** | **2** | **(Current liabilities)** | | **203** |
| 12 | 2 | Account payable | 1600.00 | 204 |
| **13** | **3** | **(Owners' capital)** | - | **303** |
| 14 | 3 | Budgets capital | 46145.52 | 304 |
| 15 | 3 | Retained earnings | 0 | 306 |
| **16** | **4** | **(Revenues)** | - | **403** |
| 17 | 4 | Sales (received budgets) | 0 | 404 |
| **18** | **5** | **(Cost)** | - | **431** |
| 19 | 5 | Cost of goods sold | 0 | 432 |
| **20** | **5** | **(Operating and administrative expenses)** | - | **453** |
| 21 | 5 | Travelling expenses | 0 | 454 |
| 22 | 5 | Other expenses | 0 | 456 |
| 23 | 5 | Office supplies expenses | 0 | 458 |
| 24 | 5 | Salary expenses | 0 | 460 |
| 25 | 5 | Amortization expenses | 0 | 462 |
| 26 | 5 | Interest expenses | 0 | 464 |
| **27** | **4** | **(Other income)** | - | **475** |
| 28 | 4 | Investment incomes | 0 | 476 |
| 29 | 4 | Deposits interest incomes | 0 | 478 |

Figure 2.2-9   Central Bank Converting Reference Table

From the Figure 2.2-9, there are total 20 accounts among which the balances of the Sales account, the Cost of goods sold account, and all expenses accounts are zero.

The Cash account has three-level subaccounts which are the identity IDs' of the opposite side, such as a customer's or a supplier's identity ID.

The Supplies account has not any subaccount. The Budgets Capital account has one

one-level subaccount of the "Central Bank".

The Central Bank once bought two bonds, so the Bonds account has two one-level subaccounts of the "Bond-xx1" and the "Bond-xx2" which may have their two-level subaccounts or three-level subaccounts respectively. Now, its balance is zero. Accordingly, the Investment income account has two-level subaccounts of the "Accrued interest income-bond-xx1 <Bonds" and the "Accrued interest income-bond-xx2 <Bonds". Their balances are zero prior to the conversion.

The Central Bank has one truck1 (five years, straight line, 30 months) and one car1 (five years, straight line, 30 months), so the multi-subaccount names of the Vehicle parent account are the "Truck11 < Truck1 < Truck" and the "Car11 < Car1 < Car" respectively. Their balances are $45,000and $40,000 respectively. Accordingly, the multi-subaccount names of the Accumulated amortization: Vehicle account, which is a contra account of the Vehicle account, are the "Truck11-accumulated amortization < Truck1-accumulated amortization < Truck-accumulated amortization" and the "Car11-accumulated amortization < Car1-accumulated amortization < Car-accumulated amortization". Their balances are -$22,500 and -$20,000 respectively.

The Central Bank has one computer server1 (two years, straight line, 20 months), one computer1" (two years, straight line, 20 months), and one computer2" (two years, straight line, 20 months), so the multi-subaccount names of the Computer parent account are the "Computer server11 < Computer server1 < Computer server", the "Computer11 < Computer1", and the "Computer21 < Computer2" respectively. Their balances are $2,800, $1,600, and $1,500 respectively. Accordingly, the multi-subaccount names of the Accumulated amortization: Computer account, which is a contra account of the Computer account, are the "Computer server11-accumulated amortization < Computer server1-accumulated amortization < Computer server-accumulated amortization", the "Computer11-accumulated amortization < Computer1-accumulated amortization", and the "Computer21-accumulated amortization < Computer2-accumulated amortization". Their balances are respectively -$2,333.33, -$1,333.33, and -$1,250.

The Travelling expenses account has a general two-level subaccount name of the

"Employee ID-travelling < Different department-travelling" and its balance is zero prior to the conversion.

The Other expenses account has also a general two-level subaccount name of the "Employee ID-other < Different department-other" and its balance is zero prior to the conversion.

The Salary expenses account has a general two-level subaccount name of the "Employee ID-salary < Different department-salary" and its balance is zero prior to the conversion.

At the ending of each fiscal year, the amount of the net income will transfer to the "Budgets capital" account for simplification. In other words, the balance of the Retained earnings is always zero.

Following above information, I can build a table of the multi-subaccount names, seeing the Figure 2.2-10 on this page and the next page.

| Order | Class | Multi-subaccount Name | Parent Name | Lowest Subaccount Balance |
|-------|-------|----------------------|-------------|---------------------------|
| 1 | 1 | 88-654301 ¢ budgets ¢ Cash receipts from central bank budgets < Financial activities | Cash | 685000.00 |
| 2 | 1 | 88-654304-c-interest of investment bond-xx1 < Cash receipts from investments < Investing activities | Cash | 0 |
| 3 | 1 | 88-654305-c-interest of investment bond-xx2 < Cash receipts from investments < Investing activities | Cash | 0 |
| 4 | 1 | 88-654306-t-truck2 < Cash payments for machinery < Operating activities | Cash | -45000.00 |
| 5 | 1 | 88-654306-t-car1 < Cash payments for machinery < Operating activities | Cash | -40000.00 |
| 6 | 1 | 88-654306-t-computer server1 < Cash payments for machinery < Operating activities | Cash | -2800.00 |
| 7 | 1 | 88-654306-t-computer1 < Cash payments for machinery < Operating activities | Cash | -1600.00 |
| 8 | 1 | 88-654306-t-computer2 < Cash payments for machinery < Operating activities | Cash | -1500.00 |
| 9 | 1 | Cash payments for operating expenses < Operating activities | Cash | -197854.41 |
| 10 | 1 | Cash payments for operating expenses < Operating activities | Cash | -196722.75 |
| 11 | 1 | Cash payments for operating expenses < Operating activities | Cash | -195432.19 |
| 12 | 1 | 88-654304-n-investment bondxx1 < Cash payments for investments < Investing activities | Cash | 0 |
| 13 | 1 | 88-654305-n-investment bondxx2 < Cash payments for investments < Investing activities | Cash | 0 |
| 14 | 1 | n | Supplies | 171.53 |
| 15 | 1 | Bondxx1 | Bonds | 0 |
| 16 | 1 | Bondxx2 | Bonds | 0 |

| | | | | |
|---|---|---|---|---|
| 17 | 1 | Truck11 < Truck1 < Truck | Vehicle | 45000.00 |
| 18 | 1 | Car11 < Car1 < Car | Vehicle | 40000.00 |
| 19 | 1 | Truck11-accumulated amortization < Truck1-accumulated amortization < Truck-accumulated amortization | Accumulated amortization: Vehicle | -22500.00 |
| 20 | 1 | Car11-accumulated amortization < Car1-accumulated amortization < Car-accumulated amortization | Accumulated amortization: Vehicle | -20000.00 |
| 21 | 1 | Computer server11 < Computer server1 < Computer server | Computer | 2800.00 |
| 22 | 1 | Computer11 < Computer1 | Computer | 1600.00 |
| 23 | 1 | Computer21 < Computer2 | Computer | 1500.00 |
| 24 | 1 | Computer server11-accumulated amortization < Computer server1-accumulated amortization < Computer server-accumulated amortization | Accumulated amortization: Computer | -2333.33 |
| 25 | 1 | Computer11-accumulated amortization < Computer1-accumulated amortization | Accumulated amortization: Computer | -1333.33 |
| 26 | 1 | Computer21-accumulated amortization < Computer2-accumulated amortization | Accumulated amortization: Computer | -1250.00 |
| 27 | 2 | 123456784 | Account payable | 1400.00 |
| 28 | 2 | 123456783 | Account payable | 0 |
| 29 | 2 | 123456782 | Account payable | 200.00 |
| 30 | 2 | 123456781 | Account payable | 0 |
| 31 | 3 | Central Bank | Budgets capital | 46145.52 |
| 32 | 4 | n | Sales (received budgets) | 0 |
| 33 | 5 | n | Supplies expenses | 0 |
| 34 | 5 | 909876501-travelling < Office department-travelling | Travelling expenses | 0 |
| 35 | 5 | 909876501-other < Office department-other | Other expenses | 0 |
| 36 | 5 | 909876502-travelling < Operation department-travelling | Travelling expenses | 0 |
| 37 | 5 | 909876502-other < Operation department-other | Other expenses | 0 |
| 38 | 5 | 909876501-salary < Office department-salary | Salary expenses | 0 |
| 39 | 5 | 909876502-salary < Operation department-salary | Salary expenses | 0 |
| 40 | 5 | Truck11-amortization < Truck1-amortization < Vehicle-truck-amortization | Amortization expenses | 0 |
| 41 | 5 | Car11-amortization < Car1-amortization < Vehicle-Car-amortization | Amortization expenses | 0 |
| 42 | 5 | Computer server11-amortization < Computer server1-amortization < Computer-computer server-amortization | Amortization expenses | 0 |
| 43 | 5 | Computer11-amortization < Computer1-amortization < Computer-amortization | Amortization expenses | 0 |
| 44 | 5 | Computer21-amortization < Computer2-amortization < Computer-amortization | Amortization expenses | 0 |
| 45 | 4 | Accrued interest income-bond-xx1 < Bonds | Investment incomes | 0 |
| 46 | 4 | Accrued interest income-bond-xx2 < Bonds | Investment incomes | 0 |
| 47 | 4 | n | Deposits interest income | 0 |

Figure 2.2-10   Central Bank Converting Multi-Subaccount Names Table

From the above Figure 2.2-9 and the Figure 2.2-10, the dynamic accounting equation on

December 31, 2015 must be divided to the N transaction sub-equations because of the restriction of the MathAccounting software. Every sub-equation has maximum twelve items. All converting transaction sub-equations can be designed and written as the followings.

- I first build a transaction sub-equation for the Account payable accounts. The transaction sub-equation includes the Account payable account with the Order 27 and the Order 29, the part of the Cash account with the Order 1, and initializations of the Account receivable account, the Sales account, and the Cost of goods sold account. The first transaction sub-equation is:

Cash (1): 1600 + Account receivable (1): 0 = Account payable (2): 1400 + Account payable (2): 200 + Sales (4): 0 + Cost of goods sold (5): 0

After entering this transaction, the new balance of the Cash account with the Order 1 is $683,400 (= $685,000 - $1,600).

- The transaction sub-equation includes the Cash account with the Order 4 to the Order 8, the Vehicle account with the Order 17 and the Order 18, and the Computer account with the Order 21 to the Order 23. The second transaction sub-equation is:

Cash (1): -45000 + Cash (1): -40000 + Cash (1): -2800 + Cash (1): -1600 + Cash (1): -1500 + Vehicle (1): 45000 + Vehicle (1): 40000 + Computer (1): 2800 + Computer (1): 1600 + Computer (1): 1500 = 0

- The transaction sub-equation includes the part of the Cash account with the Order 1, the Cash account with the Order 9 to the Order 11, the Supplies account with the Order 14, and the Budgets capital account with the Order 31. The third transaction sub-equation is:

Cash (1): 635983.34+ Cash (1): -197854.41 + Cash (1): -196722.75 + Cash (1): - 195432.19 + Supplies (1): 171.53 = Budgets capital (3): 46145.52

After entering this transaction, the new balance of the Cash account with the Order 1 is $47,416.66 (= $683,400 - $-635,983.34).

- The transaction sub-equation includes the rest ($47,416.66) of the Cash account with the Order 1, the Accumulated amortization: Vehicle account with the Order 19 and the Order 20, and the Accumulated amortization: Computer account with the Order 24 to the Order 26. The fourth transaction sub-equation is:

Cash (1): 47416.66 + Accumulated amortization: Vehicle (1): -22500 + Accumulated amortization: Vehicle (1): -20000 + Accumulated amortization: Computer (1): -2333.33 + Accumulated amortization: Computer (1): -1333.33 + Accumulated amortization: Computer (1): -1250 = 0

After completing this transaction, the dynamic accounting equation of the Central Bank on December 31, 2015 has entered into the database dcj022.

### 2.2.2.2 Brief Summary of the Central Bank

The Figure 2.2-11 on the next page shows an entering interface of a shareholder profile.

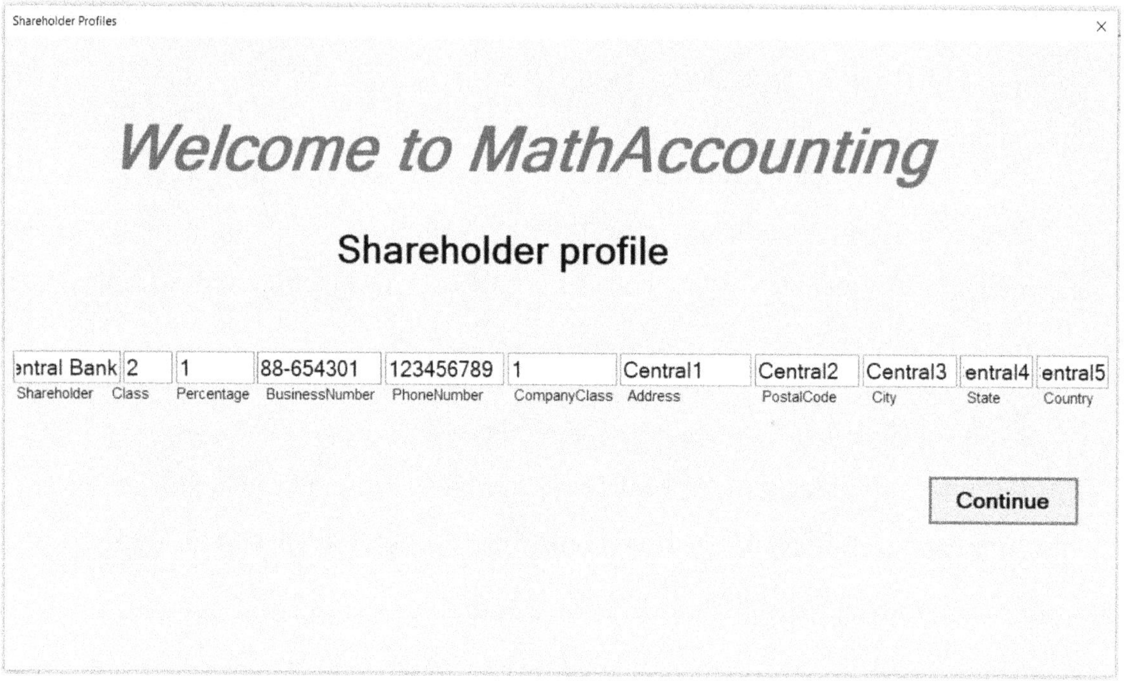
Shareholder Profiles
Welcome to MathAccounting
Shareholder profile
entral Bank
2
1
88-654301
123456789
1
Central1
Central2
Central3
entral4
entral5
Shareholder
Class
Percentage
BusinessNumber
PhoneNumber
CompanyClass
Address
PostalCode
City
State
Country
Continue

Figure 2.2-11 Central Bank Shareholder Profile Interface

The Figure 2.2-12 on the next page shows detail information of cash received or paid by other social members in the public database dcj100. The Figure 2.2-13 on the next page shows cash account table of the Central Bank on December 31, 2015. The Figure 2.2-14 on the page 38 shows balance sheet table of the Central Bank on December 31, 2015.

```
SQLQuery1.sql - LIU...SS.dcj100 (sa (53))*  ×

 use dcj100

 select sum(amount) as sum0 from CashByMembers where Recorder='88-654301'

 select * from CashByMembers where Recorder='88-654301'


100 %   ▼
 Results   Messages
1    -4090.65
```

| | IDM | Amount | Symbol | MultiSubaccount | Recorder | TransDate |
|---|---|---|---|---|---|---|
| 1 | 88-654300 | -1600.00 | c | 88-654300-c-budgets < Cash receipts from central bank budgets < Financial activities | 88-654301 | 2015-12-31 |
| 2 | 88-654306 | 45000.00 | t | 88-654306-t-truck1 < Cash payments for machinery < Operating activities | 88-654301 | 2015-12-31 |
| 3 | 88-654306 | 40000.00 | t | 88-654306-t-car1 < Cash payments for machinery < Operating activities | 88-654301 | 2015-12-31 |
| 4 | 88-654306 | 2800.00 | t | 88-654306-t-computer server1 < Cash payments for machinery < Operating activities | 88-654301 | 2015-12-31 |
| 5 | 88-654306 | 1600.00 | t | 88-654306-t-computer1 < Cash payments for machinery < Operating activities | 88-654301 | 2015-12-31 |
| 6 | 88-654306 | 1500.00 | t | 88-654306-t-computer2 < Cash payments for machinery < Operating activities | 88-654301 | 2015-12-31 |
| 7 | 88-654300 | -639270.84 | c | 88-654300-c-budgets < Cash receipts from central bank budgets < Financial activities | 88-654301 | 2015-12-31 |
| 8 | | 197854.41 | | Cash payments for operating expenses < Operating activities | 88-654301 | 2015-12-31 |
| 9 | | 196722.75 | | Cash payments for operating expenses < Operating activities | 88-654301 | 2015-12-31 |
| 10 | | 195432.19 | | Cash payments for operating expenses < Operating activities | 88-654301 | 2015-12-31 |
| 11 | 88-654300 | 3287.50 | c | 88-654300-c-budgets < Cash receipts from central bank budgets < Financial activities | 88-654301 | 2015-12-31 |
| 12 | 88-654300 | -47416.66 | c | 88-654300-c-budgets < Cash receipts from central bank budgets < Financial activities | 88-654301 | 2015-12-31 |

Figure 2.2-12    Central Bank Cash Received or Paid by Other Members

Cash

| ID | Multi-Name | Amount | Balance | General ID | Transaction Date |
|---|---|---|---|---|---|
| 1 | 88-654300-c-budgets < Cash receipts from central bank budgets < Financial activit... | $1,600.00 | $1,600.00 | 1 | 2015-12-31 |
| 2 | 88-654306-t-truck1 < Cash payments for machinery < Operating activities | -$45,000.00 | -$43,400.00 | 2 | 2015-12-31 |
| 3 | 88-654306-t-car1 < Cash payments for machinery < Operating activities | -$40,000.00 | -$83,400.00 | 2 | 2015-12-31 |
| 4 | 88-654306-t-computer server1 < Cash payments for machinery < Operating activiti... | -$2,800.00 | -$86,200.00 | 2 | 2015-12-31 |
| 5 | 88-654306-t-computer1 < Cash payments for machinery < Operating activities | -$1,600.00 | -$87,800.00 | 2 | 2015-12-31 |
| 6 | 88-654306-t-computer2 < Cash payments for machinery < Operating activities | -$1,500.00 | -$89,300.00 | 2 | 2015-12-31 |
| 7 | 88-654300-c-budgets < Cash receipts from central bank budgets < Financial activit... | $639,270.84 | $549,970.84 | 3 | 2015-12-31 |
| 8 | Cash payments for operating expenses < Operating activities | -$197,854.41 | $352,116.43 | 3 | 2015-12-31 |
| 9 | Cash payments for operating expenses < Operating activities | -$196,722.75 | $155,393.68 | 3 | 2015-12-31 |
| 10 | Cash payments for operating expenses < Operating activities | -$195,432.19 | -$40,038.51 | 3 | 2015-12-31 |
| 11 | 88-654300-c-budgets < Cash receipts from central bank budgets < Financial activit... | -$3,287.50 | -$43,326.01 | 3 | 2015-12-31 |
| 12 | 88-654300-c-budgets < Cash receipts from central bank budgets < Financial activit... | $47,416.66 | $4,090.65 | 4 | 2015-12-31 |

Figure 2.2-13    Central Bank Cash Account Table

| | As at 12/31/2015 |
|---|---|
| **ASSETS** | |
| Current assets | |
| Cash | $4,090.65 |
| Supplies | $171.53 |
| Account receivable | $0.00 |
| | $4,262.18 |
| Equipment | |
| Vehicle | $85,000.00 |
| Accumulated amortization: Vehicle | -$42,500.00 |
| Computer | $5,900.00 |
| Accumulated amortization: Computer | -$4,916.66 |
| | $43,483.34 |
| Total Assets | $47,745.52 |
| | |
| LIABILITIES | |
| Current liabilities | |
| Account payable | $1,600.00 |
| Total Liability | $1,600.00 |
| | |
| SHAREHOLDERS' EQUITY | |
| Owners capital | |
| Budgets capital | $46,145.52 |
| Retined earnings | $0.00 |
| Accumulated other comprehensive income | $0.00 |
| Total Shareholders' Equity | $46,145.52 |
| | |
| Total Liabilities and Shareholders' Equity | $47,745.52 |

Figure 2.2-14   Central Bank Balance Sheet

## 2.3 Second Rank of Social Members

The second rank of the social members is the governments at all levels and includes the Tax Bureau government. Every government pays all expenses of its employees and other expenses (including the office supplies and equipment). For simplification, it mainly has the following types of the transactions:

- Every government receives the cash of the government budget from the Central Bank (hypothesis in this book).

It is a financial activities' transaction. The every government receives the cash and the balance of the Budgets capital account increases.

- Every government pays the cash for all expenses of its employees and other expenses (including the office supplies and equipment).

  It is an operating activities' transaction. Every government pays the cash for all equipment's accounts and all expenses' accounts.

- Every government deposits the money in the business banks and can get some interest incomes.

  It is an operating transaction here. Every government receives the cash and balance of the "Interest incomes" account increases.

- One government (Tax Bureau) receives cash of the tax and will pay the cash to the Central Bank at the ending of each fiscal year.

  There are two operating activities' transactions. One is that the Tax Bureau receives the cash from the companies and the balance of the Tax receipts payable account increases. Another is that the Tax Bureau pays the cash to the Central Bank and the balance of the Tax receipts payable account decreases.

- At the ending of each fiscal year, the amount of the net income will transfer to the Budgets capital account for simplification. In other words, the balance of the Retained earnings is always zero.

There is two governments of the Government1 and the Tax Bureau in the second rank of the social members from the Figure 2.2-1 on the page 14. I will respectively introduce the samples of the two governments below.

## 2.3.1 Sample of the Government1

### 2.3.1.1 Conversion of the Government1

The Government1 will convert to the MathAccounting software on January 1, 2016, so I design the converting reference table, seeing the Figure 2.3-1 on the next page, in order to enter its dynamic accounting equation December 31, 2015 into the database dcj03.

| Order | Class | Account Name (Subtotal Name) | Balance | Row |
|---|---|---|---|---|
| **1** | **1** | **(Current assets)** | - | **103** |
| 2 | 1 | Cash | 1899.19 | 104 |
| 3 | 1 | Supplies | 122.86 | 106 |
| **4** | **1** | **(Long term investments)** | - | **141** |
| 5 | 1 | Bonds | 15000.00 | 143 |
| **6** | **1** | **(Equipment)** | - | **171** |
| 7 | 1 | Vehicle | 80000.00 | 172 |
| 8 | 1 | Accumulated amortization: vehicle | -36000.00 | 173 |
| 9 | 1 | Computer | 5900.00 | 174 |
| 10 | 1 | Accumulated amortization: computer | -1229.16 | 175 |
| **11** | **2** | **(Current liabilities)** | | **203** |
| 12 | 2 | Account payable | 500.00 | 204 |
| **13** | **3** | **(Owners' capital)** | - | **303** |
| 14 | 3 | Budgets capital | 65192.89 | 304 |
| 15 | 3 | Retained earnings | 0 | 306 |
| **16** | **4** | **(Revenues)** | - | **403** |
| 17 | 4 | Sales (received budgets) | 0 | 404 |
| **18** | **5** | **(Cost)** | - | **431** |
| 19 | 5 | Cost of goods sold | 0 | 432 |
| **20** | **5** | **(Operating and administrative expenses)** | - | **453** |
| 21 | 5 | Travelling expenses | 0 | 434 |
| 22 | 5 | Other expenses | 0 | 456 |
| 23 | 5 | Office supplies expenses | 0 | 458 |
| 24 | 5 | Salary expenses | 0 | 460 |
| 25 | 5 | Amortization expenses | 0 | 462 |
| 26 | 5 | Interest expenses | 0 | 464 |
| **27** | **4** | **(Other income)** | - | **475** |
| 28 | 4 | Investment incomes | 0 | 476 |
| 29 | 4 | Deposits interest incomes | 0 | 478 |

Figure 2.3-1   Government1 Converting Reference Table

From the Figure 2.3-1, there are total 20 accounts among which the balances of the Sales account, the Cost of goods sold account, and all expenses accounts are zero.

The Cash account has three-level subaccounts which are the identities of the opposite side, such as a customer's or supplier's identity ID.

The Supplies account has not any subaccount.

The Government1 bought two bonds, so the Bonds account has two one-level subaccounts of the "Bond11" and the "Bond21" which may have their two-level subaccounts or three-level subaccounts respectively. Their balances are $6,000 and $9,000 respectively. Accordingly, the Investment income account has two two-level subaccounts of the "Accrued interest income-bond11 < Bonds" and the "Accrued interest income-bond21 < Bonds". Their balances are zero prior to the conversion. In addition, the Government1 cannot issue any bond.

The Government1 has one truck2 (five years, straight line, 29 months) and one car1 (five years, straight line, 25 months), so the multi-subaccount names of the Vehicle parent account are the "Truck21 < Truck2 < Truck" and the "Car11 < Car1 < Car" respectively. Their balances are $40,000and $40,000 respectively. Accordingly, the multi-subaccount names of the Accumulated amortization: Vehicle account, which is a contra account of the Vehicle account, are the "Truck21-accumulated amortization < Truck2-accumulated amortization < Truck-accumulated amortization" and the "Car11-accumulated amortization < Car1-accumulated amortization < Car-accumulated amortization" respectively. Their balances are -$19,333.33 and -$16,666.67 respectively.

The Government1 has one computer server1 (two years, straight line, 5 months), one computer1" (two years, straight line, 5 months), and one computer2" (two years, straight line, 5 months), so the multi-subaccount names of the Computer parent account are the "Computer server11 < Computer server1 < Computer server", the "Computer11 < Computer1", and the "Computer21 < Computer2" respectively. Their balances are $2,800, $1,600, and $1,500 respectively. Accordingly, the multi-subaccount names of the Accumulated amortization: Computer account, which is a contra account of the Computer account, are the "Computer server11-accumulated amortization < Computer server1-accumulated amortization < Computer server-accumulated amortization", the "Computer11-accumulated amortization < Computer1-accumulated amortization", and the "Computer21-accumulated amortization < Computer2-accumulated amortization". Their balances are respectively -$583.33, -$333.33, and -$312.50.

The Travelling expenses account has a general two-level subaccount name of the

"Employee ID-travelling < Different department-travelling" and its balance is zero prior to the conversion.

The Other expenses account has a general two-level subaccount name of the "Employee ID-other < Different department-other" and its balance is zero prior to the conversion.

The Salary expenses account has a general two-level subaccount name of the "Employee ID-salary < Different department-salary" and its balance is zero prior to the conversion.

Following above information, I can build a table of the multi-subaccount names, seeing the Figure 2.3-2 on this page and the next page.

| Order | Class | Multi-subaccount Name | Parent Name | Lowest Subaccount Balance |
|---|---|---|---|---|
| 1 | 1 | 88-654301-c-budgets < Cash receipts from central bank budgets < Financial activities | Cash | 677000.00 |
| 2 | 1 | 88-654304-c-interest of investment bond11 < Cash receipts from investments < Investing activities | Cash | 460.00 |
| 3 | 1 | 88-654305-c-interest of investment bond21 < Cash receipts from investments < Investing activities | Cash | 615.00 |
| 4 | 1 | 88-654306-t-truck2 < Cash payments for machinery < Operating activities | Cash | -40000.00 |
| 5 | 1 | 88-654306-t-car1 < Cash payments for machinery < Operating activities | Cash | -40000.00 |
| 6 | 1 | 88-654306-t-computer server1 < Cash payments for machinery < Operating activities | Cash | -2800.00 |
| 7 | 1 | 88-654306-t-computer1 < Cash payments for machinery < Operating activities | Cash | -1600.00 |
| 8 | 1 | 88-654306-t-computer2 < Cash payments for machinery < Operating activities | Cash | -1500.00 |
| 9 | 1 | Cash payments for operating expenses < Operating activities | Cash | -194872.37 |
| 10 | 1 | Cash payments for operating expenses < Operating activities | Cash | -190271.95 |
| 11 | 1 | Cash payments for operating expenses < Operating activities | Cash | -190131.49 |
| 12 | 1 | 88-654304-n-investment bond11 < Cash payments for investments < Investing activities | Cash | -6000.00 |
| 13 | 1 | 88-654305-n-investment bond21 < Cash payments for investments < Investing activities | Cash | -9000.00 |
| 14 | 1 | n | Supplies | 122.86 |
| 15 | 1 | Bond11 | Bonds | 6000.00 |
| 16 | 1 | Bond21 | Bonds | 9000.00 |
| 17 | 1 | Truck21 < Truck2 < Truck | Vehicle | 40000.00 |
| 18 | 1 | Car11 < Car1 < Car | Vehicle | 40000.00 |
| 19 | 1 | Truck21-accumulated amortization < Truck2-accumulated amortization < Truck-accumulated amortization | Accumulated amortization: Vehicle | -19333.33 |
| 20 | 1 | Car11-accumulated amortization < Car1-accumulated amortization < Car-accumulated amortization | Accumulated amortization: Vehicle | -16666.67 |

| 21 | 1 | Computer server11 < Computer server1 < Computer server | Computer | 2800.00 |
|---|---|---|---|---|
| 22 | 1 | Computer11 < Computer1 | Computer | 1600.00 |
| 23 | 1 | Computer21 < Computer2 | Computer | 1500.00 |
| 24 | 1 | Computer server11-accumulated amortization < Computer server1-accumulated amortization < Computer server-accumulated amortization | Accumulated amortization: Computer | -583.33 |
| 25 | 1 | Computer11-accumulated amortization < Computer1-accumulated amortization | Accumulated amortization: Computer | -333.33 |
| 26 | 1 | Computer21-accumulated amortization < Computer2-accumulated amortization | Accumulated amortization: Computer | -312.50 |
| 27 | 2 | 123456784 | Account payable | 0 |
| 28 | 2 | 123456783 | Account payable | 500.00 |
| 29 | 2 | 123456782 | Account payable | 0 |
| 30 | 2 | 123456781 | Account payable | 0 |
| 31 | 3 | Government1 | Budgets capital | 65192.89 |
| 32 | 4 | n | Sales (received budgets) | 0 |
| 33 | 5 | n | Supplies expenses | 0 |
| 34 | 5 | 909876503-travelling < Office department-travelling | Travelling expenses | 0 |
| 35 | 5 | 909876503-other < Office department-other | Other expenses | 0 |
| 36 | 5 | 909876504-travelling < Operation department-travelling | Travelling expenses | 0 |
| 37 | 5 | 909876504-other < Operation department-other | Other expenses | 0 |
| 38 | 5 | 909876503-salary < Office department-salary | Salary expenses | 0 |
| 39 | 5 | 909876504-salary < Operation department-salary | Salary expenses | 0 |
| 40 | 5 | Truck21-amortization < Truck2-amortization < Vehicle-truck-amortization | Amortization expenses | 0 |
| 41 | 5 | Car11-amortization < Car1-amortization < Vehicle-Car-amortization | Amortization expenses | 0 |
| 42 | 5 | Computer server11-amortization < Computer server1-amortization < Computer-computer server-amortization | Amortization expenses | 0 |
| 43 | 5 | Computer11-amortization < Computer1-amortization < Computer-amortization | Amortization expenses | 0 |
| 44 | 5 | Computer21-amortization < Computer2-amortization < Computer-amortization | Amortization expenses | 0 |
| 45 | 4 | Accrued interest income-bond11 < Bonds | Investment incomes | 0 |
| 46 | 4 | Accrued interest income-bond21 < Bonds | Investment incomes | 0 |
| 47 | 4 | n | Deposits interest income | 0 |

Figure 2.3-2   Government1 Converting Multi-Subaccount Names Table

From the Figure 2.3-1 and the Figure 2.3-2, the dynamic accounting equation on December 31, 2015 must be divided to the N transaction sub-equations because of the restriction of the MathAccounting software. Every sub-equation has maximum twelve items. All converting transaction sub-equations can be designed and written as the followings.

- I first build a transaction sub-equation for the Account payable accounts. The transaction sub-equation includes the Account payable account with the Order 27 and the Order 28, the part of the Cash account with the Order 1, and initializations of the Account receivable account, the Sales account, and the Cost of goods sold account. The first transaction sub-equation is:

Cash (1): 500 + Account receivable (1): 0 = Account payable (2): 500 + Sales (received budgets) (4): 0 + Cost of goods sold (5): 0

After entering this transaction, the new balance of the Cash account with the Order 1 is $676,500 (= $677,000 - $500).

- The transaction sub-equation includes the Cash account with the Order 4 to the Order 8, the Vehicle account with the Order 17 and the Order 18, and the Computer account with the Order 21 to the Order 23. The second transaction sub-equation is:

Cash (1): -40000 + Cash (1): -40000 + Cash (1): -2800 + Cash (1): -1600 + Cash (1): -1500 + Vehicle (1): 40000 + Vehicle (1): 40000+ Computer (1): 2800 + Computer (1): 1600 + Computer (1): 1500 = 0

- The transaction sub-equation includes the Cash account with the Order 12 and the Order 13, and the Bonds account with the Order 15 and the Order 16. The third transaction sub-equation is:

Cash (1): -6000 + Cash (1): -9000 + Bonds (1): 6000 + Bonds (1): 9000 = 0

- The transaction sub-equation includes the part of the Cash account with the Order 1, the Cash account with the Order 2 and the Order 3, the Cash account with the Order 9 to the Order 11, the Supplies account with the Order 14, and the Budgets capital account with the Order 31. The fourth transaction sub-equation is:

Cash (1): 639270.84 + Cash (1): 460 + Cash (1): 615 + Cash (1): -194872.37 + Cash (1): -190271.95 + Cash (1): -190131.49 + Supplies (1): 122.86 = Budgets capital (3): 65192.89

After entering this transaction, the new balance of the Cash account with the Order 1 is $37,229.16 (= $676,500 - $639,270.84).

- The transaction sub-equation includes the rest ($37,229.16) of the Cash account with the Order 1, the Accumulated amortization: Vehicle account with the Order 19 and the Order 20, and the Accumulated amortization: Computer account with the Order 24 to the Order 26. The fifth transaction sub-equation is:

Cash (1): 37229.16 + Accumulated amortization: Vehicle (1): -19333.33 + Accumulated amortization: Vehicle (1): -16666.67 + Accumulated amortization: Computer (1): -583.33 + Accumulated amortization: Computer (1): -333.33 + Accumulated amortization: Computer (1): -312.5 = 0

After completing this transaction, the dynamic accounting equation of the Government1 on December 31, 2015 has entered into the database dcj03.

## 2.3.1.2 Brief Summary of the Government1

The Figure 2.3-3 on the next page shows cash received or paid by other members table which is in the public database dcj100. The Figure 2.3-4 on the next page shows cash account table of the Government1 on December 31, 2015. The Figure 2.3-5 on the page 47 shows balance sheet table of the Government1 on December 31, 2015.

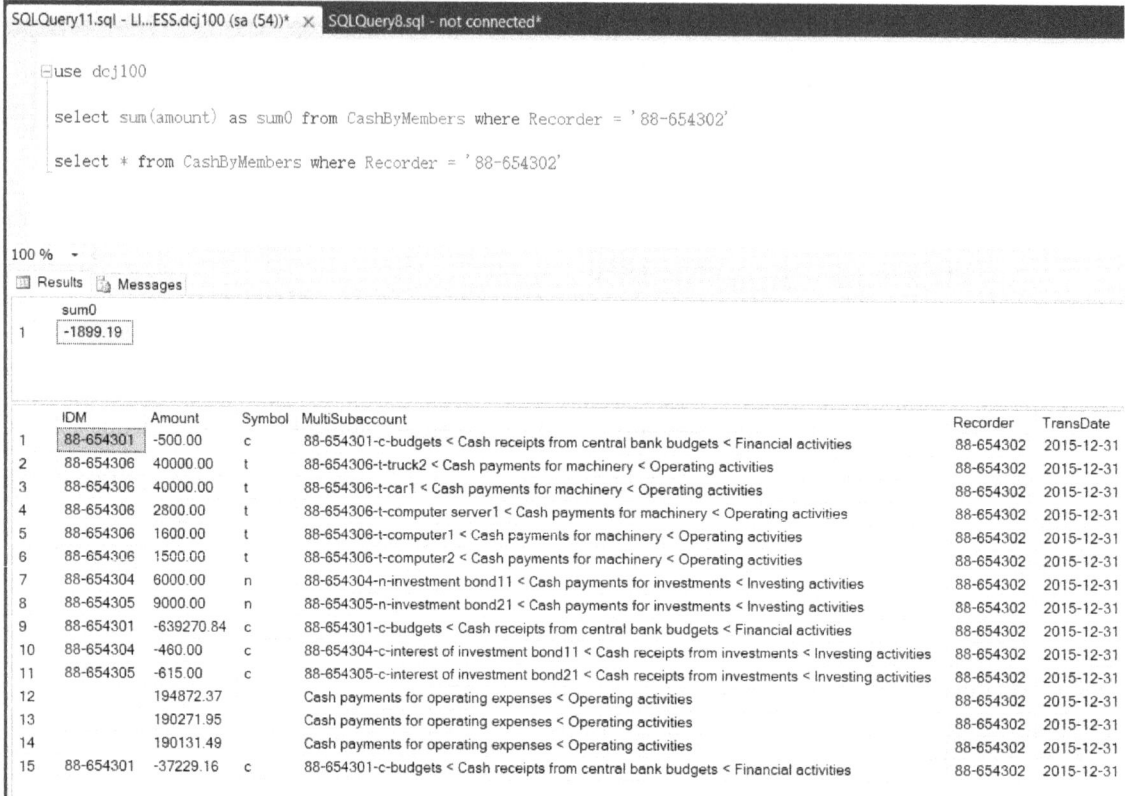

Figure 2.3-3  Governemnt1 Cash Received or Paid by Other Members

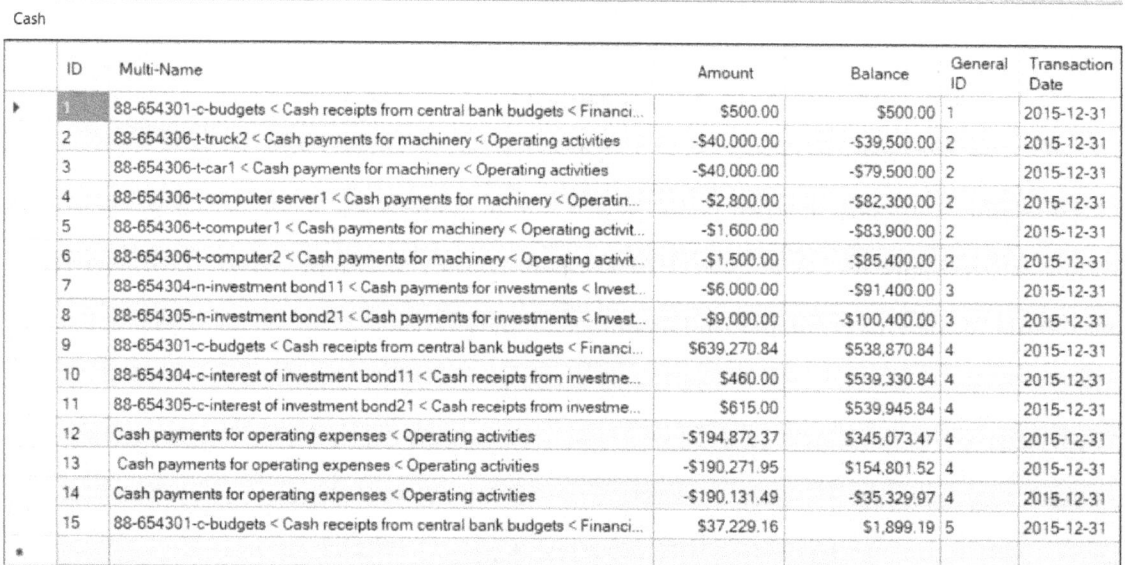

Figure 2.3-4   Government1 Cash Account Table

Balance Sheet

| | As at 12/31/2015 |
|---|---|
| **ASSETS** | |
| Current assets | |
| Cash | $1,899.19 |
| Supplies | $122.86 |
| Account receivable | $0.00 |
| | $2,022.05 |
| Long term investments | |
| Bonds | $15,000.00 |
| Equipment | |
| Vehicle | $80,000.00 |
| Accumulated amortization: Vehicle | -$36,000.00 |
| Computer | $5,900.00 |
| Accumulated amortization: Computer | -$1,229.16 |
| | $48,670.84 |
| Total Assets | $65,692.89 |
| | |
| LIABILITIES | |
| Current liabilities | |
| Account payable | $500.00 |
| Total Liability | $500.00 |
| | |
| | |
| SHAREHOLDERS' EQUITY | |
| Owners capital | |
| Budgets capital | $65,192.89 |
| Retined earnings | $0.00 |
| Accumulated other comprehensive income | $0.00 |
| Total Shareholders' Equity | $65,192.89 |
| | |
| Total Liabilities and Shareholders' Equity | $65,692.89 |

Figure 2.3-5　Government1 Balance Sheet

## 2.3.2 Sample of the Tax Bureau

### 2.3.2.1 Conversion of the Tax Bureau

The Tax Bureau will convert to the MathAccounting software on January 1, 2016, so I design a converting reference table, seeing the Figure 2.3-6 on the next page, in order to enter its dynamic accounting equation December 31, 2015 into the database dcj04.

| Order | Class | Account Name (**Subtotal Name**) | Balance | Row |
|-------|-------|-------------------------------|---------|-----|
| **1** | **1** | **(Current assets)** | - | **103** |
| 2 | 1 | Cash | 2121.68 | 104 |
| 3 | 1 | Supplies | 166.78 | 105 |
| **4** | **1** | **(Long term investments)** | - | **141** |
| 5 | 1 | Bonds | 13000.00 | 143 |
| **6** | **1** | **(Equipment)** | - | **171** |
| 7 | 1 | Vehicle | 118000.00 | 172 |
| 8 | 1 | Accumulated amortization: vehicle | -43666.67 | 173 |
| 9 | 1 | Computer | 5900 | 174 |
| 10 | 1 | Accumulated amortization: computer | -3687.50 | 175 |
| **11** | **2** | **(Current liabilities)** | | **203** |
| 12 | 2 | Account payable | 1200.00 | 204 |
| 13 | 2 | Tax receipts payable | 0 | 206 |
| **14** | **3** | **(Owners' capital)** | - | **303** |
| 15 | 3 | Budgets capital | 90634.29 | 304 |
| 16 | 3 | Retained earnings | 0 | 306 |
| **17** | **4** | **(Revenues)** | - | **403** |
| 18 | 4 | Sales (received budgets) | 0 | 404 |
| **19** | **5** | **(Cost)** | - | **431** |
| 20 | 5 | Cost of goods sold | 0 | 432 |
| **21** | **5** | **(Operating and administrative expenses)** | - | **453** |
| 22 | 5 | Travelling expenses | 0 | 454 |
| 23 | 5 | Other expenses | 0 | 456 |
| 24 | 5 | Office supplies expenses | 0 | 458 |
| 25 | 5 | Salary expenses | 0 | 460 |
| 26 | 5 | Amortization expenses | 0 | 462 |
| 27 | 5 | Interest expenses | 0 | 464 |
| **28** | **4** | **(Other income)** | - | **475** |
| 29 | 4 | Investment incomes | 0 | 476 |
| 30 | 4 | Deposits interest incomes | 0 | 478 |

Figure 2.3-6   Tax Bureau Converting Reference Table

From the Figure 2.3-6, there are total 21 accounts among which the balances of the Sales account, the Cost of goods sold account, and all expenses accounts are zero.

The Cash account has three-level subaccounts which are the identities' of the opposite side, such as a customer's or supplier's identity ID.

The Supplies account has not any subaccount.

The Tax Bureau bought two bonds, so the Bonds account has two one-level subaccounts of the "Bond11" and the "Bond21" which may have their two-level subaccounts or three-level subaccounts respectively. Their balances are $5,000 and $8,000 respectively. Accordingly, the Investment income account has two two-level subaccounts of the "Accrued interest income-bond11 < Bonds" and the "Accrued interest income-bond21 < Bonds". Their balances are zero prior to the conversion. In addition, the Tax Bureau cannot issue any bond.

The Tax Bureau has one truck2 (five years, straight line, 28 months), one car1 (five years, straight line, 28 months) and one car3 (five years, straight line, 10 months), so the multi-subaccount names of the Vehicle parent account are the "Truck21 < Truck2 < Truck", the "Car11 < Car1 < Car", and the "Car31 < Car3 < Car" respectively. Their balances are $40,000, $40,000, and $38,000 respectively. Accordingly, the multi-subaccount names of the Accumulated amortization: Vehicle account, which is a contra account of the Vehicle account, are the "Truck21-accumulated amortization < Truck2-accumulated amortization < Truck-accumulated amortization", the "Car11-accumulated amortization < Car1-accumulated amortization < Car-accumulated amortization", and the "Car31-accumulated amortization < Car3-accumulated amortization < Car-accumulated amortization" respectively. Their balances are -$18,666.67, -$18,666.67, and -$6,333.33 respectively.

The Tax Bureau has one computer server1 (two years, straight line, 15 months), one computer1" (two years, straight line, 15 months), and one computer2" (two years, straight line, 15 months), so the multi-subaccount names of the Computer parent account are the "Computer server11 < Computer server1 < Computer server", the "Computer11 < Computer1", and the "Computer21 < Computer2" respectively. Their balances are $2,800, $1,600, and $1,500 respectively. Accordingly, the multi-subaccount names of the Accumulated amortization: Computer account, which is a contra account of the Computer account, are the "Computer server11-accumulated amortization < Computer server1-accumulated amortization < Computer server-accumulated amortization", the "Computer11-accumulated amortization < Computer1-accumulated amortization", and the "Computer21-accumulated amortization < Computer2-accumulated amortization". Their balances are -

$1,750, -$1,000, and -$937.50 respectively.

The Tax receipts payable account has not any subaccount. The balance was transferred to the Central Bank on December 31, 2015. Namely, the balance of the Tax receipts payable was transferred to the Cash Management Center on December 31, 2015, so its balance is zero prior to the conversion.

The Travelling expenses account has a general two-level subaccount name of the "Employee ID-travelling < Different department-travelling" and its balance is zero prior to the conversion.

The Other expenses account has a general two-level subaccount name of the "Employee ID-other < Different department-other" and its balance is zero prior to the conversion.

The Salary expenses account has a general two-level subaccount name of the "Employee ID-salary < Different department-salary" and its balance is zero prior to the conversion.

Following above information, I can build a table of the multi-subaccount names, seeing the Figure 2.3-7 on this page and the next pages.

| Order | Class | Multi-subaccount Name | Parent Name | Lowest Subaccount Balance |
|---|---|---|---|---|
| 1 | 1 | 88-654301-c-budgets < Cash receipts from central bank < Financial activities | Cash | 718000.00 |
| 2 | 1 | 88-654304-c-tax < Cash receipts from taxation < Financial activities | Cash | 34112.53 |
| 3 | 1 | 88-654305-c-tax < Cash receipts from taxation < Financial activities | Cash | 31671.27 |
| 4 | 1 | 88-654306-c-tax < Cash receipts from taxation < Financial activities | Cash | 52674.38 |
| 5 | 1 | 88-654307-c-tax < Cash receipts from taxation < Financial activities | Cash | 71318.63 |
| 6 | 1 | 88-654308-c-tax < Cash receipts from taxation < Financial activities | Cash | 51453.71 |
| 7 | 1 | 88-654309-c-tax < Cash receipts from taxation < Financial activities | Cash | 20752.91 |
| 8 | 1 | 88-654310-c-tax < Cash receipts from taxation < Financial activities | Cash | 10079.23 |
| 9 | 1 | 88-654304-c-interest of investment bond11 < Cash receipts from investments < Investing activities | Cash | 383.33 |
| 10 | 1 | 88-654305-c-interest of investment bond21 < Cash receipts from investments < Investing activities | Cash | 546.67 |
| 11 | 1 | 88-654306-t-truck2 < Cash payments for machinery < Operating activities | Cash | -40000.00 |
| 12 | 1 | 88-654306-t-car1 < Cash payments for machinery < Operating activities | Cash | -40000.00 |
| 13 | 1 | 88-654306-t-car3 < Cash payments for machinery < Operating activities | Cash | -38000.00 |

| | | | | |
|---|---|---|---|---|
| 14 | 1 | 88-654306-t-computer server1 < Cash payments for machinery < Operating activities | Cash | -2800.00 |
| 15 | 1 | 88-654306-t-computer1 < Cash payments for machinery < Operating activities | Cash | -1600.00 |
| 16 | 1 | 88-654306-t-computer2 < Cash payments for machinery < Operating activities | Cash | -1500.00 |
| 17 | 1 | Cash payments for operating expenses < Operating activities | Cash | -195412.62 |
| 18 | 1 | Cash payments for operating expenses < Operating activities | Cash | -193578.19 |
| 19 | 1 | Cash payments for operating expenses < Operating activities | Cash | -190917.51 |
| 20 | 1 | 88-654304-n-investment bond11 < Cash payments for investments < Investing activities | Cash | -5000.00 |
| 21 | 1 | 88-654305-n-investment bond21 < Cash payments for investments < Investing activities | Cash | -8000.00 |
| 22 | 1 | 88-654301-n-tax < Cash payments to central bank < Financial activities | Cash | -272062.66 |
| 23 | 1 | n | Supplies | 166.78 |
| 24 | 1 | Bond11 | Bonds | 5000.00 |
| 25 | 1 | Bond21 | Bonds | 8000.00 |
| 26 | 1 | Truck21 < Truck2 < Truck | Vehicle | 40000.00 |
| 27 | 1 | Car11 < Car1 < Car | Vehicle | 40000.00 |
| 28 | 1 | Car31 < Car3 < Car | Vehicle | 38000.00 |
| 29 | 1 | Truck21-accumulated amortization < Truck2-accumulated amortization < Truck-accumulated amortization | Accumulated amortization: Vehicle | -18666.67 |
| 30 | 1 | Car11-accumulated amortization < Car1-accumulated amortization < Car-accumulated amortization | Accumulated amortization: Vehicle | -18666.67 |
| 31 | 1 | Car31-accumulated amortization < Car3-accumulated amortization < Car-accumulated amortization | Accumulated amortization: Vehicle | -6333.33 |
| 32 | 1 | Computer server11 < Computer server1 < Computer server | Computer | 2800.00 |
| 33 | 1 | Computer11 < Computer1 | Computer | 1600.00 |
| 34 | 1 | Computer21 < Computer2 | Computer | 1500.00 |
| 35 | 1 | Computer server11-accumulated amortization < Computer server1-accumulated amortization < Computer server-accumulated amortization | Accumulated amortization: Computer | -1750.00 |
| 36 | 1 | Computer11-accumulated amortization < Computer1-accumulated amortization | Accumulated amortization: Computer | -1000.00 |
| 37 | 1 | Computer21-accumulated amortization < Computer2-accumulated amortization | Accumulated amortization: Computer | -937.50 |
| 38 | 2 | 123456784 | Account payable | 500.00 |
| 39 | 2 | 123456783 | Account payable | 400.00 |
| 40 | 2 | 123456782 | Account payable | 300.00 |
| 41 | 2 | 123456781 | Account payable | 0 |
| 42 | 3 | Tax Bureau | Budgets capital | 90634.29 |
| 43 | 4 | n | Sales (received budgets) | 0 |
| 44 | 5 | n | Supplies expenses | 0 |
| 45 | 5 | 909876505-travelling < Office department-travelling | Travelling expenses | 0 |
| 46 | 5 | 909876505-other < Office department-other | Other expenses | 0 |
| 47 | 5 | 909876506-travelling < Operation department-travelling | Travelling expenses | 0 |
| 48 | 5 | 909876506-other < Operation department-other | Other expenses | 0 |
| 49 | 5 | 909876505-salary < Office department-salary | Salary expenses | 0 |

| 50 | 5 | 909876506-salary < Operation department-salary | Salary expenses | 0 |
|---|---|---|---|---|
| 51 | 5 | Truck21-amortization < Truck2-amortization < Vehicle-truck-amortization | Amortization expenses | 0 |
| 52 | 5 | Car11-amortization < Car1-amortization < Vehicle-Car-amortization | Amortization expenses | 0 |
| 53 | 5 | Car31-amortization < Car3-amortization < Vehicle-Car-amortization | Amortization expenses | 0 |
| 54 | 5 | Computer server11-amortization < Computer server1-amortization < Computer-computer server-amortization | Amortization expenses | 0 |
| 55 | 5 | Computer11-amortization < Computer1-amortization < Computer-computer-amortization | Amortization expenses | 0 |
| 56 | 5 | Computer21-amortization < Computer2-amortization < Computer-computer-amortization | Amortization expenses | 0 |
| 57 | 4 | Accrued interest income-bond11 < Bonds | Investment incomes | 0 |
| 58 | 4 | Accrued interest income-bond21 < Bonds | Investment incomes | 0 |
| 59 | 4 | n | Deposits interest income | 0 |

Figure 2.3-7   Tax Bureau Converting Multi-Subaccount Names Table

From the Figure 2.3-6 and the Figure 2.3-7, the dynamic accounting equation on December 31, 2015 must be divided to the N transaction sub-equations because of the restriction of the MathAccounting software. Every sub-equation has maximum twelve items. All converting transaction sub-equations can be designed and written as following.

- I first build a transaction sub-equation for the Account payable accounts. The transaction sub-equation includes the Account payable account with the Order 38 to the Order 40, and the part of the Cash account with the Order 1, and initializations of the Account receivable account, the Sales account, and the Cost of goods sold account. The first transaction sub-equation is:

  Cash (1): 1200 + Account receivable (1): 0 = Account payable (2): 500 + Account payable (2): 400 + Account payable (2): 300 + Sales (received budgets) (4): 0 + Cost of goods sold (5): 0

  After entering this transaction, the new balance of the Cash account with the Order 1 is $716,800 (= $718,000 - $1,200).

- The transaction sub-equation includes the Cash account with the Order 2 to the Order 8 and the Cash account with the 22. The second transaction sub-equation is:

Cash (1): 34112.53 + Cash (1): 31671.27 + Cash (1): 52674.38 + Cash (1): 71318.63 + Cash (1): 51453.71 + Cash (1): 20752.91+ Cash (1): 10079.23 + Cash (1): -272062.66 = 0

- The transaction sub-equation includes the Cash account with the Order 11 to the Order 16, the Vehicle account with the Order 26 and the Order 28, and the Computer account with the Order 32 to the Order 34. The third transaction sub-equation is:

Cash (1): -40000 + Cash (1): -40000 + Cash (1): -38000 + Cash (1): -2800 + Cash (1): -1600 + Cash (1): -1500 + Vehicle (1): 40000 + Vehicle (1): 40000 + Vehicle (1): 38000 + Computer (1): 2800 + Computer (1): 1600 + Computer (1): 1500 = 0

- The transaction sub-equation includes the Cash account with the Order 20 and the Order 21, and the Bonds account with the Order 24 and the Order 25. The fourth transaction sub-equation is:

Cash (1): -5000 + Cash (1): -8000 + Bonds (1): 5000 + Bonds (1): 8000 = 0

- The transaction sub-equation includes the part of the Cash account with the Order 1, the Cash account with the Order 9 and the Order 10, the Cash account with the Order 15 to the Order 17, the Supplies account with the Order 21, and the Budgets capital account with the Order 40. The fifth transaction sub-equation is:

Cash (1): 669445.83 + Cash (1): 383.33 + Cash (1): 546.67 + Cash (1): -195412.62 + Cash (1): -193578.19 + Cash (1): -190917.51 + Supplies (1): 166.78 = Budgets capital (3): 90634.29

After entering this transaction, the new balance of the Cash account with the Order 1 is $47,354.17 (= $716,800 - $669,445.83).

- The transaction sub-equation includes the rest ($47,354.17) of the Cash account with the Order 1, the Accumulated amortization: Vehicle account with the Order 29 and the Order 31, and the Accumulated amortization: Computer account with the Order 35 to the Order 37. The sixth transaction sub-equation is:

Cash (1): 47354.17 + Accumulated amortization: Vehicle (1): -18666.67 + Accumulated amortization: Vehicle (1): -18666.67 + Accumulated amortization: Vehicle (1): -6333.33 + Accumulated amortization: Computer (1): -1750 + Accumulated amortization: Computer (1): -1000 + Accumulated amortization: Computer (1): -937.5= 0

After completing this transaction, the dynamic accounting equation of the Tax Bureau on December 31, 2015 has entered into the database dcj04.

## 2.3.2.2 Brief Summary of the Tax Bureau

The Figure 2.3-8 on the next page shows cash received or paid by other members table which is in the public database dcj100. The Figure 2.3-9 on the page 56 shows cash account table of the Tax Bureau on December 31, 2015. The Figure 2.3-10 on the page 57 shows cash account table.

```
SQLQuery3.sql - LIU...SS.dcj100 (sa (54))*  ×

  -use dcj100
  select sum(amount) as sum0 from CashByMembers where Recorder='88-654303'
  select * from CashByMembers where Recorder='88-654303'

100 %  ▾

☐ Results  ☐ Messages
      sum0
1    -2121.68
```

| | IDM | Amount | Symbol | MultiSubaccount | Recorder | TransDate |
|---|---|---|---|---|---|---|
| 1 | 88-654300 | -1200.00 | c | 88-654300-c-budgets < Cash receipts from center < Financial activities | 88-654303 | 2015-12-31 |
| 2 | 88-654304 | -34112.53 | c | 88-654304-c-tax < Cash receipts from taxation < Financial activities | 88-654303 | 2015-12-31 |
| 3 | 88-654305 | -31671.27 | c | 88-654305-c-tax < Cash receipts from taxation < Financial activities | 88-654303 | 2015-12-31 |
| 4 | 88-654306 | -52674.38 | c | 88-654306-c-tax < Cash receipts from taxation < Financial activities | 88-654303 | 2015-12-31 |
| 5 | 88-654307 | -71318.63 | c | 88-654307-c-tax < Cash receipts from taxation < Financial activities | 88-654303 | 2015-12-31 |
| 6 | 88-654308 | -51453.71 | c | 88-654308-c-tax < Cash receipts from taxation < Financial activities | 88-654303 | 2015-12-31 |
| 7 | 88-654309 | -20752.91 | c | 88-654309-c-tax < Cash receipts from taxation < Financial activities | 88-654303 | 2015-12-31 |
| 8 | 88-654301 | -10079.23 | c | 88-654310-c-tax < Cash receipts from taxation < Financial activities | 88-654303 | 2015-12-31 |
| 9 | 88-654301 | 272062.66 | n | 88-654301-n-tax < Cash payments to central bank < Financial activities | 88-654303 | 2015-12-31 |
| 10 | 88-654306 | 40000.00 | t | 88-654306-t-truck2 < Cash payments for machinery < Operating activities | 88-654303 | 2015-12-31 |
| 11 | 88-654306 | 40000.00 | t | 88-654306-t-car1 < Cash payments for machinery < Operating activities | 88-654303 | 2015-12-31 |
| 12 | 88-654306 | 38000.00 | t | 88-654306-t-car3 < Cash payments for machinery < Operating activities | 88-654303 | 2015-12-31 |
| 13 | 88-654306 | 2800.00 | t | 88-654306-t-computer server1 < Cash payments for machinery < Operating activities | 88-654303 | 2015-12-31 |
| 14 | 88-654306 | 1600.00 | t | 88-654306-t-computer1 < Cash payments for machinery < Operating activities | 88-654303 | 2015-12-31 |
| 15 | 88-654306 | 1500.00 | t | 88-654306-t-computer2 < Cash payments for machinery < Operating activities | 88-654303 | 2015-12-31 |
| 16 | 88-654304 | 5000.00 | n | 88-654304-n-investment bond11 < Cash payments for investments < Investing activities | 88-654303 | 2015-12-31 |
| 17 | 88-654305 | 8000.00 | n | 88-654305-n-investment bond21 < Cash payments for investments < Investing activities | 88-654303 | 2015-12-31 |
| 18 | 88-654300 | -669445... | c | 88-654300-c-budgets < Cash receipts from center < Financial activities | 88-654303 | 2015-12-31 |
| 19 | 88-654304 | -383.33 | c | 88-654304-c-interest of investment bond11 < Cash receipts from investments < Investing activities | 88-654303 | 2015-12-31 |
| 20 | 88-654305 | -546.67 | c | 88-654305-c-interest of investment bond21 < Cash receipts from investments < Investing activities | 88-654303 | 2015-12-31 |
| 21 | | 195412.62 | | Cash payments for operating expenses < Operating activities | 88-654303 | 2015-12-31 |
| 22 | | 193578.19 | | Cash payments for operating expenses < Operating activities | 88-654303 | 2015-12-31 |
| 23 | | 190917.51 | | Cash payments for operating expenses < Operating activities | 88-654303 | 2015-12-31 |
| 24 | 88-654300 | -47354.17 | c | 88-654300-c-budgets < Cash receipts from center < Financial activities | 88-654303 | 2015-12-31 |

```
☑ Query executed successfully.                                        LIU\SQLE)
```

Figure 2.3-8   Tax Bureau Cash Received or Paid by Other Members

Cash

| ID | Multi-Name | Amount | Balance | General ID | Transaction Date |
|---|---|---|---|---|---|
| 1 | 88-654300-c-budgets < Cash receipts from center < Financial activities | $1,200.00 | $1,200.00 | 1 | 2015-12-31 |
| 2 | 88-654304-c-tax < Cash receipts from taxation < Financial activities | $34,112.53 | $35,312.53 | 2 | 2015-12-31 |
| 3 | 88-654305-c-tax < Cash receipts from taxation < Financial activities | $31,671.27 | $66,983.80 | 2 | 2015-12-31 |
| 4 | 88-654306-c-tax < Cash receipts from taxation < Financial activities | $52,674.38 | $119,658.18 | 2 | 2015-12-31 |
| 5 | 88-654307-c-tax < Cash receipts from taxation < Financial activities | $71,318.63 | $190,976.81 | 2 | 2015-12-31 |
| 6 | 88-654308-c-tax < Cash receipts from taxation < Financial activities | $51,453.71 | $242,430.52 | 2 | 2015-12-31 |
| 7 | 88-654309-c-tax < Cash receipts from taxation < Financial activities | $20,752.91 | $263,183.43 | 2 | 2015-12-31 |
| 8 | 88-654310-c-tax < Cash receipts from taxation < Financial activities | $10,079.23 | $273,262.66 | 2 | 2015-12-31 |
| 9 | 88-654301-n-tax < Cash payments to central bank < Financial activities | -$272,062.66 | $1,200.00 | 2 | 2015-12-31 |
| 10 | 88-654306-t-truck2 < Cash payments for machinery < Operating activities | -$40,000.00 | -$38,800.00 | 3 | 2015-12-31 |
| 11 | 88-654306-t-car1 < Cash payments for machinery < Operating activities | -$40,000.00 | -$78,800.00 | 3 | 2015-12-31 |
| 12 | 88-654306-t-car3 < Cash payments for machinery < Operating activities | -$38,000.00 | -$116,800.00 | 3 | 2015-12-31 |
| 13 | 88-654306-t-computer server1 < Cash payments for machinery < Operating act... | -$2,800.00 | -$119,600.00 | 3 | 2015-12-31 |
| 14 | 88-654306-t-computer1 < Cash payments for machinery < Operating activities | -$1,600.00 | -$121,200.00 | 3 | 2015-12-31 |
| 15 | 88-654306-t-computer2 < Cash payments for machinery < Operating activities | -$1,500.00 | -$122,700.00 | 3 | 2015-12-31 |
| 16 | 88-654304-n-investment bond11 < Cash payments for investments < Investing ... | -$5,000.00 | -$127,700.00 | 4 | 2015-12-31 |
| 17 | 88-654305-n-investment bond21 < Cash payments for investments < Investing ... | -$8,000.00 | -$135,700.00 | 4 | 2015-12-31 |
| 18 | 88-654300-c-budgets < Cash receipts from center < Financial activities | $669,445.83 | $533,745.83 | 5 | 2015-12-31 |
| 19 | 88-654304-c-interest of investment bond11 < Cash receipts from investments <... | $383.33 | $534,129.16 | 5 | 2015-12-31 |
| 20 | 88-654305-c-interest of investment bond21 < Cash receipts from investments <... | $546.67 | $534,675.83 | 5 | 2015-12-31 |
| 21 | Cash payments for operating expenses < Operating activities | -$195,412.62 | $339,263.21 | 5 | 2015-12-31 |
| 22 | Cash payments for operating expenses < Operating activities | -$193,578.19 | $145,685.02 | 5 | 2015-12-31 |
| 23 | Cash payments for operating expenses < Operating activities | -$190,917.51 | -$45,232.49 | 5 | 2015-12-31 |
| 24 | 88-654300-c-budgets < Cash receipts from center < Financial activities | $47,354.17 | $2,121.69 | 6 | 2015-12-31 |

Figure 2.3-9   Tax Bureau Cash Account Table

Balance Sheet

| | As at 12/31/2015 | |
|---|---|---|
| **ASSETS** | | |
| Current assets | | |
| Cash | | $2,121.68 |
| Supplies | | $166.78 |
| Account receivable | | $0.00 |
| | | $2,288.46 |
| | | |
| Long term investments | | |
| Bonds | | $13,000.00 |
| Equipment | | |
| Vehicle | | $118,000.00 |
| Accumulated amortization: Vehicle | | -$43,666.67 |
| Computer | | $5,900.00 |
| Accumulated amortization: Computer | | -$3,687.50 |
| | | $76,545.83 |
| | | |
| Total Assets | | $91,834.29 |
| | | |
| LIABILITIES | | |
| Current liabilities | | |
| Account payable | | $1,200.00 |
| Total Liability | | $1,200.00 |
| | | |
| SHAREHOLDERS' EQUITY | | |
| Owners capital | | |
| Budgets capital | | $90,634.29 |
| Retined earnings | | $0.00 |
| Accumulated other comprehensive income | | $0.00 |
| Total Shareholders' Equity | | $90,634.29 |
| | | |
| Total Liabilities and Shareholders' Equity | | $91,834.29 |

Figure 2.3-10   Tax Bureau Balance Sheet

## 2.4 Third Rank of Social Members

The third rank of the social members is all organizations or all companies (including the proprietorships). For simplification, it mainly has following types of the transactions:

- The organization or company deposits the money in the business banks and can get some interest incomes.

  It is an operating activities' transaction. The organization or company pays cash to business bank and the Deposits receivable account increases. Later, the Interest incomes account will increase.

- The organization or company purchases inventory for some cash and other on credit. It is an operating activities' transaction. The organization or company pays some cash and the Account payable increases.

- The organization or company sells inventory for some cash and other on credit.

  It is an operating activities' transaction. The organization or company receives some cash and the Account receivable increases

- The organization or company pays the cash for all expenses of its employees and the other expenses (including the office supplies and equipment).

- Only business banks lend money to the organizations or companies and earn the interest incomes.

  It is an operating activities' transaction. The business bank pays cash and the Notes receivable account increases.

There is seven companies or organizations in the third rank of the social members.

## 2.4.1 Sample of the Business Bank1

The Business Bank1 has total share capital $1,000,000 and two shareholders of the individual A7 and the individual A9. Their percentages of the share capital are 60% and 40% respectively.

## 2.4.1.1 Conversion of the Business Bank1

The Business Bank1 will convert to the MathAccounting software on January 1, 2016, so I design a converting reference table, seeing the Figure 2.4-1 on the next page, in order to enter its dynamic accounting equation on December 31, 2015 into the database dcj05.

| Order | Class | Account Name (Subtotal Name) | Balance | Row |
|-------|-------|------------------------------|---------|-----|
| **1** | **1** | **(Current assets)** | - | **103** |
| 2 | 1 | Cash | 1609115.51 | 104 |
| 3 | 1 | Supplies | 102.31 | 106 |
| 4 | 1 | Business bank reserves receivable | 0 | 108 |
| 5 | 1 | Accrued interest receivable | 0 | 110 |
| 6 | 1 | Notes receivable | 1010000.00 | 112 |
| **7** | **1** | **(Long term investments)** | - | **141** |
| 8 | 1 | Bonds | 11000.00 | 143 |
| **9** | **1** | **(Equipment)** | - | **171** |
| 10 | 1 | Vehicle | 85000.00 | 172 |
| 11 | 1 | Accumulated amortization: Vehicle | -32916.67 | 173 |
| 12 | 1 | Computer | 5600.00 | 174 |
| 13 | 1 | Accumulated amortization: Computer | -3966.67 | 175 |
| **14** | **2** | **(Current liabilities)** | - | **203** |
| 15 | 2 | Business bank reserves payable | 0 | 204 |
| 16 | 2 | Account payable | 0 | 206 |
| | 2 | Accrued interest payable | 0 | 208 |
| 17 | 2 | Deposits payable | 1528364.66 | 210 |
| 18 | 2 | Tax payable | 0 | 210 |
| **19** | **2** | **(Long term liabilities)** | - | **251** |
| 20 | 2 | Bonds payable | 150000.00 | 252 |
| **21** | **3** | **(Owners' capital)** | - | **303** |
| 22 | 3 | Share capital | 1000000.00 | 304 |
| 23 | 3 | Retained earnings (Conversion) | 5569.82 | 306 |
| **24** | **4** | **(Revenues)** | - | **403** |
| 25 | 4 | Sales (notes interest) | 0 | 404 |
| **26** | **5** | **(Cost)** | - | **431** |
| 27 | 5 | Cost of notes interest | 0 | 432 |
| **28** | **5** | **(Operating and administrative expenses)** | - | **453** |
| 29 | 5 | Travelling expenses | 0 | 454 |
| 30 | 5 | Other expenses | 0 | 456 |
| 31 | 5 | Office supplies expenses | 0 | 458 |
| 32 | 5 | Salary expenses | 0 | 460 |

| 33 | 5 | Bond interest expenses | 0 | 462 |
|----|---|------------------------|---|-----|
| 34 | 5 | Amortization expenses | 0 | 464 |
| 35 | 5 | Interest expenses | 0 | 466 |
| **36** | **4** | **(Other income)** | - | **475** |
| 37 | 4 | Investment incomes | 0 | 476 |
| 39 | 4 | Deposits fee incomes | 0 | 478 |
| **39** | **5** | **(Tax)** | - | **600** |
| 40 | 5 | Tax expenses | 0 | 602 |

Figure 2.4-1   Business Bank1 Converting Reference Table

From the Figure 2.4-1, there are total 29 accounts among which the balances of all expenses accounts are zero. Here, the Sales (notes interest) account should be actually recorded as the Accrued interest receivable (Notes) account and the Cost of notes interest account should also be recorded as the Accrued interest payable (Deposits) account at the end of every month in this book. The difference of them is gross income. For simplification, I only record the balances of the Sales (notes interest) account and Cost of notes interest account at the end of the fiscal year.

In this pure digital currency model, the balance of the Business bank reserves payable account should be zero. The balance of the Deposits payable does not include the balance of the Cash for the Business Bank1 itself. In addition, the balance of the Retained earnings should be added to the balance of the Share capital account, and its balance should be zero prior to conversion. However, for knowing the original share capital and the distinguishing retained earnings after conversion, I keep the Retained earnings account prior to conversion and give it a different name of the Retained earnings (Conversion). Later, I will build the Balance Sheet Statement of the Business Bank1 which will show the difference.

The Notes receivable account, which is put in the subtotal name of the "Current assets" for simplification, has five one-level subaccounts of the "Note11-88-654306" ($250,000, beginning on February 1, 2013, three years, annual interest rate 9%, and accrued interest $65,625.00), the "Note12-88-654307" ($140,000, beginning on March 1, 2014, four years, annual interest rate 9%, and accrued interest $23,100.00), the "Note13-88-654308" ($200,000, beginning on May 1, 2014, four years, annual interest rate 9%, and accrued interest $30,000.00), the "Note14-88-654307" ($250,000, beginning on June 1, 2014, four years, annual interest rate 9.2%, and accrued interest $36,416.67), and the "Note15-88-654306" ($170,000, beginning on October 1, 2015, three years, annual interest rate 9.5%, and accrued interest $4,037.50 ).

The Bonds account has two one-level subaccounts of the "Bond21" (issued by the Business Bank2 and purchased $6,000, beginning on May 1, 2014, five years, and annual interest rate 4.1%) and the "Bond22" (issued by the Business Bank2 and purchased $5,000, beginning on February 1, 2015, five years, and annual interest rate 4.4%). Accordingly, the balance of the Accrued interest payable account is zero prior to the conversion.

The Business Bank1 has one truck1 (five years, straight line, 27 months) and one car1 (five years, straight line, 19 months), so the multi-subaccount names of the Vehicle parent account are the "Truck11 < Truck1 < Truck" and the "Car11 < Car1 < Car" respectively. Their balances are $45,000 and $40,000 respectively. Accordingly, the multi-subaccount names of the Accumulated amortization: Vehicle account are the "Truck11-accumulated amortization < Truck1-accumulated amortization < Truck-accumulated amortization" and the "Car11-accumulated amortization < Car1-accumulated amortization < Car-accumulated amortization". Their balances are -$20,250 and -$12,666.67 respectively.

The Business Bank1 account has one computer server2 (two years, straight line, 17 months), one computer2 (two years, straight line, 17 months), and one computer3 (two years, straight line, 17 months), so the multi-subaccount names of the Computer parent account are the "Computer server21 < Computer server2 < Computer server", the "Computer21 < Computer2", and the "Computer31 < Computer3" respectively. Their balances are $2,700, $1,500, and $1,400 respectively. Accordingly, the multi-subaccount names of the Accumulated amortization: Computer account are the "Computer server21-accumulated amortization < Computer server2-accumulated amortization < Computer server-accumulated amortization", the "Computer21-accumulated amortization < Computer2 - accumulated amortization", and the "Computer31-accumulated amortization < Computer3-accumulated amortization". Their balances are respectively -$1,912.50, -$1,062.50, and -$991.61.

The balance of the Deposits payable is equal to total cash in the Business1 minus the Business Bank1's cash on December 31, 2015. The annual deposits interest rate is 0% prior to conversion. Since January 1, 2016, the annual deposits interest rate should be a percentage, such as 1%. For simplification, the business banks only pay $120 for every social member' primary account and do not pay any cash for any second account at the end of each year, seeing the following Figure 2.4-2.

| Order | Members | Primary Account | Second Account |
|-------|---------|-----------------|----------------|
| 1 | Organizations | $120 | - |
| 2 | Individuals | $120 | - |

Figure 2.4-2   Deposits Accrued Interest

The Business Bank1 issued three bonds, so the Bonds payable account has three one-level subaccounts of the "Bond11-payable" ($60,000, beginning on February 1, 2014, five years, and annual interest rate 4%), the "Bond12-payable" ($40,000, beginning on July 1, 2014, five years, and annual interest rate 4.2%), and the "Bond13-payable" ($50,000, beginning on September 1, 2015, six years, and annual interest rate 4.5%). Of course, the Bonds payable account has also many two-level subaccounts, seeing the Figure 2.4-3 on this page and the next page, which shows the detail information of the issued bonds.

| Order | Bond | Amount | Term | Purchaser Name | Identity |
|-------|------|--------|------|----------------|----------|
| 1 | Bond11 | 6000 | February 1, 2014, Five years, 4% annually | Government1 | 88-654302 |
| 2 | Bond11 | 5000 | February 1, 2014, Five years, 4% annually | Tax Bureau | 88-654303 |
| 3 | Bond11 | 7000 | February 1, 2014, Five years, 4% annually | Business Bank2 | 88-654305 |
| 4 | Bond11 | 10000 | February 1, 2014, Five years, 4% annually | Company1 | 88-654306 |
| 5 | Bond11 | 8000 | February 1, 2014, Five years, 4% annually | Company3 | 88-654308 |
| 6 | Bond11 | 5000 | February 1, 2014, Five years, 4% annually | Proprietorship1 | 88-654309 |
| 7 | Bond11 | 9000 | February 1, 2014, Five years, 4% annually | A7 | 909876507 |
| 8 | Bond11 | 6000 | February 1, 2014, Five years, 4% annually | A9 | 909876509 |
| 9 | Bond11 | 3000 | February 1, 2014, Five years, 4% annually | A13 | 909876513 |
| 10 | Bond11 | 1000 | February 1, 2014, Five years, 4% annually | A14 | 909876514 |

| | | | | | |
|---|---|---|---|---|---|
| 11 | Bond12 | 3000 | July 1, 2014, Five years, 4.2% annually | Business Bank2 | 88-654305 |
| 12 | Bond12 | 8000 | July 1, 2014, Five years, 4.2% annually | Company2 | 88-654307 |
| 13 | Bond12 | 3000 | July 1, 2014, Five years, 4.2% annually | Proprietorship1 | 88-654309 |
| 14 | Bond12 | 6000 | July 1, 2014, Five years, 4.2% annually | Proprietorship2 | 88-654310 |
| 15 | Bond12 | 5000 | July 1, 2014, Five years, 4.2% annually | A1 | 909876501 |
| 16 | Bond12 | 2000 | July 1, 2014, Five years, 4.2% annually | A2 | 909876502 |
| 17 | Bond12 | 7000 | July 1, 2014, Five years, 4.2% annually | A4 | 909876504 |
| 18 | Bond12 | 6000 | July 1, 2014, Five years, 4.2% annually | A21 | 909876521 |
| 19 | Bond13 | 6000 | September 1, 2015, Six years, 4.5% annually | Business Bank2 | 88-654305 |
| 20 | Bond13 | 3000 | September 1, 2015, Six years, 4.5% annually | Company1 | 88-654306 |
| 21 | Bond13 | 2000 | September 1, 2015, Six years, 4.5% annually | Proprietorship1 | 88-654309 |
| 22 | Bond13 | 6000 | September 1, 2015, Six years, 4.5% annually | A3 | 909876503 |
| 23 | Bond13 | 4000 | September 1, 2015, Six years, 4.5% annually | A5 | 909876505 |
| 24 | Bond13 | 7000 | September 1, 2015, Six years, 4.5% annually | A6 | 909876506 |
| 25 | Bond13 | 4000 | September 1, 2015, Six years, 4.5% annually | A15 | 909876515 |
| 26 | Bond13 | 5000 | September 1, 2015, Six years, 4.5% annually | A17 | 909876517 |
| 27 | Bond13 | 3000 | September 1, 2015, Six years, 4.5% annually | A18 | 909876518 |
| 28 | Bond13 | 6000 | September 1, 2015, Six years, 4.5% annually | A19 | 909876519 |
| 29 | Bond13 | 4000 | September 1, 2015, Six years, 4.5% annually | A21 | 909876521 |
| **30** | **Total** | **150000** | | | |

Figure 2.4-3   Business Bank1 Issued Bonds Information Table

Following above information, I can build a table of the multi-subaccount names, seeing the Figure 2.4-4 on this page and the next pages.

| Order | Class | Multi-subaccount Name | Parent Name | Lowest Subaccount Balance |
|---|---|---|---|---|
| 1 | 1 | 909876507-i-owners < Cash receipts from owners < Financial activities | Cash | 600000.00 |
| 2 | 1 | 909876509-i-owners < Cash receipts from owners < Financial activities | Cash | 400000.00 |
| 3 | 1 | 909876501-d-deposits < Cash receipts from customers deposits < Operating activities | Cash | 15900.10 |
| 4 | 1 | 909876502-d-deposits < Cash receipts from customers deposits < Operating activities | Cash | 12200.11 |
| 5 | 1 | 909876503-d-deposits < Cash receipts from customers deposits < Operating activities | Cash | 11800.23 |

| | | | | |
|---|---|---|---|---|
| 6 | 1 | 909876504-d-deposits < Cash receipts from customers deposits < Operating activities | Cash | 17230.03 |
| 7 | 1 | 909876505-d-deposits < Cash receipts from customers deposits < Operating activities | Cash | 15960.96 |
| 8 | 1 | 909876506-d-deposits < Cash receipts from customers deposits < Operating activities | Cash | 17200.52 |
| 9 | 1 | 909876507-d-deposits < Cash receipts from customers deposits < Operating activities | Cash | 28500.03 |
| 10 | 1 | 909876508-d-deposits < Cash receipts from customers deposits < Operating activities | Cash | 15620.65 |
| 11 | 1 | 909876509-d-deposits < Cash receipts from customers deposits < Operating activities | Cash | 27700.11 |
| 12 | 1 | 909876510-d-deposits < Cash receipts from customers deposits < Operating activities | Cash | 0 |
| 13 | 1 | 909876511-d-deposits < Cash receipts from customers deposits < Operating activities | Cash | 11710.41 |
| 14 | 1 | 909876512-d-deposits < Cash receipts from customers deposits < Operating activities | Cash | 15720.23 |
| 15 | 1 | 909876513-d-deposits < Cash receipts from customers deposits < Operating activities | Cash | 16510.35 |
| 16 | 1 | 909876514-d-deposits < Cash receipts from customers deposits < Operating activities | Cash | 17980.41 |
| 17 | 1 | 909876515-d-deposits < Cash receipts from customers deposits < Operating activities | Cash | 26250.27 |
| 18 | 1 | 909876516-d-deposits < Cash receipts from customers deposits < Operating activities | Cash | 18790.58 |
| 19 | 1 | 909876517-d-deposits < Cash receipts from customers deposits < Operating activities | Cash | 0 |
| 20 | 1 | 909876518-d-deposits < Cash receipts from customers deposits < Operating activities | Cash | 18260.63 |
| 21 | 1 | 909876519-d-deposits < Cash receipts from customers deposits < Operating activities | Cash | 11230.11 |
| 22 | 1 | 909876520-d-deposits < Cash receipts from customers deposits < Operating activities | Cash | 11082.23 |
| 23 | 1 | 909876521-d-deposits < Cash receipts from customers deposits < Operating activities | Cash | 0 |
| 24 | 1 | 909876522-d-deposits < Cash receipts from customers deposits < Operating activities | Cash | 16510.03 |
| 25 | 1 | 909876523-d-deposits < Cash receipts from customers deposits < Operating activities | Cash | 11960.84 |
| 26 | 1 | 909876524-d-deposits < Cash receipts from customers deposits < Operating activities | Cash | 28100.25 |
| 27 | 1 | 909876525-d-deposits < Cash receipts from customers deposits < Operating activities | Cash | 11230.32 |
| 28 | 1 | 88-654300-d-deposits < Cash receipts from customers deposits < Operating activities | Cash | 1058058.20 |
| 29 | 1 | 88-654302-d-deposits < Cash receipts from customers deposits < Operating activities | Cash | 1289.11 |
| 30 | 1 | 88-654303-d-deposits < Cash receipts from customers deposits < Operating activities | Cash | 1003.72 |
| 31 | 1 | 88-654304-d-deposits < Cash receipts from customers deposits < Operating activities | Cash | 0 |
| 32 | 1 | 88-654305-d-deposits < Cash receipts from customers deposits < Operating activities | Cash | 0 |
| 33 | 1 | 88-654306-d-deposits < Cash receipts from customers deposits < Operating activities | Cash | 67873.98 |
| 34 | 1 | 88-654307-d-deposits < Cash receipts from customers deposits < Operating activities | Cash | 0 |
| 35 | 1 | 88-654308-d-deposits < Cash receipts from customers deposits < Operating activities | Cash | 3906.47 |
| 36 | 1 | 88-654309-d-deposits < Cash receipts from customers deposits < Operating activities | Cash | 18783.78 |
| 37 | 1 | 88-654310-d-deposits < Cash receipts from customers deposits < Operating activities | Cash | 0 |

| 38 | 1 | 88-654302-i-bond11 < Cash receipts from issued bonds < Financial activities | Cash | 6000.00 |
|---|---|---|---|---|
| 39 | 1 | 88-654303-i-bond11 < Cash receipts from issued bonds < Financial activities | Cash | 5000.00 |
| 40 | 1 | 88-654305-i-bond11 < Cash receipts from issued bonds < Financial activities | Cash | 7000.00 |
| 41 | 1 | 88-654306-i-bond11 < Cash receipts from issued bonds < Financial activities | Cash | 10000.00 |
| 42 | 1 | 88-654308-i-bond11 < Cash receipts from issued bonds < Financial activities | Cash | 8000.00 |
| 43 | 1 | 88-654309-i-bond11 < Cash receipts from issued bonds < Financial activities | Cash | 5000.00 |
| 44 | 1 | 909876507-i-bond11 < Cash receipts from issued bonds < Financial activities | Cash | 9000.00 |
| 45 | 1 | 909876509-i-bond11 < Cash receipts from issued bonds < Financial activities | Cash | 6000.00 |
| 46 | 1 | 909876513-i-bond11 < Cash receipts from issued bonds < Financial activities | Cash | 3000.00 |
| 47 | 1 | 909876514-i-bond11 < Cash receipts from issued bonds < Financial activities | Cash | 1000.00 |
| 48 | 1 | 88-654305-i-bond12 < Cash receipts from issued bonds < Financial activities | Cash | 3000.00 |
| 49 | 1 | 88-654307-i-bond12 < Cash receipts from issued bonds < Financial activities | Cash | 8000.00 |
| 50 | 1 | 88-654309-i-bond12 < Cash receipts from issued bonds < Financial activities | Cash | 3000.00 |
| 51 | 1 | 88-654310-i-bond12 < Cash receipts from issued bonds < Financial activities | Cash | 6000.00 |
| 52 | 1 | 909876501-i-bond12 < Cash receipts from issued bonds < Financial activities | Cash | 5000.00 |
| 53 | 1 | 909876502-i-bond12 < Cash receipts from issued bonds < Financial activities | Cash | 2000.00 |
| 54 | 1 | 909876504-i-bond12 < Cash receipts from issued bonds < Financial activities | Cash | 7000.00 |
| 55 | 1 | 909876521-i-bond12 < Cash receipts from issued bonds < Financial activities | Cash | 6000.00 |
| 56 | 1 | 88-654305-i-bond13 < Cash receipts from issued bonds < Financial activities | Cash | 6000.00 |
| 57 | 1 | 88-654306-i-bond13 < Cash receipts from issued bonds < Financial activities | Cash | 3000.00 |
| 58 | 1 | 88-654309-i-bond13 < Cash receipts from issued bonds < Financial activities | Cash | 2000.00 |
| 59 | 1 | 909876503-i-bond13 < Cash receipts from issued bonds < Financial activities | Cash | 6000.00 |
| 60 | 1 | 909876505-i-bond13 < Cash receipts from issued bonds < Financial activities | Cash | 4000.00 |
| 61 | 1 | 909876506-i-bond13 < Cash receipts from issued bonds < Financial activities | Cash | 7000.00 |
| 62 | 1 | 909876515-i-bond13 < Cash receipts from issued bonds < Financial activities | Cash | 4000.00 |
| 63 | 1 | 909876517-i-bond13 < Cash receipts from issued bonds < Financial activities | Cash | 5000.00 |
| 64 | 1 | 909876518-i-bond13 < Cash receipts from issued bonds < Financial activities | Cash | 3000.00 |
| 65 | 1 | 909876519-i-bond13 < Cash receipts from issued bonds < Financial activities | Cash | 6000.00 |
| 66 | 1 | 909876521-i-bond13 < Cash receipts from issued bonds < Financial activities | Cash | 4000.00 |
| 67 | 1 | 88-654306-c-accrued interest < Cash receipts from note accrued interest (customers) < Operating activities | Cash | 65625.00 |
| 68 | 1 | 88-654307-c-accrued interest < Cash receipts from note accrued interest (customers) < Operating activities | Cash | 23100.00 |

| | | | | |
|---|---|---|---|---|
| 69 | 1 | 88-654308-c-accrued interest < Cash receipts from note accrued interest (customers) < Operating activities | Cash | 30000.00 |
| 70 | 1 | 88-654307-c-accrued interest < Cash receipts from note accrued interest (customers) < Operating activities | Cash | 36416.67 |
| 71 | 1 | 88-654306-c-accrued interest < Cash receipts from note accrued interest (customers) < Operating activities | Cash | 4037.50 |
| 72 | 1 | 88-654305-c-interest of investment bond21 < Cash receipts from investments < Investing activities | Cash | 410.00 |
| 73 | 1 | 88-654305-c-interest of investment bond22 < Cash receipts from investments < Investing activities | Cash | 201.67 |
| 74 | 1 | 88-654306-t-truck1 < Cash payments for machinery < Operating activities | Cash | -45000.00 |
| 75 | 1 | 88-654306-t-car1 < Cash payments for machinery < Operating activities | Cash | -40000.00 |
| 76 | 1 | 88-654306-t-computer server2 < Cash payments for machinery < Operating activities | Cash | -2700.00 |
| 77 | 1 | 88-654306-t-computer2 < Cash payments for machinery < Operating activities | Cash | -1500.00 |
| 78 | 1 | 88-654306-t-computer3 < Cash payments for machinery < Operating activities | Cash | -1400.00 |
| 79 | 1 | Cash payments for operating expenses < Operating activities | Cash | -28061.55 |
| 80 | 1 | Cash payments for operating expenses < Operating activities | Cash | -27953.14 |
| 81 | 1 | Cash payments for operating expenses < Operating activities | Cash | -27312.77 |
| 82 | 1 | 88-654303-n-tax < Cash payments for operating expenses < Operating activities | Cash | -34112.53 |
| 83 | 1 | 88-654306-n-notes1 < Cash payments to notes lenders < Operating activities | Cash | -250000.00 |
| 84 | 1 | 88-654307-n-notes2 < Cash payments to notes lenders < Operating activities | Cash | -140000.00 |
| 85 | 1 | 88-654308-n-notes3 < Cash payments to notes lenders < Operating activities | Cash | -200000.00 |
| 86 | 1 | 88-654307-n-notes4 < Cash payments to notes lenders < Operating activities | Cash | -250000.00 |
| 87 | 1 | 88-654306-n-notes5 < Cash payments to notes lenders < Operating activities | Cash | -170000.00 |
| 88 | 1 | 88-654305-n-investment bond21 < Cash payments for investments < Investing activities | Cash | -6000.00 |
| 89 | 1 | 88-654305-n-investment bond22 < Cash payments for investments < Investing activities | Cash | -5000.00 |
| 90 | 1 | n | Supplies | 102.31 |
| 91 | 1 | Note11-88-654306 | Notes receivable | 250000.00 |
| 92 | 1 | Note12-88-654307 | Notes receivable | 140000.00 |
| 93 | 1 | Note13-88-654308 | Notes receivable | 200000.00 |
| 94 | 1 | Note14-88-654307 | Notes receivable | 250000.00 |
| 95 | 1 | Note15-88-654306 | Notes receivable | 170000.00 |
| 96 | 1 | Bond21 | Bonds | 6000.00 |
| 97 | 1 | Bond22 | Bonds | 5000.00 |
| 98 | 1 | Truck11 < Truck1 < Truck | Vehicle | 45000.00 |
| 99 | 1 | Car11 < Car1 < Car | Vehicle | 40000.00 |
| 100 | 1 | Truck11-accumulated amortization < Truck1-accumulated amortization < Truck-accumulated amortization | Accumulated amortization: Vehicle | -20250.00 |

| 101 | 1 | Car11-accumulated amortization < Car1-accumulated amortization < Car-accumulated amortization | Accumulated amortization: Vehicle | -12666.67 |
|---|---|---|---|---|
| 102 | 1 | Computer server21 < Computer server2 < Computer server | Computer | 2700.00 |
| 103 | 1 | Computer21 < Computer2 | Computer | 1500.00 |
| 104 | 1 | Computer31 < Computer3 | Computer | 1400.00 |
| 105 | 1 | Computer server21-accumulated amortization < Computer server2-accumulated amortization < Computer server-accumulated amortization | Accumulated amortization: Computer | -1912.5 |
| 106 | 1 | Computer21-accumulated amortization < Computer2-accumulated amortization | Accumulated amortization: Computer | -1062.5 |
| 107 | 1 | Computer31-accumulated amortization < Computer3-accumulated amortization | Accumulated amortization: Computer | -991.67 |
| 108 | 2 | Deposits-909876501 | Deposits payable | 15900.10 |
| 109 | 2 | Deposits-909876502 | Deposits payable | 12200.11 |
| 110 | 2 | Deposits-909876503 | Deposits payable | 11800.23 |
| 111 | 2 | Deposits-909876504 | Deposits payable | 17230.03 |
| 112 | 2 | Deposits-909876505 | Deposits payable | 15960.96 |
| 113 | 2 | Deposits-909876506 | Deposits payable | 17200.52 |
| 114 | 2 | Deposits-909876507 | Deposits payable | 28500.03 |
| 115 | 2 | Deposits-909876508 | Deposits payable | 15620.65 |
| 116 | 2 | Deposits-909876509 | Deposits payable | 27700.11 |
| 117 | 2 | Deposits-909876510 | Deposits payable | 0 |
| 118 | 2 | Deposits-909876511 | Deposits payable | 11710.41 |
| 119 | 2 | Deposits-909876512 | Deposits payable | 15720.23 |
| 120 | 2 | Deposits-909876513 | Deposits payable | 16510.35 |
| 121 | 2 | Deposits-909876514 | Deposits payable | 17980.41 |
| 122 | 2 | Deposits-909876515 | Deposits payable | 26250.27 |
| 123 | 2 | Deposits-909876516 | Deposits payable | 18790.58 |
| 124 | 2 | Deposits-909876517 | Deposits payable | 0 |
| 125 | 2 | Deposits-909876518 | Deposits payable | 18260.63 |
| 126 | 2 | Deposits-909876519 | Deposits payable | 11230.11 |
| 127 | 2 | Deposits-909876520 | Deposits payable | 11082.23 |
| 128 | 2 | Deposits-909876521 | Deposits payable | 0 |
| 129 | 2 | Deposits-909876522 | Deposits payable | 16510.03 |
| 130 | 2 | Deposits-909876523 | Deposits payable | 11960.84 |
| 131 | 2 | Deposits-909876524 | Deposits payable | 28100.25 |
| 132 | 2 | Deposits-909876525 | Deposits payable | 11230.32 |
| 133 | 2 | Deposits-88-654300 | Deposits payable | 1058058.2 |
| 134 | 2 | Deposits-88-654302 | Deposits payable | 1289.11 |
| 135 | 2 | Deposits-88-654303 | Deposits payable | 1003.72 |
| 136 | 2 | Deposits-88-654304 | Deposits payable | 0 |
| 137 | 2 | Deposits-88-654305 | Deposits payable | 0 |
| 138 | 2 | Deposits-88-654306 | Deposits payable | 67873.98 |

| 139 | 2 | Deposits-88-654307 | Deposits payable | 0 |
|---|---|---|---|---|
| 140 | 2 | Deposits-88-654308 | Deposits payable | 3906.47 |
| 141 | 2 | Deposits-88-654309 | Deposits payable | 18783.78 |
| 142 | 2 | Deposits-88-654310 | Deposits payable | 0 |
| 143 | 2 | Bond11-88-654302 < Bond11 | Bonds payable | 6000.00 |
| 144 | 2 | Bond11-88-654303 < Bond11 | Bonds payable | 5000.00 |
| 145 | 2 | Bond11-88-654305 < Bond11 | Bonds payable | 7000.00 |
| 146 | 2 | Bond11-88-654306 < Bond11 | Bonds payable | 10000.00 |
| 147 | 2 | Bond11-88-654308 < Bond11 | Bonds payable | 8000.00 |
| 148 | 2 | Bond11-88-654309 < Bond11 | Bonds payable | 5000.00 |
| 149 | 2 | Bond11-909876507 < Bond11 | Bonds payable | 9000.00 |
| 150 | 2 | Bond11-909876509 < Bond11 | Bonds payable | 6000.00 |
| 151 | 2 | Bond11-909876513 < Bond11 | Bonds payable | 3000.00 |
| 152 | 2 | Bond11-909876514 < Bond11 | Bonds payable | 1000.00 |
| 153 | 2 | Bond12-88-654305 < Bond12 | Bonds payable | 3000.00 |
| 154 | 2 | Bond12-88-654307 < Bond12 | Bonds payable | 8000.00 |
| 155 | 2 | Bond12-88-654309 < Bond12 | Bonds payable | 3000.00 |
| 156 | 2 | Bond12-88-654310 < Bond12 | Bonds payable | 6000.00 |
| 157 | 2 | Bond12-909876501 < Bond12 | Bonds payable | 5000.00 |
| 158 | 2 | Bond12-909876502 < Bond12 | Bonds payable | 2000.00 |
| 159 | 2 | Bond12-909876504 < Bond12 | Bonds payable | 7000.00 |
| 160 | 2 | Bond12-909876521 < Bond12 | Bonds payable | 6000.00 |
| 161 | 2 | Bond13-88-654305 < Bond13 | Bonds payable | 6000.00 |
| 162 | 2 | Bond13-88-654306 < Bond13 | Bonds payable | 3000.00 |
| 163 | 2 | Bond13-88-654309 < Bond13 | Bonds payable | 2000.00 |
| 164 | 2 | Bond13-909876503 < Bond13 | Bonds payable | 6000.00 |
| 165 | 2 | Bond13-909876505 < Bond13 | Bonds payable | 4000.00 |
| 166 | 2 | Bond13-909876506 < Bond13 | Bonds payable | 7000.00 |
| 167 | 2 | Bond13-909876515 < Bond13 | Bonds payable | 4000.00 |
| 168 | 2 | Bond13-909876517 < Bond13 | Bonds payable | 5000.00 |
| 169 | 2 | Bond13-909876518 < Bond13 | Bonds payable | 3000.00 |
| 170 | 2 | Bond13-909876519 < Bond13 | Bonds payable | 6000.00 |
| 171 | 2 | Bond13-909876521 < Bond13 | Bonds payable | 4000.00 |
| 172 | 3 | Capital-909876507 | Share capital | 600000.00 |
| 173 | 3 | Capital-909876509 | Share capital | 400000.00 |
| 174 | 3 | n | Retained earnings (Conversion) | 5569.82 |
| 175 | 4 | Note11-interest income | Sales (notes interest) | 0 |
| 176 | 4 | Note12-interest income | Sales (notes interest) | 0 |
| 177 | 4 | Note13-interest income | Sales (notes interest) | 0 |
| 178 | 4 | Note14-interest income | Sales (notes interest) | 0 |

| 179 | 4 | Note15-interest income | Sales (notes interest) | 0 |
|-----|---|------------------------|------------------------|---|
| 180 | 5 | Deposit interest expenses | Cost of notes interest | 0 |
| 181 | 5 | 909876509-travelling < Sales department-travelling | Travelling expenses | 0 |
| 182 | 5 | 909876508-other < Purchase department-other | Other expenses | 0 |
| 183 | 5 | 909876507-salary < Office department-salary | Salary expenses | 0 |
| 184 | 5 | Bond11-interest expenses | Bond interest expenses | 0 |
| 185 | 5 | Bond12-interest expenses | Bond interest expenses | 0 |
| 186 | 5 | Bond13-interest expenses | Bond interest expenses | 0 |
| 187 | 5 | Truck11-amortization < Truck1-amortization < Vehicle-truck-amortization | Amortization expenses | 0 |
| 188 | 5 | Car11-amortization < Car1-amortization < Vehicle-car-amortization | Amortization expenses | 0 |
| 189 | 5 | Computer server21-amortization < Computer server2-amortization < Computer-amortization | Amortization expenses | 0 |
| 190 | 5 | Computer21-amortization < Computer2-amortization < Computer-amortization | Amortization expenses | 0 |
| 191 | 5 | Computer31-amortization < Computer3-amortization < Computer-amortization | Amortization expenses | 0 |
| 192 | 4 | Accrued interest income-bond21 <Bonds | Investment incomes | 0 |
| 193 | 4 | Accrued interest income-bond22 <Bonds | Investment incomes | 0 |
| 194 | 4 | n | Deposits fee incomes | 0 |

Figure 2.4-4   Business Bank1 Converting Multi-Subaccount Names Table

From the Figure 2.4-4, there are some accounts whose balances are zero. Their "MultiSubaccount name" forms all are the "n" during the conversion even if they should have the multi-subaccount names. Later, their multi-subaccount names can be entered following the need. Of course, you can choice not to enter these accounts during the conversion.

Please pay attention here. The lowest subaccounts of all parent accounts are sole, so the "MultiSubaccount name" form is the same "n" for all parent accounts without any subaccount. Therefore, there should be only one "n" in the Figure 2.4-4. However, I write all possible parent accounts, which have not any subaccount, into the table to provide detail information to readers.

If I do not need to understand the details of some three-level subaccounts of the Cash account or I cannot get the details of some three-level subaccounts of the Cash account during the conversion, then these multi-subaccount names cannot have any three-level subaccount and can have only two-level subaccounts. For example, the multi-subaccount name with the "Order 81" is the "Cash payments for operating expenses < Operating activities" and its balance is -$34,112.53 which is equal to the sum of the Tax expenses (cash paid), the Supplies (cash paid), and so on for the previous years.

Before entering the dynamic accounting equation on December 31, 2015 into the database dcj05, I first enter two initialization sub-equations.

Account receivable (1): 0 = Account payable (2): 0

0 = Sales (notes interest) (4): 0 – Cost of notes interest (5):0

From the Figure 2.4-1 and the Figure 2.4-4, the dynamic accounting equation on December 31, 2015 must be divided to the N transaction sub-equations because of the limitation of the MathAccounting software. Every sub-equation has maximum twelve items. The all converting transaction sub-equations can be designed and written as following.

- The transaction sub-equation includes the Cash account with the Order 3 to the Order 8 and the Deposits payable account with the Order 108 to the Order 113. The first transaction sub-equation is:

  Cash (1): 15900.1 + Cash (1): 12200.11 + Cash (1): 11800.23 + Cash (1): 17230.03 + Cash (1): 15960.96 + Cash (1): 17200.52 = Deposits payable (2): 15900.1 + Deposits payable (2): 12200.11 + Deposits payable (2): 11800.23 + Deposits payable (2): 17230.03 + Deposits payable (2): 15960.96 + Deposits payable (2): 17200.52

- The transaction sub-equation includes the Cash account with the Order 9 to the Order 15 and the Deposits payable account with the Order 114 to the Order 120. Because the balances of the Cash account with the Order 12 and the Order 117 are zero, the second transaction sub-equation is:

  Cash (1): 28500.03 + Cash (1): 15620.65 + Cash (1): 27700.11+ Cash (1):

11710.41 + Cash (1): 15720.23 + Cash (1): 16510.35 = Deposits payable (2): 28500.03 + Deposits payable (2): 15620.65 + Deposits payable (2): 27700.11+ Deposits payable (2): 11710.41 + Deposits payable (2): 15720.23 + Deposits payable (2): 16510.35

- The transaction sub-equation includes the Cash account with the Order 16 to the Order 22 and the Deposits payable account with the Order 121 to the Order 127. Because the balances of the Cash account with the Order 19 and the Order 124 are zero, the third transaction sub-equation is:

Cash (1): 17980.41 + Cash (1): 26250.27 + Cash (1): 18790.58 + Cash (1): 18260.63 + Cash (1): 11230.11 + Cash (1): 11082.23 = Deposits payable (2): 17980.41+ Deposits payable (2): 26250.27 + Deposits payable (2): 18790.58 + Deposits payable (2): 18260.63 + Deposits payable (2): 11230.11 + Deposits payable (2): 11082.23

- The transaction sub-equation includes the Cash account with the Order 23 to the Order 29 and the Deposits payable account with the Order 128 to the Order 134. Because the balances of the Cash account with the Order 23 and the Order 128 are zero, the fourth transaction sub-equation is:

Cash (1): 16510.03 + Cash (1): 11960.84 + Cash (1): 28100.25 + Cash (1): 11230.32 + Cash (1): 1058058.2 + Cash (1): 1289.11 = Deposits payable (2): 16510.03 + Deposits payable (2): 11960.84 + Deposits payable (2): 28100.25 + Deposits payable (2): 11230.32 + Deposits payable (2): 1058058.2 + Deposits payable (2): 1289.11

- The transaction sub-equation includes the Cash account with the Order 2, 30, 33, 35, and 36 , the Share capital account with the Order 173, and the Deposits payable account with the Order 135, 138, 140, and 141. The fifth transaction sub-equation is:

Cash (1): 400000 + Cash (1): 1003.72 + Cash (1): 67873.98 + Cash (1): 3906.47 + Cash (1): 18783.78 = Share capital (3): 400000 + Deposits payable (2): 1003.72 + Deposits payable (2): 67873.98 + Deposits payable (2): 3906.47+ Deposits payable (2): 18783.78

- The transaction sub-equation includes the Cash account with the Order 38 to the Order 43 and the Bonds payable account with the Order 143 to the Order 148. The sixth transaction sub-equation is:

Cash (1): 6000 + Cash (1): 5000 + Cash (1): 7000 + Cash (1): 10000 + Cash (1): 8000 + Cash (1): 5000 = Bonds payable (2): 6000 + Bonds payable (2): 5000 + Bonds payable (2): 7000 + Bonds payable (2): 10000 + Bonds payable (2): 8000 + Bonds payable (2): 5000

- The transaction sub-equation includes the Cash account with the Order 44 to the Order 49 and the Bonds payable account with the Order 149 to the Order 154. The seventh transaction sub-equation is:

Cash (1): 9000 + Cash (1): 6000 + Cash (1): 3000 + Cash (1): 1000 + Cash (1): 3000 + Cash (1): 8000 = Bonds payable (2): 9000 + Bonds payable (2): 6000 + Bonds payable (2): 3000 + Bonds payable (2): 1000 + Bonds payable (2): 3000 + Bonds payable (2): 8000

- The transaction sub-equation includes the Cash account with the Order 50 to the Order 55 and the Bonds payable account with the Order 155 to the Order 160. The eighth transaction sub-equation is:

Cash (1): 3000 + Cash (1): 6000 + Cash (1): 5000 + Cash (1): 2000 + Cash (1): 7000 + Cash (1): 6000 = Bonds payable (2): 3000 + Bonds payable (2): 6000 + Bonds payable (2): 5000 + Bonds payable (2): 2000 + Bonds payable (2): 7000 + Bonds payable (2): 6000

- The transaction sub-equation includes the Cash account with the Order 56 to the Order 61 and the Bonds payable account with the Order 161 to the Order 166. The ninth transaction sub-equation is:

  Cash (1): 6000 + Cash (1): 3000 + Cash (1): 2000 + Cash (1): 6000 + Cash (1): 4000 + Cash (1): 7000 = Bonds payable (2): 6000 + Bonds payable (2): 3000 + Bonds payable (2): 2000 + Bonds payable (2): 6000 + Bonds payable (2): 4000 + Bonds payable (2): 7000

- The transaction sub-equation includes the Cash account with the Order 62 to the Order 66 and the Bonds payable account with the Order 167 to the Order 171. The tenth transaction sub-equation is:

  Cash (1): 4000 + Cash (1): 5000 + Cash (1): 3000 + Cash (1): 6000 + Cash (1): 4000 = Bonds payable (2): 6000 + Bonds payable (2): 3000 + Bonds payable (2): 2000 + Bonds payable (2): 6000 + Bonds payable (2): 4000

- The transaction sub-equation includes the Cash account with the Order 67 to the Order 75 and the part of the Share capital account with the Order 172. The eleventh transaction sub-equation is:

  Cash (1): 65625 + Cash (1): 23100 + Cash (1): 30000 + Cash (1): 36416.67 + Cash (1): 4037.5 + Cash (1): 410 + Cash (1): 201.67 + Cash (1): -45000 + Cash (1): -40000 = Share capital (3): 74790.84

  After entering this transaction, the new balance of the Share capital account with the Order 171 is $525,209.16 (= $600,000 - $74,790.84).

- The transaction sub-equation includes the Cash account with the Order 79 to the Order 82 and the Order 88 to the Order 89, the Bonds with the Order 96 to the Order 97, and the part of the Cash account with the Order 1. The twelfth  transaction sub-equation is:

Cash (1): -28061.55 + Cash (1): -27953.14 + Cash (1): -27312.77 + Cash (1): -34112.53 + Cash (1): -6000 + Cash (1): -5000 + Bonds (1): 6000 + Bonds (1): 5000 + Cash (1): 117439.99 = 0

After entering this transaction, the new balance of the Cash account with the Order 1 is $482,560.01 (= $600,000 - $117,439.99).

- The transaction sub-equation includes the Cash account with the Order 83 to the Order 88, the Supplies account with the Order 90, the Notes receivable account with the Order 91 to the Order 95, and the part of the Share capital account with the Order 170. The thirteenth transaction sub-equation is:

Cash (1): -250000 + Cash (1): -140000 + Cash (1): -200000 + Cash (1): -250000 + Cash (1): -170000 + Supplies (1): 102.31 + Notes receivable (1): 250000 + Notes receivable (1): 140000 + Notes receivable (1): 200000 + Notes receivable (1): 250000 + Notes receivable (1): 170000 = Share capital (3): 102.31

After entering this transaction, the new balance of the Share capital account with the Order 171 is $525,106.85 (= $525,209.16 - $102.31)

- The transaction sub-equation includes the Vehicle account with the Order 98 and 99, the Accumulated amortization: Vehicle account with the Order 100 and 101, the Computer account with the Order 102 to the Order 104, the Accumulated amortization: Computer account with the Order 105 and the Order 107, and the part of the Share capital account with the Order 172. The fourteenth transaction sub-equation is:

Vehicle (1): 45000 + Vehicle (1): 40000 + Accumulated amortization: Vehicle (1): -20250 + Accumulated amortization: Vehicle (1): -12666.67 + Computer (1): 2700

+ Computer (1): 1500 + Computer (1): 1400 + Accumulated amortization: Computer (1): -1912.5 + Accumulated amortization: Computer (1): -1062.5 + Accumulated amortization: Computer (1): -991.67 = Share capital (3): 53716.66

After entering this transaction, the new balance of the Share capital account with the Order 172 is \$471,390.19 (= \$525,106.85 - \$53,716.66)

- The transaction sub-equation includes the Cash account with the Order 76 to the Order 78, the rest (\$482,560.01) of the Cash account with the Order 1, the rest (\$471,390.13) of the Share capital account with the Order 171, and the Retained earnings (Conversion) account with the balance \$5,569.88. The fifteenth transaction sub-equation is:

Cash (1): -2700 + Cash (1): -1500 + Cash (1): -1400 + Cash (1): 482560.01 = Share capital (3): 471390.19 + Retained earnings (Conversion) (3): 5569.82

After completing this transaction, the dynamic accounting equation of the Business Bank1 on December 31, 2015 has entered into the database dcj05.

## 2.4.1.2 Brief Summary of the Business Bank1

The Figure 2.4-5 on the next pages shows cash received or paid by other members table which is in the public database dcj100. The Figure 2.4-6 on the page 78 shows cash flow statement of the Business Bank1 on December 31, 2015. The Figure 2.4-7 on the page 79 and page 80 shows cash account table of the Business Bank1 on December 31, 2015. The Figure 2.4-8 on the page 81 shows balance sheet table of the Business Bank1 on December 31, 2015.

```
SQLQuery1.sql - LIU...SS.dcj100 (sa (52))*  ×
  ⊟use dcj100
   select sum(amount) as sum0 from CashByMembers where Recorder='88-654304'
   select * from CashByMembers where Recorder='88-654304'
```

100 %  ▾

▦ Results ▤ Messages

| | sum0 |
|---|---|
| 1 | -1609115.51 |

| | IDM | Amount | Symbol | MultiSubaccount | Recorder | TransDate |
|---|---|---|---|---|---|---|
| 1 | 909876501 | -15900.10 | d | 909876501-d-deposits < Cash receipts from customers deposits < ... | 88-654304 | 2015-12-31 |
| 2 | 909876502 | -12200.11 | d | 909876502-d-deposits < Cash receipts from customers deposits < ... | 88-654304 | 2015-12-31 |
| 3 | 909876503 | -11800.23 | d | 909876503-d-deposits < Cash receipts from customers deposits < ... | 88-654304 | 2015-12-31 |
| 4 | 909876504 | -17230.03 | d | 909876504-d-deposits < Cash receipts from customers deposits < ... | 88-654304 | 2015-12-31 |
| 5 | 909876505 | -15960.96 | d | 909876505-d-deposits < Cash receipts from customers deposits < ... | 88-654304 | 2015-12-31 |
| 6 | 909876506 | -17200.52 | d | 909876506-d-deposits < Cash receipts from customers deposits < ... | 88-654304 | 2015-12-31 |
| 7 | 909876507 | -28500.03 | d | 909876507-d-deposits < Cash receipts from customers deposits < ... | 88-654304 | 2015-12-31 |
| 8 | 909876508 | -15620.65 | d | 909876508-d-deposits < Cash receipts from customers deposits < ... | 88-654304 | 2015-12-31 |
| 9 | 909876509 | -27700.11 | d | 909876509-d-deposits < Cash receipts from customers deposits < ... | 88-654304 | 2015-12-31 |
| 10 | 909876511 | -11710.41 | d | 909876511-d-deposits < Cash receipts from customers deposits < ... | 88-654304 | 2015-12-31 |
| 11 | 909876512 | -15720.23 | d | 909876512-d-deposits < Cash receipts from customers deposits < ... | 88-654304 | 2015-12-31 |
| 12 | 909876513 | -16510.35 | d | 909876513-d-deposits < Cash receipts from customers deposits < ... | 88-654304 | 2015-12-31 |
| 13 | 909876514 | -17980.41 | d | 909876514-d-deposits < Cash receipts from customers deposits < ... | 88-654304 | 2015-12-31 |
| 14 | 909876515 | -26250.27 | d | 909876515-d-deposits < Cash receipts from customers deposits < ... | 88-654304 | 2015-12-31 |
| 15 | 909876516 | -18790.58 | d | 909876516-d-deposits < Cash receipts from customers deposits < ... | 88-654304 | 2015-12-31 |
| 16 | 909876518 | -18260.63 | d | 909876518-d-deposits < Cash receipts from customers deposits < ... | 88-654304 | 2015-12-31 |
| 17 | 909876519 | -11230.11 | d | 909876519-d-deposits < Cash receipts from customers deposits < ... | 88-654304 | 2015-12-31 |
| 18 | 909876520 | -11082.23 | d | 909876520-d-deposits < Cash receipts from customers deposits < ... | 88-654304 | 2015-12-31 |
| 19 | 909876522 | -16510.03 | d | 909876522-d-deposits < Cash receipts from customers deposits < ... | 88-654304 | 2015-12-31 |
| 20 | 909876523 | -11960.84 | d | 909876523-d-deposits < Cash receipts from customers deposits < ... | 88-654304 | 2015-12-31 |
| 21 | 909876524 | -28100.25 | d | 909876524-d-deposits < Cash receipts from customers deposits < ... | 88-654304 | 2015-12-31 |
| 22 | 909876525 | -11230.32 | d | 909876525-d-deposits < Cash receipts from customers deposits < ... | 88-654304 | 2015-12-31 |
| 23 | 88-654300 | -2900.52 | d | 88-654300-d-deposits < Cash receipts from customers deposits < ... | 88-654304 | 2015-12-31 |
| 24 | 88-654302 | -1289.11 | d | 88-654302-d-deposits < Cash receipts from customers deposits < ... | 88-654304 | 2015-12-31 |
| 25 | 909876509 | -400000.00 | i | 909876509-i-owners < Cash receipts from owners < Financial activi... | 88-654304 | 2015-12-31 |
| 26 | 88-654303 | -1003.72 | d | 88-654303-d-deposits < Cash receipts from customers deposits < ... | 88-654304 | 2015-12-31 |
| 27 | 88-654306 | -67873.98 | d | 88-654306-d-deposits < Cash receipts from customers deposits < ... | 88-654304 | 2015-12-31 |

 Query executed successfully.

Figure 2.4-5   Business Bank1Cash Received or Paid by Other Members (Continue)

```
SQLQuery1.sql - LIU...SS.dcj100 (sa (52))*  ×
   -use dcj100
    select sum(amount) as sum0 from CashByMembers where Recorder='88-654304'
    select * from CashByMembers where Recorder='88-654304'
```

100 %   ▾

☐ Results  ⌐ Messages

| | sum0 |
|---|---|
| 1 | -1609115.51 |

| | IDM | Amount | Symbol | MultiSubaccount | Recorder | TransDate |
|---|---|---|---|---|---|---|
| 58 | 909876521 | -4000.00 | i | 909876521-i-bond13 < Cash receipts from issued bonds < Financi... | 88-654304 | 2015-12-31 |
| 59 | 88-654306 | -65625.00 | c | 88-654306-c-accrued interest < Cash receipts from note accrued i... | 88-654304 | 2015-12-31 |
| 60 | 88-654307 | -23100.00 | c | 88-654307-c-accrued interest < Cash receipts from note accrued i... | 88-654304 | 2015-12-31 |
| 61 | 88-654308 | -30000.00 | c | 88-654308-c-accrued interest < Cash receipts from note accrued i... | 88-654304 | 2015-12-31 |
| 62 | 88-654307 | -36416.67 | c | 88-654307-c-accrued interest < Cash receipts from note accrued i... | 88-654304 | 2015-12-31 |
| 63 | 88-654306 | -4037.50 | c | 88-654306-c-accrued interest < Cash receipts from note accrued i... | 88-654304 | 2015-12-31 |
| 64 | 88-654305 | -410.00 | c | 88-654305-c-interest of investment bond21 < Cash receipts from in... | 88-654304 | 2015-12-31 |
| 65 | 88-654305 | -201.67 | c | 88-654305-c-interest of investment bond22 < Cash receipts from in... | 88-654304 | 2015-12-31 |
| 66 | 88-654306 | 45000.00 | t | 88-654306-t-truck1 < Cash payments for machinery < Operating a... | 88-654304 | 2015-12-31 |
| 67 | 88-654306 | 40000.00 | t | 88-654306-t-car1 < Cash payments for machinery < Operating acti... | 88-654304 | 2015-12-31 |
| 68 | | 28061.55 | | Cash payments for operating expenses < Operating activities | 88-654304 | 2015-12-31 |
| 69 | | 27953.14 | | Cash payments for operating expenses < Operating activities | 88-654304 | 2015-12-31 |
| 70 | | 27312.77 | | Cash payments for operating expenses < Operating activities | 88-654304 | 2015-12-31 |
| 71 | 88-654303 | 34112.53 | n | 88-654303-n-tax < Cash payments for operating expenses < Oper... | 88-654304 | 2015-12-31 |
| 72 | 88-654305 | 6000.00 | n | 88-654305-n-investment bond21 < Cash payments for investments... | 88-654304 | 2015-12-31 |
| 73 | 88-654305 | 5000.00 | n | 88-654305-n-investment bond22 < Cash payments for investments... | 88-654304 | 2015-12-31 |
| 74 | 909876507 | -117439.99 | i | 909876507-i-owners < Cash receipts from owners < Financial activi... | 88-654304 | 2015-12-31 |
| 75 | 88-654306 | 250000.00 | n | 88-654306-n-notes1 < Cash payments to notes lenders < Operatin... | 88-654304 | 2015-12-31 |
| 76 | 88-654307 | 140000.00 | n | 88-654307-n-notes2 < Cash payments to notes lenders < Operatin... | 88-654304 | 2015-12-31 |
| 77 | 88-654308 | 200000.00 | n | 88-654308-n-notes3 < Cash payments to notes lenders < Operatin... | 88-654304 | 2015-12-31 |
| 78 | 88-654307 | 250000.00 | n | 88-654307-n-notes4 < Cash payments to notes lenders < Operatin... | 88-654304 | 2015-12-31 |
| 79 | 88-654306 | 170000.00 | n | 88-654306-n-notes5 < Cash payments to notes lenders < Operatin... | 88-654304 | 2015-12-31 |
| 80 | 88-654306 | 2700.00 | t | 88-654306-t-computer server2 < Cash payments for machinery < ... | 88-654304 | 2015-12-31 |
| 81 | 88-654306 | 1500.00 | t | 88-654306-t-computer2 < Cash payments for machinery < Operati... | 88-654304 | 2015-12-31 |
| 82 | 88-654306 | 1400.00 | t | 88-654306-t-computer3 < Cash payments for machinery < Operati... | 88-654304 | 2015-12-31 |
| 83 | 909876507 | -482560.01 | i | 909876507-i-owners < Cash receipts from owners < Financial activi... | 88-654304 | 2015-12-31 |
| 84 | 88-654300 | -1055157.68 | d | 88-654300-d-deposits < Cash receipts from customers deposits < ... | 88-654304 | 2015-12-31 |

⊘ Query executed successfully.

Figure 2.4-5  Business Bank1 Cash Received or Paid by Other Members

Cash Flow Statement

| Cash Flows Statement Year Ended 2015-12-31 | |
|---|---|
| **Operating activities** | |
| Cash payments for machinery | -$90,600.00 |
| Cash payments for operating expenses | -$117,439.99 |
| Cash payments to notes lenders | -$1,010,000.00 |
| Cash receipts from customers deposits | $1,528,364.66 |
| Cash receipts from note accrued interest (customers) | $159,179.17 |
| Net cash provided by Operating activities | $469,503.84 |
| | |
| Investing activities | |
| Cash payments for investments | -$11,000.00 |
| Cash receipts from investments | $611.67 |
| Net cash provided by Investing activities | -$10,388.33 |
| | |
| Financial activities | |
| Cash receipts from issued bonds | $150,000.00 |
| Cash receipts from owners | $1,000,000.00 |
| Net cash provided by Financial activities | $1,150,000.00 |
| | |
| Net change in cash | $1,609,115.51 |
| Cash, Begining | $0.00 |
| Cash, Ending | $1,609,115.51 |

Figure 2.4-6   Business Bank1 Cash Flows Statement

Cash

| | ID | Multi-Name | Amount | Balance | General ID | Transaction Date |
|---|---|---|---|---|---|---|
| ▸ | 1 | 909876501-d-deposits < Cash receipts from customers deposits < Operating ... | $15,900.10 | $15,900.10 | 3 | 2015-12-31 |
| | 2 | 909876502-d-deposits < Cash receipts from customers deposits < Operating ... | $12,200.11 | $28,100.21 | 3 | 2015-12-31 |
| | 3 | 909876503-d-deposits < Cash receipts from customers deposits < Operating ... | $11,800.23 | $39,900.44 | 3 | 2015-12-31 |
| | 4 | 909876504-d-deposits < Cash receipts from customers deposits < Operating ... | $17,230.03 | $57,130.47 | 3 | 2015-12-31 |
| | 5 | 909876505-d-deposits < Cash receipts from customers deposits < Operating ... | $15,960.96 | $73,091.43 | 3 | 2015-12-31 |
| | 6 | 909876506-d-deposits < Cash receipts from customers deposits < Operating ... | $17,200.52 | $90,291.95 | 3 | 2015-12-31 |
| | 7 | 909876507-d-deposits < Cash receipts from customers deposits < Operating ... | $28,500.03 | $118,791.98 | 5 | 2015-12-31 |
| | 8 | 909876508-d-deposits < Cash receipts from customers deposits < Operating ... | $15,620.65 | $134,412.63 | 5 | 2015-12-31 |
| | 9 | 909876509-d-deposits < Cash receipts from customers deposits < Operating ... | $27,700.11 | $162,112.74 | 5 | 2015-12-31 |
| | 10 | 909876511-d-deposits < Cash receipts from customers deposits < Operating ... | $11,710.41 | $173,823.15 | 5 | 2015-12-31 |
| | 11 | 909876512-d-deposits < Cash receipts from customers deposits < Operating ... | $15,720.23 | $189,543.38 | 5 | 2015-12-31 |
| | 12 | 909876513-d-deposits < Cash receipts from customers deposits < Operating ... | $16,510.35 | $206,053.73 | 5 | 2015-12-31 |
| | 13 | 909876514-d-deposits < Cash receipts from customers deposits < Operating ... | $17,980.41 | $224,034.14 | 6 | 2015-12-31 |
| | 14 | 909876515-d-deposits < Cash receipts from customers deposits < Operating ... | $26,250.27 | $250,284.41 | 6 | 2015-12-31 |
| | 15 | 909876516-d-deposits < Cash receipts from customers deposits < Operating ... | $18,790.58 | $269,074.99 | 6 | 2015-12-31 |
| | 16 | 909876518-d-deposits < Cash receipts from customers deposits < Operating ... | $18,260.63 | $287,335.62 | 6 | 2015-12-31 |
| | 17 | 909876519-d-deposits < Cash receipts from customers deposits < Operating ... | $11,230.11 | $298,565.73 | 6 | 2015-12-31 |
| | 18 | 909876520-d-deposits < Cash receipts from customers deposits < Operating ... | $11,082.23 | $309,647.96 | 6 | 2015-12-31 |
| | 19 | 909876522-d-deposits < Cash receipts from customers deposits < Operating ... | $16,510.03 | $326,157.99 | 7 | 2015-12-31 |
| | 20 | 909876523-d-deposits < Cash receipts from customers deposits < Operating ... | $11,960.84 | $338,118.83 | 7 | 2015-12-31 |
| | 21 | 909876524-d-deposits < Cash receipts from customers deposits < Operating ... | $28,100.25 | $366,219.08 | 7 | 2015-12-31 |
| | 22 | 909876525-d-deposits < Cash receipts from customers deposits < Operating ... | $11,230.32 | $377,449.40 | 7 | 2015-12-31 |
| | 23 | 88-654300-d-deposits < Cash receipts from customers deposits < Operating a... | $2,900.52 | $380,349.92 | 7 | 2015-12-31 |
| | 24 | 88-654302-d-deposits < Cash receipts from customers deposits < Operating a... | $1,289.11 | $381,639.03 | 7 | 2015-12-31 |

Figure 2.4-7   Business Bank1 Cash Account Table (Continue)

Cash

| ID | Multi-Name | Amount | Balance | General ID | Transaction Date |
|----|-----------|--------|---------|------------|------------------|
| 61 | 88-654308-c-accrued interest < Cash receipts from note accrued interest (cust... | $30,000.00 | $1,141,931.98 | 14 | 2015-12-31 |
| 62 | 88-654307-c-accrued interest < Cash receipts from note accrued interest (cust... | $36,416.67 | $1,178,348.65 | 14 | 2015-12-31 |
| 63 | 88-654306-c-accrued interest < Cash receipts from note accrued interest (cust.. | $4,037.50 | $1,182,386.15 | 14 | 2015-12-31 |
| 64 | 88-654305-c-interest of investment bond21 < Cash receipts from investments ... | $410.00 | $1,182,796.15 | 14 | 2015-12-31 |
| 65 | 88-654305-c-interest of investment bond22 < Cash receipts from investments ... | $201.67 | $1,182,997.82 | 14 | 2015-12-31 |
| 66 | 88-654306-t-truck1 < Cash payments for machinery < Operating activities | -$45,000.00 | $1,137,997.82 | 14 | 2015-12-31 |
| 67 | 88-654306-t-car1 < Cash payments for machinery < Operating activities | -$40,000.00 | $1,097,997.82 | 14 | 2015-12-31 |
| 68 | Cash payments for operating expenses < Operating activities | -$28,061.55 | $1,069,936.27 | 15 | 2015-12-31 |
| 69 | Cash payments for operating expenses < Operating activities | -$27,953.14 | $1,041,983.13 | 15 | 2015-12-31 |
| 70 | Cash payments for operating expenses < Operating activities | -$27,312.77 | $1,014,670.36 | 15 | 2015-12-31 |
| 71 | 88-654303-n-tax < Cash payments for operating expenses < Operating activiti... | -$34,112.53 | $980,557.83 | 15 | 2015-12-31 |
| 72 | 88-654305-n-investment bond21 < Cash payments for investments < Investing... | -$6,000.00 | $974,557.83 | 15 | 2015-12-31 |
| 73 | 88-654305-n-investment bond22 < Cash payments for investments < Investing... | -$5,000.00 | $969,557.83 | 15 | 2015-12-31 |
| 74 | 909876507-i-owners < Cash receipts from owners < Financial activities | $117,439.99 | $1,086,997.82 | 15 | 2015-12-31 |
| 75 | 88-654306-n-notes1 < Cash payments to notes lenders < Operating activities | -$250,000.00 | $836,997.82 | 16 | 2015-12-31 |
| 76 | 88-654307-n-notes2 < Cash payments to notes lenders < Operating activities | -$140,000.00 | $696,997.82 | 16 | 2015-12-31 |
| 77 | 88-654308-n-notes3 < Cash payments to notes lenders < Operating activities | -$200,000.00 | $496,997.82 | 16 | 2015-12-31 |
| 78 | 88-654307-n-notes4 < Cash payments to notes lenders < Operating activities | -$250,000.00 | $246,997.82 | 16 | 2015-12-31 |
| 79 | 88-654306-n-notes5 < Cash payments to notes lenders < Operating activities | -$170,000.00 | $76,997.82 | 16 | 2015-12-31 |
| 80 | 88-654306-t-computer server2 < Cash payments for machinery < Operating a... | -$2,700.00 | $74,297.82 | 18 | 2015-12-31 |
| 81 | 88-654306-t-computer2 < Cash payments for machinery < Operating activities | -$1,500.00 | $72,797.82 | 18 | 2015-12-31 |
| 82 | 88-654306-t-computer3 < Cash payments for machinery < Operating activities | -$1,400.00 | $71,397.82 | 18 | 2015-12-31 |
| 83 | 909876507-i-owners < Cash receipts from owners < Financial activities | $482,560.01 | $553,957.83 | 18 | 2015-12-31 |
| 84 | 88-654300-d-deposits < Cash receipts from customers deposits < Operating a... | $1,055,157.68 | $1,609,115.51 | 19 | 2015-12-31 |

Figure 2.4-7   Business Bank1 Cash Account Table

Balance Sheet

| | As at 12/31/2015 |
|---|---|
| **ASSETS** | |
| Current assets | |
| Cash | $1,609,115.51 |
| Supplies | $102.31 |
| Notes receivable | $1,010,000.00 |
| Account receivable | $0.00 |
| | $2,619,217.82 |
| Long term investments | |
| Bonds | $11,000.00 |
| Equipment | |
| Vehicle | $85,000.00 |
| Accumulated amortization: Vehicle | -$32,916.67 |
| Computer | $5,600.00 |
| Accumulated amortization: Computer | -$3,966.67 |
| | $53,716.66 |
| Total Assets | $2,683,934.48 |
| LIABILITIES | |
| Current liabilities | |
| Account payable | $0.00 |
| Deposits payable | $1,528,364.66 |
| | $1,528,364.66 |
| Long term liabilities | |
| Bonds payable | $150,000.00 |
| Total Liability | $1,678,364.66 |
| SHAREHOLDERS' EQUITY | |
| Owners capital | |
| Share capital | $1,000,000.00 |
| Retained earnings (Conversion) | $5,569.82 |
| | $1,005,569.82 |
| Retined earnings | $0.00 |
| Accumulated other comprehensive income | $0.00 |
| Total Shareholders' Equity | $1,005,569.82 |
| Total Liabilities and Shareholders' Equity | $2,683,934.48 |

Figure 2.4-8　Business Bank1 Balance Sheet Statement

## 2.4.2 Sample of the Business Bank2

The Business Bank2 has total share capital $900,000 and three shareholders of the individual A11, the individual A17, and the Business Bank1. Their percentages of the share capital are 40%, 25%, and 35% respectively.

## 2.4.2.1 Conversion of the Business Bank2

The Business Bank2 will convert to the MathAccounting software on January 1, 2016, so I design a reference table, seeing the Figure 2.4-9 on this page and the next page, in order to enter its dynamic accounting equation on December 31, 2015 into the database dcj06.

| Order | Class | Account Name (**Subtotal Name**) | Balance | Row |
|---|---|---|---|---|
| **1** | **1** | **(Current assets)** | - | **103** |
| 2 | 1 | Cash | 390884.49 | 104 |
| 3 | 1 | Supplies | 84.16 | 106 |
| 4 | 1 | Business bank reserves receivable | 0 | 108 |
| 5 | 1 | Accrued interest receivable | 0 | 110 |
| 6 | 1 | Notes receivable | 960000.00 | 112 |
| **7** | **1** | **(Long term investments)** | - | **141** |
| 8 | 1 | Bonds | 29000.00 | 143 |
| **9** | **1** | **(Equipment)** | - | **171** |
| 10 | 1 | Vehicle | 78000.00 | 172 |
| 11 | 1 | Accumulated amortization: Vehicle | -28066.67 | 173 |
| 12 | 1 | Computer | 5900.00 | 174 |
| 13 | 1 | Accumulated amortization: Computer | -3687.5 | 175 |
| **14** | **2** | **(Current liabilities)** | - | **203** |
| 15 | 2 | Business bank reserves payable | 0 | 204 |
| 16 | 2 | Deposits payable | 387783.31 | 206 |
| 17 | 2 | Accrued interest payable | 0 | 208 |
| 18 | 2 | Account payable | 0 | 210 |
| 19 | 2 | Tax payable | 0 | 212 |
| **20** | **2** | **(Long term liabilities)** | - | **251** |
| 21 | 2 | Bonds payable | 140000.00 | 252 |
| **22** | **3** | **(Owners' capital)** | - | **303** |
| 23 | 3 | Share capital | 900000.00 | 304 |
| 24 | 3 | Retained earnings (Conversion) | 4331.17 | 306 |
| **25** | **4** | **(Revenues)** | - | **403** |
| 26 | 4 | Sales (notes interest) | 0 | 404 |
| **27** | **5** | **(Cost)** | - | **431** |
| 28 | 5 | Cost of notes interest | 0 | 432 |
| **29** | **5** | **(Operating and administrative expenses)** | - | **453** |
| 30 | 5 | Travelling expenses | 0 | 454 |
| 31 | 5 | Other expenses | 0 | 456 |
| 32 | 5 | Office supplies expenses | 0 | 458 |
| 33 | 5 | Salary expenses | 0 | 460 |

| 34 | 5 | Bond interest expenses | 0 | 462 |
|---|---|---|---|---|
| 35 | 5 | Amortization expenses | 0 | 464 |
| 36 | 5 | Interest expenses | 0 | 466 |
| **37** | **4** | **(Other income)** | - | **475** |
| 38 | 4 | Investment incomes | 0 | 476 |
| **39** | **5** | **(Tax)** | - | **600** |
| 40 | 5 | Tax expenses | 0 | 602 |

Figure 2.4-9    Business Bank2 Converting Reference Table

From the Figure 2.4-9, there are total 29 accounts among which the balances of all expenses accounts are zero. Here, the Sales (notes interest) account should be actually recorded as the Accrued interest receivable (Notes) account and the Cost of notes interest account should also be recorded as the Accrued interest payable (Deposits) account at the end of every month in this book. The difference of them is gross income. For simplification, I only record the balances of the Sales (notes interest) account and Cost of notes interest account at the end of the fiscal year.

In this pure digital currency model, the balance of the Business bank reserves payable account should be zero. The balance of the Deposits payable does not include the balance of the Cash itself for the Business Bank2. In addition, the balance of the Retained earnings should be added to the balance of the Share capital, and its balance should be zero prior to conversion. However, for knowing the original share capital and the distinguishing retained earnings after conversion, I keep the Retained earnings account prior to conversion and give it a different name of the Retained earnings (Conversion).

The Notes receivable, which is put in the subtotal name of the "Current assets" for simplification, has three one-level subaccounts of the "Note21-88-654306" ($220,000, beginning on March 1, 2013, three years, annual interest rate 9%, and accrued interest $56,100.00), the "Note22-88-654307" ($240,000, beginning on May 1, 2014, five years, annual interest rate 9%, and accrued interest $36,000.00), the "Note23-88-654308" ($180,000, beginning on June 1, 2014, four years, annual interest rate 9%, and accrued interest $25,650.00), the "Note24-88-654308" ($200,000, beginning on July 1, 2014, four years, annual interest rate 9.1%, and accrued interest $27,300.00), and the "Note25-88-654309" ($120,000, beginning on September 1, 2015, three years, annual interest rate 9.4%, and accrued interest $3,760).

The Bonds account has five one-level subaccounts of the "Bond11 (issued by the Business Bank1 and purchased $7,000, beginning on February 1, 2014, five years, and annual interest rate 4%), the "Bond12" (issued by the Business Bank1 and purchased $3,000, beginning on July 1, 2014, five years, and annual interest rate 4.2%), the "Bond13" (issued by the Business Bank1 and purchased $6,000, beginning on September 1, 2015, six years, and annual interest rate 4.5%), the "Bond31" (issued by the Company1 and purchased $5,000, beginning on July 1, 2014, five years, and annual interest rate 4.2%), and the "Bond41" (issued by the Company2 and purchased $8,000, beginning on September 1, 2015, six years, and annual interest rate 4.5%). Accordingly, the balance of the Accrued interest payable account is zero prior to the conversion.

The Business Bank2 has one truck2 (five years, straight line, 27 months) and one car2 (five years, straight line, 18 months), so the multi-subaccount names of the Vehicle parent account are the "Truck21 < Truck2 < Truck" and the "Car21 < Car2 < Car" respectively. Their balances are $40,000 and $38,000 respectively. Accordingly, the multi-subaccount names of the Accumulated amortization: Vehicle account are the "Truck21-accumulated amortization < Truck2-accumulated amortization < Truck-accumulated amortization" and the "Car21-accumulated amortization < Car2-accumulated amortization < Car-accumulated amortization". Their balances are -$16,666.67 and -$11,400 respectively.

The Business Bank2 has one computer server1 (two years, straight line, 15 months), one computer1 (two years, straight line, 15 months), and one computer2 (two years, straight line, 15 months), so the multi-subaccount names of the Computer parent account are the "Computer server11 < Computer server1 < Computer server", the "Computer11 < Computer1", and the "Computer21 < Computer2" respectively. Their balances are $2,800, $1,600, and $1,500 respectively. Accordingly, the multi-subaccount names of the Accumulated amortization: Computer account are the "Computer server21-accumulated amortization < Computer server2-accumulated amortization < Computer server-accumulated amortization", the "Computer21-accumulated amortization < Computer2 - accumulated amortization", and the "Computer31-accumulated amortization < Computer3-accumulated amortization". Their balances are respectively -$1,750, -$1,000, and -$937.5.

The balance of the Deposits payable account is equal to total cash in the Business2 minus the Business Bank2's cash itself on January 1, 2016. The Business Bank2 only pays $120 for every social member' primary account at the end of each year.

The Business Bank2 issued two bonds, so the Bonds payable has two one-level subaccounts of the "Bond21-payable" ($80,000, beginning on May 1, 2014, five years, and annual interest rate 4.1%) and the "Bond22-payable" ($60,000, beginning on February 1, 2015, five years, and annual interest rate 4.4%). Of course, the Bonds payable account has also many two-level subaccounts, seeing the Figure 2.4-10 on this page and the next page, which shows the detail information of the issued bonds.

| Order | Bond | Amount | Term | Purchaser Name | Identity |
|-------|------|--------|------|----------------|----------|
| 1 | Bond21 | 9000 | May 1, 2014, Five years, 4.1% annually | Government1 | 88-654302 |
| 2 | Bond21 | 8000 | May 1, 2014, Five years, 4.1% annually | Tax Bureau | 88-654303 |
| 3 | Bond21 | 6000 | May 1, 2014, Five years, 4.1% annually | Business Bank1 | 88-654304 |
| 4 | Bond21 | 9000 | May 1, 2014, Five years, 4.1% annually | Company1 | 88-654306 |
| 5 | Bond21 | 12000 | May 1, 2014, Five years, 4.1% annually | Company3 | 88-654308 |
| 6 | Bond21 | 7000 | May 1, 2014, Five years, 4.1% annually | Proprietorship2 | 88-654310 |
| 7 | Bond21 | 4000 | May 1, 2014, Five years, 4.1% annually | A7 | 909876507 |
| 8 | Bond21 | 6000 | May 1, 2014, Five years, 4.1% annually | A9 | 909876509 |
| 9 | Bond21 | 3000 | May 1, 2014, Five years, 4.1% annually | A13 | 909876513 |
| 10 | Bond21 | 5000 | May 1, 2014, Five years, 4.1% annually | A14 | 909876514 |
| 11 | Bond21 | 3000 | May 1, 2014, Five years, 4.1% annually | A18 | 909876518 |
| 12 | Bond21 | 8000 | May 1, 2014, Five years, 4.1% annually | A20 | 909876520 |
| 13 | Bond22 | 5000 | February 1, 2015, Five years, 4.4% annually | Business Bank1 | 88-654304 |
| 14 | Bond22 | 6000 | February 1, 2015, Five years, 4.4% annually | Company2 | 88-654307 |
| 15 | Bond22 | 8000 | February 1, 2015, Five years, 4.4% annually | Proprietorship1 | 88-654309 |
| 16 | Bond22 | 4000 | February 1, 2015, Five years, 4.4% annually | Proprietorship2 | 88-654310 |
| 17 | Bond22 | 6000 | February 1, 2015, Five years, 4.4% annually | A3 | 909876503 |

| | | February 1, 2015, Five years, 4.4% | | |
|---|---|---|---|---|
| 18 | Bond22 | 7000 | February 1, 2015, Five years, 4.4% annually | A4 | 909876504 |
| 19 | Bond22 | 6000 | February 1, 2015, Five years, 4.4% annually | A6 | 909876506 |
| 20 | Bond22 | 8000 | February 1, 2015, Five years, 4.4% annually | A11 | 909876511 |
| 21 | Bond22 | 3000 | February 1, 2015, Five years, 4.4% annually | A19 | 909876519 |
| 22 | Bond22 | 7000 | February 1, 2015, Five years, 4.4% annually | A21 | 909876521 |
| **23** | **Total** | **140000** | | | |

Figure 2.4-10   Business Bank2 Issued Bonds Information Table

Following above information, I can build a table of the multi-subaccount names, seeing the Figure 2.4-11 on this page and the next pages.

| Order | Class | Multi-subaccount Name | Parent Name | Lowest Subaccount Balance |
|---|---|---|---|---|
| 1 | 1 | 909876511-i-owners < Cash receipts from owners < Financial activities | Cash | 360000.00 |
| 2 | 1 | 909876517-i-owners < Cash receipts from owners < Financial activities | Cash | 225000.00 |
| 3 | 1 | 88-654304-i-owners < Cash receipts from owners < Financial activities | Cash | 315000.00 |
| 4 | 1 | 909876501-d-deposits < Cash receipts from customers deposits < Operating activities | Cash | 12000.15 |
| 5 | 1 | 909876502-d-deposits < Cash receipts from customers deposits < Operating activities | Cash | 16500.55 |
| 6 | 1 | 909876503-d-deposits < Cash receipts from customers deposits < Operating activities | Cash | 16260.10 |
| 7 | 1 | 909876504-d-deposits < Cash receipts from customers deposits < Operating activities | Cash | 11400.61 |
| 8 | 1 | 909876505-d-deposits < Cash receipts from customers deposits < Operating activities | Cash | 11970.23 |
| 9 | 1 | 909876506-d-deposits < Cash receipts from customers deposits < Operating activities | Cash | 11100.54 |
| 10 | 1 | 909876507-d-deposits < Cash receipts from customers deposits < Operating activities | Cash | 0 |
| 11 | 1 | 909876508-d-deposits < Cash receipts from customers deposits < Operating activities | Cash | 11000.11 |
| 12 | 1 | 909876509-d-deposits < Cash receipts from customers deposits < Operating activities | Cash | 0 |
| 13 | 1 | 909876510-d-deposits < Cash receipts from customers deposits < Operating activities | Cash | 28600.21 |
| 14 | 1 | 909876511-d-deposits < Cash receipts from customers deposits < Operating activities | Cash | 14520.56 |
| 15 | 1 | 909876512-d-deposits < Cash receipts from customers deposits < Operating activities | Cash | 11680.34 |
| 16 | 1 | 909876513-d-deposits < Cash receipts from customers deposits < Operating activities | Cash | 11810.18 |
| 17 | 1 | 909876514-d-deposits < Cash receipts from customers deposits < Operating activities | Cash | 12200.45 |
| 18 | 1 | 909876515-d-deposits < Cash receipts from customers deposits < Operating activities | Cash | 0 |
| 19 | 1 | 909876516-d-deposits < Cash receipts from customers deposits < Operating activities | Cash | 11300.74 |
| 20 | 1 | 909876517-d-deposits < Cash receipts from customers deposits < Operating activities | Cash | 26150.88 |

| 21 | 1 | 909876518-d-deposits < Cash receipts from customers deposits < Operating activities | Cash | 10510.99 |
|---|---|---|---|---|
| 22 | 1 | 909876519-d-deposits < Cash receipts from customers deposits < Operating activities | Cash | 16910.92 |
| 23 | 1 | 909876520-d-deposits < Cash receipts from customers deposits < Operating activities | Cash | 15900.51 |
| 24 | 1 | 909876521-d-deposits < Cash receipts from customers deposits < Operating activities | Cash | 26210.18 |
| 25 | 1 | 909876522-d-deposits < Cash receipts from customers deposits < Operating activities | Cash | 11720.14 |
| 26 | 1 | 909876523-d-deposits < Cash receipts from customers deposits < Operating activities | Cash | 15150.21 |
| 27 | 1 | 909876524-d-deposits < Cash receipts from customers deposits < Operating activities | Cash | 0 |
| 28 | 1 | 909876525-d-deposits < Cash receipts from customers deposits < Operating activities | Cash | 16150.25 |
| 29 | 1 | 88-654301-d-deposits < Cash receipts from customers deposits < Operating activities | Cash | 4090.65 |
| 30 | 1 | 88-654302-d-deposits < Cash receipts from customers deposits < Operating activities | Cash | 610.08 |
| 31 | 1 | 88-654303-d-deposits < Cash receipts from customers deposits < Operating activities | Cash | 1117.96 |
| 32 | 1 | 88-654304-d-deposits < Cash receipts from customers deposits < Operating activities | Cash | 0 |
| 33 | 1 | 88-654305-d-deposits < Cash receipts from customers deposits < Operating activities | Cash | 0 |
| 34 | 1 | 88-654306-d-deposits < Cash receipts from customers deposits < Operating activities | Cash | 0 |
| 35 | 1 | 88-654307-d-deposits < Cash receipts from customers deposits < Operating activities | Cash | 47393.19 |
| 36 | 1 | 88-654308-d-deposits < Cash receipts from customers deposits < Operating activities | Cash | 6753.89 |
| 37 | 1 | 88-654309-d-deposits < Cash receipts from customers deposits < Operating activities | Cash | 0 |
| 38 | 1 | 88-654310-d-deposits < Cash receipts from customers deposits < Operating activities | Cash | 8768.69 |
| 39 | 1 | 88-654302-i-bond21 < Cash receipts from issued bonds < Financial activities | Cash | 9000.00 |
| 40 | 1 | 88-654303-i-bond21 < Cash receipts from issued bonds < Financial activities | Cash | 8000.00 |
| 41 | 1 | 88-654304-i-bond21 < Cash receipts from issued bonds < Financial activities | Cash | 6000.00 |
| 42 | 1 | 88-654306-i-bond21 < Cash receipts from issued bonds < Financial activities | Cash | 9000.00 |
| 43 | 1 | 88-654308-i-bond21 < Cash receipts from issued bonds < Financial activities | Cash | 12000.00 |
| 44 | 1 | 88-654310-i-bond21 < Cash receipts from issued bonds < Financial activities | Cash | 7000.00 |
| 45 | 1 | 909876507-i-bond21 < Cash receipts from issued bonds < Financial activities | Cash | 4000.00 |
| 46 | 1 | 909876509-i-bond21 < Cash receipts from issued bonds < Financial activities | Cash | 6000.00 |
| 47 | 1 | 909876513-i-bond21 < Cash receipts from issued bonds < Financial activities | Cash | 3000.00 |
| 48 | 1 | 909876514-i-bond21 < Cash receipts from issued bonds < Financial activities | Cash | 5000.00 |
| 49 | 1 | 909876518-i-bond21 < Cash receipts from issued bonds < Financial activities | Cash | 3000.00 |
| 50 | 1 | 909876520-i-bond21 < Cash receipts from issued bonds < Financial activities | Cash | 8000.00 |
| 51 | 1 | 88-654304-i-bond22 < Cash receipts from issued bonds < Financial activities | Cash | 5000.00 |
| 52 | 1 | 88-654307-i-bond22 < Cash receipts from issued bonds < Financial activities | Cash | 6000.00 |

| | | | | |
|---|---|---|---|---|
| 53 | 1 | 88-654309-i-bond22 < Cash receipts from issued bonds < Financial activities | Cash | 8000.00 |
| 54 | 1 | 88-654310-i-bond22 < Cash receipts from issued bonds < Financial activities | Cash | 4000.00 |
| 55 | 1 | 909876503-i-bond22 < Cash receipts from issued bonds < Financial activities | Cash | 6000.00 |
| 56 | 1 | 909876504-i-bond22 < Cash receipts from issued bonds < Financial activities | Cash | 7000.00 |
| 57 | 1 | 909876506-i-bond22 < Cash receipts from issued bonds < Financial activities | Cash | 6000.00 |
| 58 | 1 | 909876511-i-bond22 < Cash receipts from issued bonds < Financial activities | Cash | 8000.00 |
| 59 | 1 | 909876519-i-bond22 < Cash receipts from issued bonds < Financial activities | Cash | 3000.00 |
| 60 | 1 | 909876521-i-bond22 < Cash receipts from issued bonds < Financial activities | Cash | 7000.00 |
| 61 | 1 | 88-654306-c-accrued interest < Cash receipts from note accrued interest (customers) < Operating activities | Cash | 56100.00 |
| 62 | 1 | 88-654307-c-accrued interest < Cash receipts from note accrued interest (customers) < Operating activities | Cash | 36000.00 |
| 63 | 1 | 88-654308-c-accrued interest < Cash receipts from note accrued interest (customers) < Operating activities | Cash | 25650.00 |
| 64 | 1 | 88-654307-c-accrued interest < Cash receipts from note accrued interest (customers) < Operating activities | Cash | 27300.00 |
| 65 | 1 | 88-654306-c-accrued interest < Cash receipts from note accrued interest (customers) < Operating activities | Cash | 3760.00 |
| 66 | 1 | 88-654304-c-interest of investment bond11 < Cash receipts from investments < Investing activities | Cash | 536.67 |
| 67 | 1 | 88-654304-c-interest of investment bond12 < Cash receipts from Investments < Investing activities | Cash | 189.00 |
| 68 | 1 | 88-654304-c-interest of investment bond13 < Cash receipts from investments < Investing activities | Cash | 90.00 |
| 69 | 1 | 88-654306-c-interest of investment bond31 < Cash receipts from investments < Investing activities | Cash | 268.33 |
| 70 | 1 | 88-654307-c-interest of investment bond41 < Cash receipts from investments < Investing activities | Cash | 313.33 |
| 71 | 1 | 88-654306-t-truck2 < Cash payments for machinery < Operating activities | Cash | -40000.00 |
| 72 | 1 | 88-654306-t-car3 < Cash payments for machinery < Operating activities | Cash | -38000.00 |
| 73 | 1 | 88-654306-t-computer server1 < Cash payments for machinery < Operating activities | Cash | -2800.00 |
| 74 | 1 | 88-654306-t-computer1 < Cash payments for machinery < Operating activities | Cash | -1600.00 |
| 75 | 1 | 88-654306-t-computer2 < Cash payments for machinery < Operating activities | Cash | -1500.00 |
| 76 | 1 | Cash payments for operating expenses < Operating activities | Cash | -27634.61 |
| 77 | 1 | Cash payments for operating expenses < Operating activities | Cash | -26587.92 |
| 78 | 1 | Cash payments for operating expenses < Operating activities | Cash | -28312.35 |
| 79 | 1 | 88-654303-n-tax < Cash payments for operating expenses < Operating activities | Cash | -31671.27 |
| 80 | 1 | 88-654306-n-notes1 < Cash payments to notes lenders < Operating activities | Cash | -220000.00 |
| 81 | 1 | 88-654307-n-notes2 < Cash payments to notes lenders < Operating activities | Cash | -240000.00 |

| 82 | 1 | 88-654308-n-notes3 < Cash payments to notes lenders < Operating activities | Cash | -180000.00 |
|---|---|---|---|---|
| 83 | 1 | 88-654308-n-notes4 < Cash payments to notes lenders < Operating activities | Cash | -200000.00 |
| 84 | 1 | 88-654309-n-notes5 < Cash payments to notes lenders < Operating activities | Cash | -120000.00 |
| 85 | 1 | 88-654304-n-investment bond11 < Cash payments for investments < Investing activities | Cash | -7000.00 |
| 86 | 1 | 88-654304-n-investment bond12 < Cash payments for investments < Investing activities | Cash | -3000.00 |
| 87 | 1 | 88-654304-n-investment bond13 < Cash payments for investments < Investing activities | Cash | -6000.00 |
| 88 | 1 | 88-654306-n-investment bond31 < Cash payments for investments < Investing activities | Cash | -5000.00 |
| 89 | 1 | 88-654307-n-investment bond41 < Cash payments for investments < Investing activities | Cash | -8000.00 |
| 90 | 1 | n | Supplies | 84.16 |
| 91 | 1 | Note11-88-654306 | Notes receivable | 220000.00 |
| 92 | 1 | Note12-88-654307 | Notes receivable | 240000.00 |
| 93 | 1 | Note13-88-654308 | Notes receivable | 180000.00 |
| 94 | 1 | Note14-88-654308 | Notes receivable | 200000.00 |
| 95 | 1 | Note15-88-654309 | Notes receivable | 120000.00 |
| 96 | 1 | Bond11 | Bonds | 7000.00 |
| 97 | 1 | Bond12 | Bonds | 3000.00 |
| 98 | 1 | Bond13 | Bonds | 6000.00 |
| 99 | 1 | Bond31 | Bonds | 5000.00 |
| 100 | 1 | Bond41 | Bonds | 8000.00 |
| 101 | 1 | Truck21 < Truck2 < Truck | Vehicle | 40000.00 |
| 102 | 1 | Car31 < Car3 < Car | Vehicle | 38000.00 |
| 103 | 1 | Truck21-accumulated amortization < Truck2-accumulated amortization < Truck-accumulated amortization | Accumulated amortization: Vehicle | -16666.67 |
| 104 | 1 | Car31-accumulated amortization < Car3-accumulated amortization < Car-accumulated amortization | Accumulated amortization: Vehicle | -11400.00 |
| 105 | 1 | Computer server11 < Computer server1 < Computer server | Computer | 2800.00 |
| 106 | 1 | Computer11 < Computer1 | Computer | 1600.00 |
| 107 | 1 | Computer21 < Computer2 | Computer | 1500.00 |
| 108 | 1 | Computer server11-accumulated amortization < Computer server1-accumulated amortization < Computer server-accumulated amortization | Accumulated amortization: Computer | -1750.00 |
| 109 | 1 | Computer11-accumulated amortization < Computer1-accumulated amortization | Accumulated amortization: Computer | -1000.00 |
| 110 | 1 | Computer21-accumulated amortization < Computer2-accumulated amortization | Accumulated amortization: Computer | -937.50 |
| 111 | 2 | Deposits-909876501 | Deposits payable | 12000.15 |
| 112 | 2 | Deposits-909876502 | Deposits payable | 16500.55 |
| 113 | 2 | Deposits-909876503 | Deposits payable | 16260.10 |
| 114 | 2 | Deposits-909876504 | Deposits payable | 11400.61 |
| 115 | 2 | Deposits-909876505 | Deposits payable | 11970.23 |
| 116 | 2 | Deposits-909876506 | Deposits payable | 11100.54 |

| 117 | 2 | Deposits-909876507 | Deposits payable | 0 |
|-----|---|--------------------|--------------------|-------|
| 118 | 2 | Deposits-909876508 | Deposits payable | 11000.11 |
| 119 | 2 | Deposits-909876509 | Deposits payable | 0 |
| 120 | 2 | Deposits-909876510 | Deposits payable | 28600.21 |
| 121 | 2 | Deposits-909876511 | Deposits payable | 14520.56 |
| 122 | 2 | Deposits-909876512 | Deposits payable | 11680.34 |
| 123 | 2 | Deposits-909876513 | Deposits payable | 11810.18 |
| 124 | 2 | Deposits-909876514 | Deposits payable | 12200.45 |
| 125 | 2 | Deposits-909876515 | Deposits payable | 0 |
| 126 | 2 | Deposits-909876516 | Deposits payable | 11300.74 |
| 127 | 2 | Deposits-909876517 | Deposits payable | 26150.88 |
| 128 | 2 | Deposits-909876518 | Deposits payable | 10510.99 |
| 129 | 2 | Deposits-909876519 | Deposits payable | 16910.92 |
| 130 | 2 | Deposits-909876520 | Deposits payable | 15900.51 |
| 131 | 2 | Deposits-909876521 | Deposits payable | 26210.18 |
| 132 | 2 | Deposits-909876522 | Deposits payable | 11720.14 |
| 133 | 2 | Deposits-909876523 | Deposits payable | 15150.21 |
| 134 | 2 | Deposits-909876524 | Deposits payable | 0 |
| 135 | 2 | Deposits-909876525 | Deposits payable | 16150.25 |
| 136 | 2 | Deposits-88-654301 | Deposits payable | 4090.63 |
| 137 | 2 | Deposits-88-654302 | Deposits payable | 610.08 |
| 138 | 2 | Deposits 88 654303 | Deposits payable | 1117.96 |
| 139 | 2 | Deposits-88-654304 | Deposits payable | 0 |
| 140 | 2 | Deposits-88-654305 | Deposits payable | 0 |
| 141 | 2 | Deposits-88-654306 | Deposits payable | 0 |
| 142 | 2 | Deposits-88-654307 | Deposits payable | 47393.19 |
| 143 | 2 | Deposits-88-654308 | Deposits payable | 6753.89 |
| 144 | 2 | Deposits-88-654309 | Deposits payable | 0 |
| 145 | 2 | Deposits-88-654310 | Deposits payable | 8768.69 |
| 146 | 2 | Bond 21-88-654302 < Bond21 | Bonds payable | 9000.00 |
| 147 | 2 | Bond21-88-654303 < Bond21 | Bonds payable | 8000.00 |
| 148 | 2 | Bond21-88-654305 < Bond21 | Bonds payable | 6000.00 |
| 149 | 2 | Bond21-88-654306 < Bond21 | Bonds payable | 9000.00 |
| 150 | 2 | Bond21-88-654308 < Bond21 | Bonds payable | 12000.00 |
| 151 | 2 | Bond21-88-654309 < Bond21 | Bonds payable | 7000.00 |
| 152 | 2 | Bond21-909876507 < Bond21 | Bonds payable | 4000.00 |
| 153 | 2 | Bond21-909876509 < Bond21 | Bonds payable | 6000.00 |
| 154 | 2 | Bond21-909876513 < Bond21 | Bonds payable | 3000.00 |
| 155 | 2 | Bond21-909876514 < Bond21 | Bonds payable | 5000.00 |
| 156 | 2 | Bond21-909876518 < Bond21 | Bonds payable | 3000.00 |

| 157 | 2 | Bond21-909876520 < Bond21 | Bonds payable | 8000.00 |
|---|---|---|---|---|
| 158 | 2 | Band22-88-654305 < Band22 | Bonds payable | 5000.00 |
| 159 | 2 | Bond22-88-654307 < Bond22 | Bonds payable | 6000.00 |
| 160 | 2 | Bond22-88-654309 < Bond22 | Bonds payable | 8000.00 |
| 161 | 2 | Bond22-88-654310 < Bond22 | Bonds payable | 4000.00 |
| 162 | 2 | Bond22-909876503 < Bond22 | Bonds payable | 6000.00 |
| 163 | 2 | Bond22-909876504 < Bond22 | Bonds payable | 7000.00 |
| 164 | 2 | Bond22-909876506 < Bond22 | Bonds payable | 6000.00 |
| 165 | 2 | Bond22-909876511 < Bond22 | Bonds payable | 8000.00 |
| 166 | 2 | Bond22-909876519 < Bond22 | Bonds payable | 3000.00 |
| 167 | 2 | Bond22-909876521 < Bond22 | Bonds payable | 7000.00 |
| 168 | 3 | Capital-909876511 | Share capital | 360000.00 |
| 169 | 3 | Capital-909876517 | Share capital | 225000.00 |
| 170 | 3 | Capital-88-654304 | Share capital | 315000.00 |
| 171 | 3 | n | Retained earnings (Conversion) | 4331.17 |
| 172 | 4 | Note21-interest incomes | Sales (notes interest) | 0 |
| 173 | 4 | Note22-interest incomes | Sales (notes interest) | 0 |
| 174 | 4 | Note23-interest incomes | Sales (notes interest) | 0 |
| 175 | 4 | Note24-interest incomes | Sales (notes interest) | 0 |
| 176 | 4 | Note25-interest incomes | Sales (notes interest) | 0 |
| 177 | 5 | Deposit interest expenses | Cost of notes interest | 0 |
| 178 | 5 | 909876512-travelling < Sales department-travelling | Travelling expenses | 0 |
| 179 | 5 | 909876511-other < Purchase department-other | Other expenses | 0 |
| 180 | 5 | 909876510-salary < Office department-salary | Salary expenses | 0 |
| 181 | 5 | Bond21-interest expenses | Bond interest expenses | 0 |
| 182 | 5 | Bond22-interest expenses | Bond interest expenses | 0 |
| 183 | 5 | Bond23-interest expenses | Bond interest expenses | 0 |
| 184 | 5 | Truck21-amortization < Truck2-amortization < Vehicle-truck-amortization | Amortization expenses | 0 |
| 185 | 5 | Car31-amortization < Car3-amortization < Vehicle-car-amortization | Amortization expenses | 0 |
| 186 | 5 | Computer server11-amortization < Computer server2-amortization < Computer-amortization | Amortization expenses | 0 |
| 187 | 5 | Computer11-amortization < Computer1-amortization < Computer-amortization | Amortization expenses | 0 |
| 188 | 5 | Computer21-amortization < Computer2-amortization < Computer-amortization | Amortization expenses | 0 |
| 189 | 4 | Accrued interest income-bond11 < Bonds | Investment incomes | 0 |
| 190 | 4 | Accrued interest income-bond12 < Bonds | Investment incomes | 0 |
| 191 | 4 | Accrued interest income-bond13 < Bonds | Investment incomes | 0 |
| 192 | 4 | Accrued interest income-bond31 < Bonds | Investment incomes | 0 |
| 193 | 4 | Accrued interest income-bond41 < Bonds | Investment incomes | 0 |

Figure 2.4-11   Business Bank2 Converting Multi-Subaccount Names Table

From the Figure 2.4-11, there are some accounts whose balances are zero. Their "MultiSubaccount name" forms all are the "n" during the conversion even if they should have the multi-subaccount names. Later, their multi-subaccount names can be entered following the need. Of course, you can choice not to enter these accounts during the conversion.

Please pay attention here. The lowest subaccounts of all parent accounts are sole, so the "MultiSubaccount name" form is the same "n" for all parent accounts without any subaccount. Therefore, there is only one "n" in in the Figure 2.4-11. However, I write all possible parent accounts, which have not any subaccount, into the table to provide detail information to readers.

If I do not need to understand the details of some three-level subaccounts of the Cash account or I cannot get the details of some three-level subaccounts of the Cash account during the conversion, then these multi-subaccount names cannot have any three-level subaccount and can have only two-level subaccounts. For example, amount of the multi-subaccount name with the Order 75 is the "Cash payments for operating expenses<Operating activities" and its balance is -$31,671.27 which is equal to the sum of the Tax expenses (cash paid), the Supplies (cash paid), and so on for the previous years.

Before entering the dynamic accounting equation on December 31, 2015 into the database dcj05, I first enter three initialization sub-equations.

Cash (1): 0 = Share capital (3): 0

Account receivable (1): 0 = Account payable (2): 0

0 = Sales (notes interest) (4): 0 – Cost of notes interest (5):0

From the Figure 2.4-9 and the Figure 2.4-11, the dynamic accounting equation on January 1, 2016 must be divided to the N transaction sub-equations because of the limitation of the MathAccounting software. Every sub-equation has maximum twelve items. All converting transaction sub-equations can be designed and written as following.

- The transaction sub-equation includes the Cash account with the Order 4 to the Order 10 and the Deposits payable account with the Order 111 to the Order 117. Because the balances of the Cash account with the Order 10 and the Order 117 are zero, the first transaction sub-equation is:

Cash (1): 12000.15 + Cash (1): 16500.55 + Cash (1): 16260.1 + Cash (1): 11400.61 + Cash (1): 11970.23 + Cash (1): 11100.54 = Deposits payable (2): 12000.15 + Deposits payable (2): 16500.55 + Deposits payable (2): 16260.1 + Deposits payable (2): 11400.61 + Deposits payable (2): 11970.23 + Deposits payable (2): 11100.54

- The transaction sub-equation includes the Cash account with the Order 11 to the Order 17 and the Deposits payable account with the Order 118 to the Order 124. Because the balances of the Cash with the Order 12 and the Order 119 are zero, the second transaction sub-equation is:

Cash (1): 11000.11 + Cash (1): 28600.21 + Cash (1): 14520.56 + Cash (1): 11680.34 + Cash (1): 11810.18 + Cash (1): 12200.45 = Deposits payable (2): 11000.11 + Deposits payable (2): 28600.21 + Deposits payable (2): 14520.56 + Deposits payable (2): 11680.34 + Deposits payable (2): 11810.18 + Deposits payable (2): 12200.45

- The transaction sub-equation includes the Cash account with the Order 18 to the Order 24 and the Deposits payable account with the Order 125 to the Order 131. Because the balances of the Cash account with the Order 18 and the Order 125 are zero, the third transaction sub-equation is:

Cash (1): 11300.74 + Cash (1): 26150.88 + Cash (1): 10510.99 + Cash (1): 16910.92 + Cash (1): 15900.51 + Cash (1): 26210.18 = Deposits payable (2): 11300.74 + Deposits payable (2): 26150.88 + Deposits payable (2): 10510.99 + Deposits payable (2): 16910.92 + Deposits payable (2): 15900.51+ Deposits payable (2): 26210.18

- The transaction sub-equation includes the Cash account with the Order 25 to the Order 31 and the Deposits payable account with the Order 132 to the Order 138. Because the balances of the Cash account with the Order 27 and the Order 134 are zero, the fourth transaction sub-equation is:

  Cash (1): 11720.14 + Cash (1): 15150.21 + Cash (1): 16150.25 + Cash (1): 4090.65 + Cash (1): 610.08 + Cash (1): 1117.96 = Deposits payable (2): 11720.14 + Deposits payable (2): 15150.21 + Deposits payable (2): 16150.25 + Deposits payable (2): 4090.65 + Deposits payable (2): 610.08 + Deposits payable (2): 1117.96

- The transaction sub-equation includes the Cash account with the Order 32 to the Order 38 and the Deposits payable account with the Order 139 to the Order 145. Because the balances of the Cash account with the Order 32 to the Order 34, the Order 37, the Order 139 to the Order 141, and the Order 144 are zero, the fifth transaction sub-equation is:

  Cash (1): 47393.19 + Cash (1): 6753.89 + Cash (1): 8768.69 = Deposits payable (2): 47393.19 + Deposits payable (2): 6753.89 + Deposits payable (2): 8768.69

- The transaction sub-equation includes the Cash account with the Order 39 to the Order 44 and the Bonds payable account with the Order 146 to the Order 151. The sixth transaction sub-equation is:

  Cash (1): 9000 + Cash (1): 8000 + Cash (1): 6000 + Cash (1): 9000 + Cash (1): 12000 + Cash (1): 7000 = Bonds payable (2): 9000 + Bonds payable (2): 8000 + Bonds payable (2): 6000 + Bonds payable (2): 9000 + Bonds payable (2): 12000 + Bonds payable (2): 7000

- The transaction sub-equation includes the Cash account with the Order 45 to the Order 50 and the Bonds payable account with the Order 152 to the Order 157. The seventh transaction sub-equation is:

  Cash (1): 4000 + Cash (1): 6000 + Cash (1): 3000 + Cash (1): 5000 + Cash (1): 3000 + Cash (1): 8000 = Bonds payable (2): 4000 + Bonds payable (2): 6000 + Bonds payable (2): 3000 + Bonds payable (2): 5000 + Bonds payable (2): 3000 + Bonds payable (2): 8000

- The transaction sub-equation includes the Cash account with the Order 51 to the Order 56 and the Bonds payable account with the Order 158 to the Order 163. The eighth transaction sub-equation is:

  Cash (1): 5000 + Cash (1): 6000 + Cash (1): 8000 + Cash (1): 4000 + Cash (1): 6000 + Cash (1): 7000 = Bonds payable (2): 5000 + Bonds payable (2): 6000 + Bonds payable (2): 8000 + Bonds payable (2): 4000 + Bonds payable (2): 6000+ Bonds payable (2): 7000

- The transaction sub-equation includes the Cash account with the Order 57 to the Order 60 and the Bonds payable account with the Order 164 to the Order 167. The ninth transaction sub-equation is:

  Cash (1): 6000 + Cash (1): 8000 + Cash (1): 3000 + Cash (1): 7000 = Bonds payable (2): 6000 + Bonds payable (2): 8000 + Bonds payable (2): 3000 + Bonds payable (2): 7000

- The transaction sub-equation includes the Cash account with the Order 61 to the Order 70 and the part of the Share capital account with the Order 168. The tenth transaction sub-equation is:

  Cash (1): 56100 + Cash (1): 36000 + Cash (1): 25650 + Cash (1): 27300 + Cash

(1): 3760 + Cash (1): 536.67 + Cash (1): 189 + Cash (1): 90 + Cash (1): 268.33 + Cash (1): 313.33 = Share capital (3): 150207.33

After entering this transaction, the new balance of the Share capital account with the Order 168 is $209,792.67 (= $360,000 - $150,207.33).

- The transaction sub-equation includes the Cash account with the Order 71, the Order 72, the Order 76 to the Order 79, the Order 85 to the Order 89, and the part of the Cash account with the Order 1. The eleventh transaction sub-equation is:

Cash (1): -40000 + Cash (1): -38000 + Cash (1): -27634.61 + Cash (1): -26587.92 + Cash (1): -28312.35 + Cash (1): -31671.27 + Cash (1): -7000 + Cash (1): -3000 + Cash (1): -6000 + Cash (1): -5000 + Cash (1): -8000 + Cash (1): 221206.15 = 0

After entering this transaction, the new balance of the Cash account with the Order 1 is $138,793.85 (= $360,000 - $221,206.15).

- The transaction sub-equation includes the Cash account with the Order 80 to the Order 84, the Supplies account with the Order 90, the Notes receivable account with the Order 91 to the Order 95, and the part of the Share capital account with the Order 168. The twelfth transaction sub-equation is:

Cash (1): -220000 + Cash (1): -240000 + Cash (1): -180000 + Cash (1): -200000 + Cash (1): -120000 + Supplies (1): 84.16 + Notes receivable (1): 250000 + Notes receivable (1): 240000 + Notes receivable (1): 180000 + Notes receivable (1): 200000 + Notes receivable (1): 120000 = Share capital (3): 84.16

After entering this transaction, the balance of the Share capital account with the Order 168 is $209,708.51 (= $209,792.67 - $84.16)

- The transaction sub-equation includes the Cash account with the Order 2 and the Order 3, Bonds account with the Order 96 to the Order 100, the Share capital account with the Order 169 and the Order 170, the and the part of the Share capital account with the Order 168. The thirteenth transaction sub-equation is:

Cash (1): 225000 + Cash (1): 315000 + Bonds (1): 7000 + Bonds (1): 3000 + Bonds (1): 6000 + Bonds (1): 5000 + Bonds (1): 8000 = Share capital (3): 225000 + Share capital (3): 315000 + Share capital (3): 29000

After entering this transaction, the balance of the Share capital account with the Order 168 is $180,708.51 (= $209,708.51 - $29,000)

- The transaction sub-equation includes the Vehicle account with the Order 101 and the Order 102, the Accumulated amortization: Vehicle account with the Order 103 and the Order 104, the Computer account with the Order 105 to the Order 107, the Accumulated amortization: Computer account with the Order 108 and the Order 110, and the part of the Share capital account with the Order 168. The fourteenth transaction sub-equation is:

Vehicle (1): 40000 + Vehicle (1): 38000 + Accumulated amortization: Vehicle (1): -16666.67 + Accumulated amortization: Vehicle (1): -11400 + Computer (1): 2800 + Computer (1): 1500 + Computer (1): 1600 + Accumulated amortization: Computer (1): -1750 + Accumulated amortization: Computer (1): -1000 + Accumulated amortization: Computer (1): -937.5 = Share capital (3): 52145.83

After entering this transaction, the balance of the Share capital account with the Order 168 is $128,562.68 (= $180,708.51 - $52,145.83)

- The transaction sub-equation includes the Cash account with the Order 73 to the Order 75, the rest ($138,793.85) of the Cash account with the Order 1, the rest ($128,562.68) of the Share capital account with the Order 168, and the Retained earnings (Conversion) account with the balance $24,331.17. The fifteenth transaction sub-equation is:

Cash (1): -2800 + Cash (1): -1600 + Cash (1): -1500 + Cash (1): 138793.85 =

Share capital (3): 128562.68 + Retained earnings (Conversion) (3): 4331.17

After completing this transaction, the dynamic accounting equation of the Business Bank2 on December 31, 2015 has entered into the database dcj06.

## 2.4.2.2 Brief Summary of the Business Bank2

The Figure 2.4-12 on this page and the next page shows cash received or paid by other members table which is in the public database dcj100.

| | IDM | Amount | Symbol | MultiSubaccount | Recorder | TransDate |
|---|---|---|---|---|---|---|
| 1 | 909876507 | -4000.00 | i | 909876507-i-bond21 < Cash receipts from issued bonds < Financial activities | 88-654305 | 2015-12-31 |
| 2 | 909876509 | -6000.00 | i | 909876509-i-bond21 < Cash receipts from issued bonds < Financial activities | 88-654305 | 2015-12-31 |
| 3 | 909876513 | -3000.00 | i | 909876513-i-bond21 < Cash receipts from issued bonds < Financial activities | 88-654305 | 2015-12-31 |
| 4 | 909876514 | -1000.00 | i | 909876514-i-bond21 < Cash receipts from issued bonds < Financial activities | 88-654305 | 2015-12-31 |
| 5 | 909876518 | -3000.00 | i | 909876518-i-bond21 < Cash receipts from issued bonds < Financial activities | 88-654305 | 2015-12-31 |
| 6 | 909876520 | -8000.00 | i | 909876520-i-bond21 < Cash receipts from issued bonds < Financial activities | 88-654305 | 2015-12-31 |
| 7 | 88-654304 | -5000.00 | i | 88-654304-i-bond22 < Cash receipts from issued bonds < Financial activities | 88-654305 | 2015-12-31 |
| 8 | 88-654307 | -6000.00 | i | 88-654307-i-bond22 < Cash receipts from issued bonds < Financial activities | 88-654305 | 2015-12-31 |
| 9 | 88-654309 | -8000.00 | i | 88-654309-i-bond22 < Cash receipts from issued bonds < Financial activities | 88-654305 | 2015-12-31 |
| 10 | 88-654310 | -4000.00 | i | 88-654310-i-bond22 < Cash receipts from issued bonds < Financial activities | 88-654305 | 2015-12-31 |
| 11 | 909876503 | -6000.00 | i | 909876503-i-bond22 < Cash receipts from issued bonds < Financial activities | 88-654305 | 2015-12-31 |
| 12 | 909876504 | -7000.00 | i | 909876504-i-bond22 < Cash receipts from issued bonds < Financial activities | 88-654305 | 2015-12-31 |
| 13 | 909876506 | -6000.00 | i | 909876506-i-bond22 < Cash receipts from issued bonds < Financial activities | 88-654305 | 2015-12-31 |
| 14 | 909876511 | -8000.00 | i | 909876511-i-bond22 < Cash receipts from issued bonds < Financial activities | 88-654305 | 2015-12-31 |
| 15 | 909876519 | -3000.00 | i | 909876519-i-bond22 < Cash receipts from issued bonds < Financial activities | 88-654305 | 2015-12-31 |
| 16 | 909876521 | -7000.00 | i | 909876521-i-bond22 < Cash receipts from issued bonds < Financial activities | 88-654305 | 2015-12-31 |
| 17 | 88-654306 | -56100... | c | 88-654306-c-accrued interest < Cash receipts from note accrued interest (customers) < Operating act... | 88-654305 | 2015-12-31 |
| 18 | 88-654307 | -36000... | c | 88-654307-c-accrued interest < Cash receipts from note accrued interest (customers) < Operating act... | 88-654305 | 2015-12-31 |
| 19 | 88-654308 | -25650... | c | 88-654308-c-accrued interest < Cash receipts from note accrued interest (customers) < Operating act... | 88-654305 | 2015-12-31 |
| 20 | 88-654307 | -27300... | c | 88-654307-c-accrued interest < Cash receipts from note accrued interest (customers) < Operating act... | 88-654305 | 2015-12-31 |
| 21 | 88-654306 | -3760.00 | c | 88-654306-c-accrued interest < Cash receipts from note accrued interest (customers) < Operating act... | 88-654305 | 2015-12-31 |
| 22 | 88-654304 | -536.67 | c | 88-654304-c-interest of investment bond11 < Cash receipts from investments < Investing activities | 88-654305 | 2015-12-31 |
| 23 | 88-654304 | -189.00 | c | 88-654304-c-interest of investment bond12 < Cash receipts from investments < Investing activities | 88-654305 | 2015-12-31 |
| 24 | 88-654304 | -90.00 | c | 88-654304-c-interest of investment bond13 < Cash receipts from investments < Investing activities | 88-654305 | 2015-12-31 |
| 25 | 88-654306 | -268.33 | c | 88-654306-c-interest of investment bond31 < Cash receipts from investments < Investing activities | 88-654305 | 2015-12-31 |
| 26 | 88-654307 | -313.33 | c | 88-654307-c-interest of investment bond41 < Cash receipts from investments < Investing activities | 88-654305 | 2015-12-31 |

Figure 2.4-12   Business Bank2 Cash Received or Paid by Other Members (Continue)

```
 use dcj100
 select sum(amount) as sum0 from CashByMembers where Recorder='88-654305'
 select * from CashByMembers where Recorder='88-654305'
```

100 %   ▾

☐ Results  ▤ Messages

| | sum0 |
|---|---|
| 1 | -390884.49 |

| | IDM | Amount | Symbol | MultiSubaccount | Recorder | TransDate |
|---|---|---|---|---|---|---|
| 57 | 909876510 | -28600... | d | 909876510-d-deposits < Cash receipts from customers deposits < Operating activities | 88-654305 | 2015-12-31 |
| 58 | 909876511 | -14520... | d | 909876511-d-deposits < Cash receipts from customers deposits < Operating activities | 88-654305 | 2015-12-31 |
| 59 | 909876512 | -11680... | d | 909876512-d-deposits < Cash receipts from customers deposits < Operating activities | 88-654305 | 2015-12-31 |
| 60 | 909876513 | -11810... | d | 909876513-d-deposits < Cash receipts from customers deposits < Operating activities | 88-654305 | 2015-12-31 |
| 61 | 909876514 | -12200... | d | 909876514-d-deposits < Cash receipts from customers deposits < Operating activities | 88-654305 | 2015-12-31 |
| 62 | 909876516 | -11300... | d | 909876516-d-deposits < Cash receipts from customers deposits < Operating activities | 88-654305 | 2015-12-31 |
| 63 | 909876517 | -26150... | d | 909876517-d-deposits < Cash receipts from customers deposits < Operating activities | 88-654305 | 2015-12-31 |
| 64 | 909876518 | -10510... | d | 909876518-d-deposits < Cash receipts from customers deposits < Operating activities | 88-654305 | 2015-12-31 |
| 65 | 909876519 | -16910... | d | 909876519-d-deposits < Cash receipts from customers deposits < Operating activities | 88-654305 | 2015-12-31 |
| 66 | 909876520 | -15900... | d | 909876520-d-deposits < Cash receipts from customers deposits < Operating activities | 88-654305 | 2015-12-31 |
| 67 | 909876521 | -26210... | d | 909876521-d-deposits < Cash receipts from customers deposits < Operating activities | 88-654305 | 2015-12-31 |
| 68 | 909876522 | -11720... | d | 909876522-d-deposits < Cash receipts from customers deposits < Operating activities | 88-654305 | 2015-12-31 |
| 69 | 909876523 | -15150... | d | 909876523-d-deposits < Cash receipts from customers deposits < Operating activities | 88-654305 | 2015-12-31 |
| 70 | 909876525 | -16150... | d | 909876525-d-deposits < Cash receipts from customers deposits < Operating activities | 88-654305 | 2015-12-31 |
| 71 | 88-654301 | -4090.65 | d | 88-654301-d-deposits < Cash receipts from customers deposits < Operating activities | 88-654305 | 2015-12-31 |
| 72 | 88-654302 | -610.08 | d | 88-654302-d-deposits < Cash receipts from customers deposits < Operating activities | 88-654305 | 2015-12-31 |
| 73 | 88-654303 | -1117.96 | d | 88-654303-d-deposits < Cash receipts from customers deposits < Operating activities | 88-654305 | 2015-12-31 |
| 74 | 88-654307 | -47393... | d | 88-654307-d-deposits < Cash receipts from customers deposits < Operating activities | 88-654305 | 2015-12-31 |
| 75 | 88-654308 | -6753.89 | d | 88-654308-d-deposits < Cash receipts from customers deposits < Operating activities | 88-654305 | 2015-12-31 |
| 76 | 88-654310 | -8768.69 | d | 88-654310-d-deposits < Cash receipts from customers deposits < Operating activities | 88-654305 | 2015-12-31 |
| 77 | 88-654302 | -9000.00 | i | 88-654302-i-bond21 < Cash receipts from issued bonds < Financial activities | 88-654305 | 2015-12-31 |
| 78 | 88-654303 | -8000.00 | i | 88-654303-i-bond21 < Cash receipts from issued bonds < Financial activities | 88-654305 | 2015-12-31 |
| 79 | 88-654304 | -6000.00 | i | 88-654304-i-bond21 < Cash receipts from issued bonds < Financial activities | 88-654305 | 2015-12-31 |
| 80 | 88-654306 | -9000.00 | i | 88-654306-i-bond21 < Cash receipts from issued bonds < Financial activities | 88-654305 | 2015-12-31 |
| 81 | 88-654308 | -12000... | i | 88-654308-i-bond21 < Cash receipts from issued bonds < Financial activities | 88-654305 | 2015-12-31 |
| 82 | 88-654309 | -7000.00 | i | 88-654309-i-bond21 < Cash receipts from issued bonds < Financial activities | 88-654305 | 2015-12-31 |

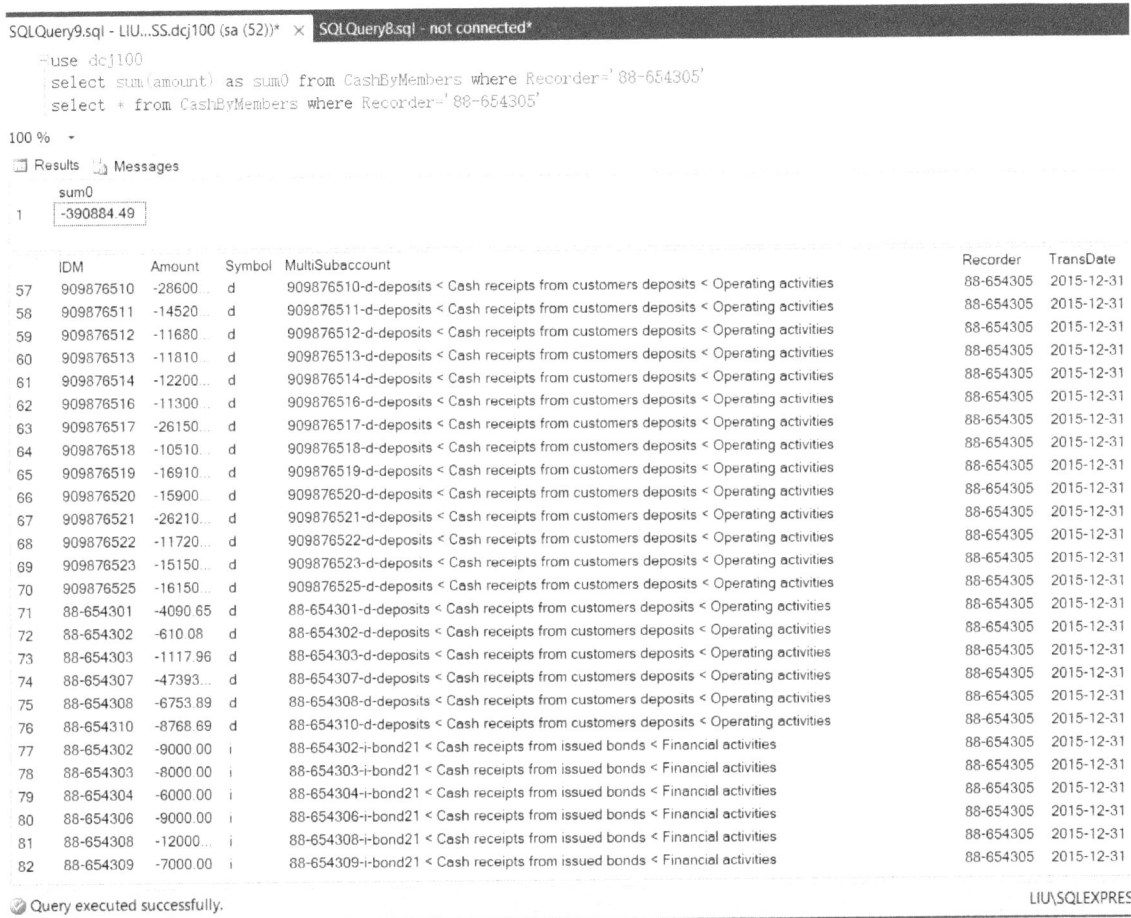

Figure 2.4-12   Business Bank2 Cash Received or Paid by Other Members

The Figure 2.4-13 on the next page shows cash flows statement of the Business Bank2 on December 31, 2015.

Cash Flow Statement

| Cash Flows Statement Year Ended 2015-12-31 | |
|---|---|
| **Operating activities** | |
| Cash payments for machinery | -$83,900.00 |
| Cash payments for operating expenses | -$114,206.15 |
| Cash payments to notes lenders | -$960,000.00 |
| Cash receipts from customers deposits | $387,783.31 |
| Cash receipts from note accrued interest (customers) | $148,810.00 |
| Net cash provided by Operating activities | -$621,512.84 |
| | |
| Investing activities | |
| Cash payments for investments | -$29,000.00 |
| Cash receipts from investments | $1,397.33 |
| Net cash provided by Investing activities | -$27,602.67 |
| | |
| Financial activities | |
| Cash receipts from issued bonds | $140,000.00 |
| Cash receipts from owners | $900,000.00 |
| Net cash provided by Financial activities | $1,040,000.00 |
| | |
| Net change in cash | $390,884.49 |
| Cash, Begining | $0.00 |
| Cash, Ending | $390,884.49 |

Figure 2.4-13   Business Bank2 Cash Flows Statement

The Figure 2.4-14 on the next pages shows cash account table of the Business Bank2 on December 31, 2015.

Cash

| ID | Multi-Name | Amount | Balance | General ID | Transaction Date |
|---|---|---|---|---|---|
| 1 | 909876501-d-deposits < Cash receipts from customers deposits < Opera... | $12,000.15 | $12,000.15 | 3 | 2015-12-31 |
| 2 | 909876502-d-deposits < Cash receipts from customers deposits < Opera... | $16,500.55 | $28,500.70 | 3 | 2015-12-31 |
| 3 | 909876503-d-deposits < Cash receipts from customers deposits < Opera... | $16,260.10 | $44,760.80 | 3 | 2015-12-31 |
| 4 | 909876504-d-deposits < Cash receipts from customers deposits < Opera... | $11,400.61 | $56,161.41 | 3 | 2015-12-31 |
| 5 | 909876505-d-deposits < Cash receipts from customers deposits < Opera... | $11,970.23 | $68,131.64 | 3 | 2015-12-31 |
| 6 | 909876506-d-deposits < Cash receipts from customers deposits < Opera... | $11,100.54 | $79,232.18 | 3 | 2015-12-31 |
| 7 | 909876507-d-deposits < Cash receipts from customers deposits < Opera... | $0.00 | $79,232.18 | 4 | 2015-12-31 |
| 8 | 909876508-d-deposits < Cash receipts from customers deposits < Opera... | $11,000.11 | $90,232.29 | 5 | 2015-12-31 |
| 9 | 909876510-d-deposits < Cash receipts from customers deposits < Opera... | $28,600.21 | $118,832.50 | 5 | 2015-12-31 |
| 10 | 909876511-d-deposits < Cash receipts from customers deposits < Opera... | $14,520.56 | $133,353.06 | 5 | 2015-12-31 |
| 11 | 909876512-d-deposits < Cash receipts from customers deposits < Opera... | $11,680.34 | $145,033.40 | 5 | 2015-12-31 |
| 12 | 909876513-d-deposits < Cash receipts from customers deposits < Opera... | $11,810.18 | $156,843.58 | 5 | 2015-12-31 |
| 13 | 909876514-d-deposits < Cash receipts from customers deposits < Opera... | $12,200.45 | $169,044.03 | 5 | 2015-12-31 |
| 14 | 909876516-d-deposits < Cash receipts from customers deposits < Opera... | $11,300.74 | $180,344.77 | 6 | 2015-12-31 |
| 15 | 909876517-d-deposits < Cash receipts from customers deposits < Opera... | $26,150.88 | $206,495.65 | 6 | 2015-12-31 |
| 16 | 909876518-d-deposits < Cash receipts from customers deposits < Opera... | $10,510.99 | $217,006.64 | 6 | 2015-12-31 |
| 17 | 909876519-d-deposits < Cash receipts from customers deposits < Opera... | $16,910.92 | $233,917.56 | 6 | 2015-12-31 |
| 18 | 909876520-d-deposits < Cash receipts from customers deposits < Opera... | $15,900.51 | $249,818.07 | 6 | 2015-12-31 |
| 19 | 909876521-d-deposits < Cash receipts from customers deposits < Opera... | $26,210.18 | $276,028.25 | 6 | 2015-12-31 |
| 20 | 909876522-d-deposits < Cash receipts from customers deposits < Opera... | $11,720.14 | $287,748.39 | 7 | 2015-12-31 |
| 21 | 909876523-d-deposits < Cash receipts from customers deposits < Opera... | $15,150.21 | $302,898.60 | 7 | 2015-12-31 |
| 22 | 909876525-d-deposits < Cash receipts from customers deposits < Opera... | $16,150.25 | $319,048.85 | 7 | 2015-12-31 |
| 23 | 88-654301-d-deposits < Cash receipts from customers deposits < Operat... | $4,090.65 | $323,139.50 | 7 | 2015-12-31 |
| 24 | 88-654302-d-deposits < Cash receipts from customers deposits < Operat... | $610.08 | $323,749.58 | 7 | 2015-12-31 |

Figure 2.4-14   Business Bank2 Cash Account Table (Continue)

Cash

| ID | Multi-Name | Amount | Balance | General ID | Transaction Date |
|---|---|---|---|---|---|
| 62 | 88-654306-t-car2 < Cash payments for machinery < Operating activities | -$38,000.00 | $599,990.64 | 14 | 2015-12-31 |
| 63 | Cash payments for operating expenses < Operating activities | -$27,634.61 | $572,356.03 | 14 | 2015-12-31 |
| 64 | Cash payments for operating expenses < Operating activities | -$26,587.92 | $545,768.11 | 14 | 2015-12-31 |
| 65 | Cash payments for operating expenses < Operating activities | -$28,312.35 | $517,455.76 | 14 | 2015-12-31 |
| 66 | 88-654303-n-tax < Cash payments for operating expenses < Operating a... | -$31,671.27 | $485,784.49 | 14 | 2015-12-31 |
| 67 | 88-654304-n-investment bond11 < Cash payments for investments < Inve... | -$7,000.00 | $478,784.49 | 14 | 2015-12-31 |
| 68 | 88-654304-n-investment bond12 < Cash payments for investments < Inve... | -$3,000.00 | $475,784.49 | 14 | 2015-12-31 |
| 69 | 88-654304-n-investment bond13 < Cash payments for investments < Inve... | -$6,000.00 | $469,784.49 | 14 | 2015-12-31 |
| 70 | 88-654306-n-investment bond31 < Cash payments for investments < Inve... | -$5,000.00 | $464,784.49 | 14 | 2015-12-31 |
| 71 | 88-654307-n-investment bond41 < Cash payments for investments < Inve... | -$8,000.00 | $456,784.49 | 14 | 2015-12-31 |
| 72 | 909876511-i-owners < Cash receipts from owners < Financial activities | $221,206.15 | $677,990.64 | 14 | 2015-12-31 |
| 73 | 88-654306-n-notes1 < Cash payments to notes lenders < Operating activi... | -$220,000.00 | $457,990.64 | 15 | 2015-12-31 |
| 74 | 88-654307-n-notes2 < Cash payments to notes lenders < Operating activi... | -$240,000.00 | $217,990.64 | 15 | 2015-12-31 |
| 75 | 88-654308-n-notes3 < Cash payments to notes lenders < Operating activi... | -$180,000.00 | $37,990.64 | 15 | 2015-12-31 |
| 76 | 88-654308-n-notes4 < Cash payments to notes lenders < Operating activi... | -$200,000.00 | -$162,009.36 | 15 | 2015-12-31 |
| 77 | 88-654309-n-notes5 < Cash payments to notes lenders < Operating activi... | -$120,000.00 | -$282,009.36 | 15 | 2015-12-31 |
| 78 | 909876517-i-owners < Cash receipts from owners < Financial activities | $225,000.00 | -$57,009.36 | 16 | 2015-12-31 |
| 79 | 88-654304-i-owners < Cash receipts from owners < Financial activities | $315,000.00 | $257,990.64 | 16 | 2015-12-31 |
| 80 | 88-654306-t-computer server1 < Cash payments for machinery < Operati... | -$2,800.00 | $255,190.64 | 18 | 2015-12-31 |
| 81 | 88-654306-t-computer1 < Cash payments for machinery < Operating acti... | -$1,600.00 | $253,590.64 | 18 | 2015-12-31 |
| 82 | 88-654306-t-computer2 < Cash payments for machinery < Operating acti... | -$1,500.00 | $252,090.64 | 18 | 2015-12-31 |
| 83 | 909876511-i-owners < Cash receipts from owners < Financial activities | $138,793.85 | $390,884.49 | 18 | 2015-12-31 |

Figure 2.4-14　Business Bank2 Cash Account Table

Because the one-level subaccount "Capital-909876511" of the Share capital account is divided many times during conversion, the detail information of the one-level subaccount "Capital-909876511" is showed in the following Figure 2.4-15.

Share capital: Capital-909876511

| ID | Multi-Name | Amount | Unit | General ID | Transaction Date |
|---|---|---|---|---|---|
| 2 | Capital-909876511 | $150,207.33 | 1 | 13 | 2015-12-31 |
| 3 | Capital-909876511 | $84.16 | 1 | 15 | 2015-12-31 |
| 6 | Capital-909876511 | $29,000.00 | 1 | 16 | 2015-12-31 |
| 7 | Capital-909876511 | $52,145.83 | 1 | 17 | 2015-12-31 |
| 8 | Capital-909876511 | $128,562.68 | 1 | 18 | 2015-12-31 |
| | | $360,000.00 | 5 | | |

Figure 2.4-15　Capital-909876511 Subaccount Table

The following Figure 2.4-16 shows balance sheet table of the Business Bank2 on December 31, 2015.

Balance Sheet

| | As at 12/31/2015 |
|---|---|
| **ASSETS** | |
| Current assets | |
| Cash | $390,884.49 |
| Supplies | $84.16 |
| Notes receivable | $960,000.00 |
| Account receivable | $0.00 |
| | $1,350,968.65 |
| Long term investments | |
| Bonds | $29,000.00 |
| Equipment | |
| Vehicle | $78,000.00 |
| Accumulated amortization: Vehicle | -$28,066.67 |
| Computer | $5,900.00 |
| Accumulated amortization: Computer | -$3,687.50 |
| | $52,145.83 |
| Total Assets | $1,432,114.48 |
| | |
| | |
| LIABILITIES | |
| Current liabilities | |
| Deposits payable | $387,783.31 |
| Account payable | $0.00 |
| | $387,783.31 |
| Long term liabilities | |
| Bonds payable | $140,000.00 |
| Total Liability | $527,783.31 |
| | |
| SHAREHOLDERS' EQUITY | |
| Owners capital | |
| Share capital | $900,000.00 |
| Retained earnings (Conversion) | $4,331.17 |
| | $904,331.17 |
| Retined earnings | $0.00 |
| Accumulated other comprehensive income | $0.00 |
| Total Shareholders' Equity | $904,331.17 |
| | |
| Total Liabilities and Shareholders' Equity | $1,432,114.48 |

Figure 2.4-16   Business Bank2 Balance Sheet

## 2.4.3 Sample of the Company1

The Company1 has total share capital $200,000 and three shareholders of the individual A12, the individual A15, and the individual A18. Their percentages of the share capital are 40%, 35%, and 25% respectively. The Company1 produces the vehicles and the computers. The Figure 2.4-17 shows its products and sale prices.

| Order | Product (the Lowest-level Subaccount) Names | Multi-subaccount Names | Costs | Sale Prices |
|---|---|---|---|---|
| 1 | Truck1 | Truck1 < Truck < Vehicle | 33700.00 | 45000.00 |
| 2 | Truck2 | Truck2 < Truck < Vehicle | 30000.00 | 40000.00 |
| 3 | Car1 | Car1 < Car < Vehicle | 28000.00 | 40000.00 |
| 4 | Car2 | Car2 < Car < Vehicle | 27000.00 | 39000.00 |
| 5 | Car3 | Car3 < Car < Vehicle | 26000.00 | 38000.00 |
| 6 | Computer server1 | Computer server1 < Computer server < Computer | 1600.00 | 2800.00 |
| 7 | Computer server2 | Computer server2 < Computer server < Computer | 1500.00 | 2700.00 |
| 8 | Computer1 | Computer1 < Computer | 1000.00 | 1600.00 |
| 9 | Computer2 | Computer2 < Computer | 920.00 | 1500.00 |
| 10 | Computer3 | Computer3 < Computer | 830.00 | 1400.00 |
| 11 | Computer4 | Computer4 < Computer | 770.00 | 1300.00 |
| 12 | Truck1- Service package1 | Truck1- Service package1 < Truck-service < Vehicle-service | - | 550.00 |
| 13 | Truck2- Service package2 | Truck2- Service package2 < Truck-service < Vehicle-service | - | 500.00 |
| 14 | Car1- Service package3 | Car1- Service package3 < Car-service < Vehicle-service | - | 490.00 |
| 15 | Car2- Service package4 | Car2- Service package4 < Car-service < Vehicle-service | - | 450.00 |
| 16 | Car3- Service package5 | Car3- Service package5 < Car-service < Vehicle-service | - | 410.00 |
| 17 | Computer server1- Service package6 | Computer server1- Service package6 < Computer server-service < Computer-service | - | 60.00 |
| 18 | Computer server2- Service package7 | Computer server2- Service package7 < Computer server-service < Computer-service | - | 55.00 |
| 19 | Computer1- Service package8 | Computer1- Service package8 < Computer-service | - | 50.00 |
| 20 | Computer2- Service package9 | Computer2- Service package9 < Computer-service | - | 45.00 |
| 21 | Computer3- Service package10 | Computer3- Service package10 < Computer-service | - | 40.00 |

Figure 2.4-17   Company1 Products and Sale Prices Table

For a manufacturing company, the balances of the working-in-process inventory and the cost of goods manufactured must be calculated during a fiscal year.

The Cost of goods manufactured account, which is a middle account, is consisted of the raw materials, the direct labor, and the manufacturing overhead. The manufacturing overhead includes the costs of the supervisors' salaries expenses, the indirect labor expenses, the utilities expenses (heat, light, power, and water), the amortization expenses of building and equipment, the tools expenses, patent amortization expenses, and the miscellaneous factory expenses during a fiscal year. If I need the financial statements at the end of every month, then the balance of the Cost of goods manufactured account must be transferred into the Working-in-process inventory account. In this book, the balance of the Cost of goods manufactured account must only be transferred into the Working-in-process inventory account at the ending of every fiscal year. If some products begins to be produced and are completed during one fiscal year, then the balance of the Cost of goods manufactured account must directly be transferred into the Inventory account on the completing day. Other companies and proprietorships are as the same as the Company1.

When the Company1 uses the MathAccounting software, the Working-in-process inventory account is treated as a parent account of the class 1 and the Cost of goods manufactured account is treated as the parent accounts of the class 5. For simplification, the Cost of goods manufactured account has only three one-level subaccounts of the "Supplies expenses", the "Salary expenses" for employees of A13 and A15, and the "Other general parts" in this book.

## 2.4.3.1 Conversion of the Company1

The Company1 will convert to the MathAccounting software on December 31, 2015, so I design a converting reference table, seeing the following Figure 2.4-18, in order to enter its dynamic accounting equation on December 31, 2015 into the database dcj07.

| Order | Class | Account Name (**Subtotal Name**) | Balance | Row |
|-------|-------|----------------------------------|---------|-----|
| **1** | **1** | **(Current assets)** | - | **103** |
| 2 | 1 | Cash | 67873.98 | 104 |
| 3 | 1 | Supplies | 93.79 | 106 |
| 4 | 1 | Account receivable | 6400.00 | 108 |

| | | | | |
|---|---|---|---|---|
| 5 | 1 | Inventory | 357130.00 | 110 |
| 6 | 1 | Working-in-process inventory | 367796.65 | 112 |
| **7** | **1** | **(Long term investments)** | - | **141** |
| 8 | 1 | Bonds | 22000.00 | 142 |
| 9 | 1 | Share | 36000.00 | 144 |
| **10** | **1** | **(Equipment)** | - | **171** |
| 11 | 1 | Vehicle | 121000.00 | 172 |
| 12 | 1 | Accumulated amortization: Vehicle | -48833.33 | 173 |
| 13 | 1 | Computer | 5400.00 | 174 |
| 14 | 1 | Accumulated amortization: Computer | -4275.00 | 175 |
| **15** | **2** | **(Current liabilities)** | - | **203** |
| 16 | 2 | Account payable | 27040.00 | 204 |
| 17 | 2 | Accrued interest payable | 0 | 206 |
| 18 | 2 | Tax payable | 0 | 208 |
| **19** | **2** | **(Long term liabilities)** | - | **251** |
| 20 | 2 | Bonds payable | 50000.00 | 252 |
| 21 | 2 | Note payable | 640000.00 | 254 |
| **22** | **3** | **(Owners' capital)** | - | **303** |
| 23 | 3 | Share capital | 200000.00 | 304 |
| 24 | 3 | Retained earnings (Conversion) | 13546.09 | 306 |
| **25** | **4** | **(Revenues)** | - | **403** |
| 26 | 4 | Sales | | 404 |
| **27** | **5** | **(Cost)** | - | **431** |
| 28 | 5 | Cost of goods sold | | 432 |
| **29** | **5** | **(Operating and administrative expenses)** | - | **453** |
| 30 | 5 | Travelling expenses | 0 | 454 |
| 31 | 5 | Other expenses | 0 | 455 |
| 32 | 5 | Salary expenses | 0 | 456 |
| 33 | 5 | Cost of goods manufactured | 0 | 457 |
| 34 | 5 | Bond interest expenses | 0 | 458 |
| 35 | 5 | Note interest expenses | 0 | 460 |
| 36 | 5 | Amortization expenses | 0 | 462 |
| **37** | **4** | **(Other income)** | - | **475** |
| 38 | 4 | Investment income | | 476 |
| 39 | 4 | Deposits interest income | 0 | 478 |
| 40 | 4 | Service package income | 0 | 480 |
| **41** | **5** | **(Tax)** | - | **600** |
| 42 | 5 | Tax expenses | 0 | 602 |

Figure 2.4-18   Company1 Converting Reference Table

From the Figure 2.4-18, there are total 31 accounts among which the balances of the Sales account, the Cost of goods sold account, and all expenses accounts are zero. In addition, the balance of the Retained earnings account should be added to the balance of the Share capital account and its balance should be zero prior to conversion. However, for knowing the original share capital and the distinguishing retained earnings after conversion, I keep the Retained earnings account prior to conversion and give it a different name of the Retained earnings (Conversion).

The Bonds account has three one-level subaccounts of the "Bond11 (issued by the Business Bank1 and purchased $10,000, beginning on February 1, 2014, five years, and annual interest rate 4%), the "Bond13" (issued by the Business Bank1 and purchased $3,000, beginning on September 1, 2015, six years, and annual interest rate 4.5%), and the "Bond21" (issued by the Business Bank2 and purchased $9,000, beginning on May 1, 2014, five years, and annual interest rate 4.1%).

The Company1 has one truck1 (five years, straight line, 26 months), one truck2 (five years, straight line, 26 months), and one car3 (five years, straight line, 20 months) and purchased them from itself company of the "Company1" in market price, so the multi-subaccount names of the Vehicle parent account are the "Truck11 < Truck1 < Truck", the "Truck21 < Truck2 < Truck", and the "Car31 < Car3 < Car" respectively. Their balances are $45,000, $40,000 and $36,000 respectively. Accordingly, the multi-subaccount names of the Accumulated amortization: Vehicle account are the "Truck11-accumulated amortization < Truck1-accumulated amortization < Truck-accumulated amortization", the "Truck2-accumulated amortization < Truck2-accumulated amortization < Truck-accumulated amortization", and the "Car31-accumulated amortization < Car3-accumulated amortization < Car-accumulated amortization". Their balances are -$19,500, -$17,333.33 and -$12,000 respectively.

The Company1 has one computer server2 (two years, straight line, 19 months), one computer3" (two years, straight line, 19 months), and one computer4" (two years, straight line, 19 months), so the multi-subaccount names of the Computer parent account are the "Computer server21 < Computer server2 < Computer server", the "Computer31 <

Computer3", and the "Computer41 < Computer4" respectively. Their balances are $2,700, $1,400, and $1,300 respectively. Accordingly, the multi-subaccount names of the Accumulated amortization: Computer account are the "Computer server21-accumulated amortization < Computer server2-accumulated amortization < Computer server-accumulated amortization", the "Computer31-accumulated amortization < Computer3-accumulated amortization", and the "Computer41-accumulated amortization < Computer4-accumulated amortization". Their balances are respectively -$2,137.50, -$1,108.33, and -$1,029.17.

The Company1 issued one bond, seeing the Figure 2.4-19 on this page and the next page. The Figure 2.4-19 shows the detail information of the issued bond. The Bonds payable account has one one-level subaccount of the "Bond31-payable" ($50,000, beginning on November 1, 2014, five years, and annual interest rate 4.6%). Of course, the Bonds payable account has also many two-level subaccounts. The Notes payable account has three one-level subaccounts of the "Note11" ($250,000 from the Business Bank1, beginning on February 1, 2013, three years, and annual interest rate 9%), the "Note15" ($170,000 from the Business Bank1, beginning on October 1, 2015, three years, and annual interest rate 9.5%), and the "Note21" ($220,000 from the Business Bank2, beginning on March 1, 2013, three years, and annual interest rate 9%). Therefore, the Accrued interest payable account has two one-level subaccounts of the "Bonds-interest payable" and the "Notes-interest payable". Accordingly, the balance of the Accrued interest payable account is zero prior to the conversion.

| Order | Bond | Amount | Term | Purchaser Name | Identity |
|---|---|---|---|---|---|
| 1 | Bond31 | 5000 | November 1, 2014, Five years, 4.6% annually | Business Bank2 | 88-654305 |
| 2 | Bond31 | 3000 | November 1, 2014, Five years, 4.6% annually | A1 | 909876501 |
| 3 | Bond31 | 6000 | November 1, 2014, Five years, 4.6% annually | A2 | 909876502 |
| 4 | Bond31 | 5000 | November 1, 2014, Five years, 4.6% annually | A8 | 909876508 |
| 5 | Bond31 | 7000 | November 1, 2014, Five years, 4.6% annually | A11 | 909876511 |
| 6 | Bond31 | 2000 | November 1, 2014, Five years, 4.6% annually | A14 | 909876514 |
| 7 | Bond31 | 4000 | November 1, 2014, Five years, 4.6% annually | A16 | 909876516 |

| 8 | Bond31 | 2000 | November 1, 2014, Five years, 4.6% annually | A18 | 909876518 |
| 9 | Bond31 | 3000 | November 1, 2014, Five years, 4.6% annually | A21 | 909876521 |
| 10 | Bond31 | 5000 | November 1, 2014, Five years, 4.6% annually | A22 | 909876522 |
| 11 | Bond31 | 3000 | November 1, 2014, Five years, 4.6% annually | A24 | 909876524 |
| 12 | Bond31 | 5000 | November 1, 2014, Five years, 4.6% annually | A25 | 909876525 |
| **13** | **Total** | **50000** | | | |

Figure 2.4-19　Company1 Issued Bond Information Table

The Account receivable account and the Account payable account need transaction dates during the conversion, so I assume that their transaction dates are also on December 31, 2015 for simplification.

For a society which follows the wealth conservation law, the total sum of all balances of the "Cash receipts from customers<Operating activities" and the "Cash payments to suppliers<Operating activities" should be zero, seeing the following Figure 2.4-20 and the Figure 2.4-21 on the next page. For simplification, the two Figures only include 3 companies and two proprietorships. The difference between the balance of the "Cash receipts from customers<Operating activities" and the balance of the "Cash payments to suppliers<Operating activities" for a company can be set to be a formula because I do not want to know every amount prior to the conversation and only need to get the sum of all companies' balances (differences). The sum should be zero.

| Order | Company Name | Cash Receipts From Customers | Twin Cash Paid by Customers | Balance (Difference) | Customer Name |
|---|---|---|---|---|---|
| 1 | Company1 | RC1C2 | - RC2C1 | RC1C2 - RC2C1 | Company2 |
| 2 | Company1 | RC1C3 | - RC3C1 | RC1C3 - RC3C1 | Company3 |
| 3 | Company1 | RC1P1 | - RP1C1 | RC1P1 - RP1C1 | Proprietorship1 |
| 4 | Company1 | RC1P2 | - RP2C1 | RC1P2 - RP2C1 | Proprietorship2 |
| 5 | Company2 | RC2C1 | - RC1C2 | RC2C1 - RC1C2 | Company1 |
| 6 | Company2 | RC2C3 | - RC3C2 | RC2C3 - RC3C2 | Company3 |
| 7 | Company2 | RC2P1 | - RP1C2 | RC2P1 - RP1C2 | Proprietorship1 |
| 8 | Company2 | RC2P2 | - RP2C2 | RC2P2 - RP2C2 | Proprietorship2 |
| 9 | Company3 | RC3C1 | - RC1C3 | RC3C1 - RC1C3 | Company1 |
| 10 | Company3 | RC3C2 | - RC2C3 | RC3C2 - RC2C3 | Company2 |

| 11 | Company3 | RC3P1 | - RP1C3 | RC3P1 - RP1C3 | Proprietorship1 |
| 12 | Company3 | RC3P2 | - RP2C3 | RC3P2 - RP2C3 | Proprietorship2 |
| 13 | Proprietorship1 | RP1C1 | - RC1P1 | RP1C1 - RC1P1 | Company1 |
| 14 | Proprietorship1 | RP1C2 | - RC2P1 | RP1C2 - RC2P1 | Company2 |
| 15 | Proprietorship1 | RP1C3 | - RC3P1 | RP1C3 - RC3P1 | Company3 |
| 16 | Proprietorship1 | RP1P2 | - RP2P1 | RP1P2 - RP2P1 | Proprietorship2 |
| 17 | Proprietorship2 | RP2C1 | - RC1P2 | RP2C1 - RC1P2 | Company1 |
| 18 | Proprietorship2 | RP2C2 | - RC2P2 | RP2C2 - RC2P2 | Company2 |
| 19 | Proprietorship2 | RP2C3 | - RC3P2 | RP2C3 - RC3P2 | Company3 |
| 20 | Proprietorship2 | RP2P1 | - RP1P2 | RP2P1 - RP1P2 | Proprietorship1 |
| **21** | **Total** | - | - | **0** | - |

Figure 2.4-20   Cash Receipts from Customers Table

| Order | Company Name | Cash Payments to Suppliers | Twin Cash Received by Suppliers | Balance (Difference) | Supplier Name |
|---|---|---|---|---|---|
| 1 | Company1 | - PC1C2 | PC2C1 | PC2C1 - PC1C2 | Company2 |
| 2 | Company1 | - PC1C3 | PC3C1 | PC3C1 - PC1C3 | Company3 |
| 3 | Company1 | - PC1P1 | PP1C1 | PP1C1 - PC1P1 | Proprietorship1 |
| 4 | Company1 | - PC1P2 | PP2C1 | PP2C1 - PC1P2 | Proprietorship2 |
| 5 | Company2 | - PC2C1 | PC1C2 | PC1C2 - PC2C1 | Company1 |
| 6 | Company2 | - PC2C3 | PC3C2 | PC3C2 - PC2C3 | Company3 |
| 7 | Company2 | - PC2P1 | RP1C2 | RP1C2 - PC2P1 | Proprietorship1 |
| 8 | Company2 | - PC2P2 | PP2C2 | PP2C2- PC2P2 | Proprietorship2 |
| 9 | Company3 | - PC3C1 | PC1C3 | PC1C3 - PC3C1 | Company1 |
| 10 | Company3 | - PC3C2 | PC2C3 | PC2C3 - PC3C2 | Company2 |
| 11 | Company3 | - PC3P1 | PP1C3 | PP1C3 - PC3P1 | Proprietorship1 |
| 12 | Company3 | - PC3P2 | PP2C3 | PP2C3 - PC3P2 | Proprietorship2 |
| 13 | Proprietorship1 | - PP1C1 | PC1P1 | PC1P1 - PP1C1 | Company1 |
| 14 | Proprietorship1 | - PP1C2 | PC2P1 | PC2P1 - PP1C2 | Company2 |
| 15 | Proprietorship1 | - PP1C3 | PC3P1 | PC3P1 - PP1C3 | Company3 |
| 16 | Proprietorship1 | - PP1P2 | PP2P1 | PP2P1 - PP1P2 | Proprietorship2 |
| 17 | Proprietorship2 | - PP2C1 | PC1P2 | PC1P2 - PP2C1 | Company1 |
| 18 | Proprietorship2 | - PP2C2 | PC2P2 | PC2P2 - PP2C2 | Company2 |
| 19 | Proprietorship2 | - PP2C3 | PC3P2 | PC3P2 - PP2C3 | Company3 |
| 20 | Proprietorship2 | - PP2P1 | PP1P2 | PP1P2 - PP2P1 | Proprietorship1 |
| **21** | **Total** | - | - | **0** | - |

Figure 2.4-21   Cash Payments to Suppliers Table

For the Company1, the balances of the "Cash receipts from customers<Operating activities" and the "Cash payments to suppliers<Operating activities" are respectively zero and -$30,000. The following Figure 2.4-22 shows the difference detail information of the Company1.

| Order | Supplier Company Name | Cash Payments to Suppliers | Twin Cash Received by Suppliers | Balance (Difference) |
|-------|----------------------|---------------------------|--------------------------------|----------------------|
| 1 | Company3 | -1000 | 0 | -1000 |
| 2 | Proprietorship1 | -17000 | 0 | -17000 |
| 3 | Proprietorship2 | -16000 | 0 | -16000 |
| 4 | **Total** | **-30000** | **0** | **-30000** |
| | | | | |

Figure 2.4-22   Difference Information Table

Following above information, I can build a table of the multi-subaccount names, seeing the Figure 2.4-23 on this page and the next pages.

| Order | Class | Multi-subaccount Name | Parent Name | Lowest Subaccount Balance |
|-------|-------|----------------------|-------------|---------------------------|
| 1 | 1 | 909876512-i-owners < Cash receipts from owners < Financial activities | Cash | 80000.00 |
| 2 | 1 | 909876515-i-owners < Cash receipts from owners < Financial activities | Cash | 70000.00 |
| 3 | 1 | 909876518-i-owners < Cash receipts from owners < Financial activities | Cash | 50000.00 |
| 4 | 1 | 88-654304-i-note11 < Cash receipts from banks < Financial activities | Cash | 250000.00 |
| 5 | 1 | 88-654304-i-note15 < Cash receipts from banks < Financial activities | Cash | 170000.00 |
| 6 | 1 | 88-654305-i-note21 < Cash receipts from banks < Financial activities | Cash | 220000.00 |
| 7 | 1 | Cash receipts from customers < Operating activities | Cash | 0 |
| 8 | 1 | 88-654305-i-bond31 < Cash receipts from issued bonds < Financial activities | Cash | 5000.00 |
| 9 | 1 | 909876501-i-bond31 < Cash receipts from issued bonds < Financial activities | Cash | 3000.00 |
| 10 | 1 | 909876502-i-bond31 < Cash receipts from issued bonds < Financial activities | Cash | 6000.00 |
| 11 | 1 | 909876508-i-bond31 < Cash receipts from issued bonds < Financial activities | Cash | 5000.00 |
| 12 | 1 | 909876511-i-bond31 < Cash receipts from issued bonds < Financial activities | Cash | 7000.00 |
| 13 | 1 | 909876514-i-bond31 < Cash receipts from issued bonds < Financial activities | Cash | 2000.00 |
| 14 | 1 | 909876516-i-bond31 < Cash receipts from issued bonds < Financial activities | Cash | 4000.00 |
| 15 | 1 | 909876518-i-bond31 < Cash receipts from issued bonds < Financial activities | Cash | 2000.00 |

| | | | | |
|---|---|---|---|---|
| 16 | 1 | 909876521-i-bond31 < Cash receipts from issued bonds < Financial activities | Cash | 3000.00 |
| 17 | 1 | 909876522-i-bond31 < Cash receipts from issued bonds < Financial activities | Cash | 5000.00 |
| 18 | 1 | 909876524-i-bond31 < Cash receipts from issued bonds < Financial activities | Cash | 3000.00 |
| 19 | 1 | 909876525-i-bond31 < Cash receipts from issued bonds < Financial activities | Cash | 5000.00 |
| 20 | 1 | 88-654304-c-interest of investment bond11 < Cash receipts from investments < Investing activities | Cash | 766.67 |
| 21 | 1 | 88-654304-c-interest of investment bond13 < Cash receipts from investments < Investing activities | Cash | 45.00 |
| 22 | 1 | 88-654305-c-interest of investment bond21 < Cash receipts from investments < Investing activities | Cash | 615.00 |
| 23 | 1 | 88-654306-t-truck1 < Cash payments for machinery < Operating activities | Cash | -45000.00 |
| 24 | 1 | 88-654306-t-truck2 < Cash payments for machinery < Operating activities | Cash | -40000.00 |
| 25 | 1 | 88-654306-t-car3 < Cash payments for machinery < Operating activities | Cash | -36000.00 |
| 26 | 1 | 88-654306-t-computer server2 < Cash payments for machinery < Operating activities | Cash | -2700.00 |
| 27 | 1 | 88-654306-t-computer3 < Cash payments for machinery < Operating activities | Cash | -1400.00 |
| 28 | 1 | 88-654306-t-computer4 < Cash payments for machinery < Operating activities | Cash | -1300.00 |
| 29 | 1 | Cash payments for operating expenses < Operating activities | Cash | -185721.33 |
| 30 | 1 | Cash payments for operating expenses < Operating activities | Cash | -184369.41 |
| 31 | 1 | Cash payments for operating expenses < Operating activities | Cash | -186387.57 |
| 32 | 1 | 88-654303-n-tax < Cash payments for operating expenses < Operating activities | Cash | -52674.38 |
| 33 | 1 | 88-654308-t-operating < Cash payments to suppliers<Operating activities | Cash | -1000.00 |
| 34 | 1 | 88-654309-t-operating < Cash payments to suppliers<Operating activities | Cash | -17000.00 |
| 35 | 1 | 88-654310-t-operating < Cash payments to suppliers<Operating activities | Cash | -12000.00 |
| 36 | 1 | 88-654304-n-investment bond11 < Cash payments for investments < Investing activities | Cash | -10000.00 |
| 37 | 1 | 88-654304-n-investment bond13 < Cash payments for investments < Investing activities | Cash | -3000.00 |
| 38 | 1 | 88-654305-n-investment bond21 < Cash payments for investments < Investing activities | Cash | -9000.00 |
| 39 | 1 | 88-654307-n-company2 share capital < Cash payments for investments < Investing activities | Cash | -36000.00 |
| 40 | 1 | n | Supplies | 93.79 |
| 41 | 1 | 123456789 | Account receivable | 1400.00 |
| 42 | 1 | 123456787 | Account receivable | 500.00 |
| 43 | 1 | 123456783 | Account receivable | 600.00 |
| 44 | 1 | 123456782 | Account receivable | 900.00 |
| 45 | 1 | 123456781 | Account receivable | 1000.00 |
| 46 | 1 | 123456780 | Account receivable | 2000.00 |
| 47 | 1 | Inven111 < Inven11 < Inven1 | Inventory | $10*74 = 740.00$ |
| 48 | 1 | Inven112 < Inven11 < Inven1 | Inventory | $40*95 = 3800.00$ |
| 49 | 1 | Inven121 < Inven12 < Inven1 | Inventory | $0.8*275 = 220.00$ |

| 50 | 1 | Inven122 < Inven12 < Inven1 | Inventory | $50*32 = 1600.00$ |
|---|---|---|---|---|
| 51 | 1 | Inven21 < Inven2 | Inventory | $30*90 = 2700.00$ |
| 52 | 1 | Inven221 < Inven22 < Inven2 | Inventory | $30*30 = 900.00$ |
| 53 | 1 | Inven222 < Inven22 < Inven2 | Inventory | $50*60 = 3000.00$ |
| 54 | 1 | PPUK parts < ASD parts < Inven2 | Inventory | $40*50 = 2000.00$ |
| 55 | 1 | PPGH parts < ASD parts < Inven2 | Inventory | $2*500 = 1000.00$ |
| 56 | 1 | Inven31 < Inven3 | Inventory | $10*40 = 400.00$ |
| 57 | 1 | Inven32 < Inven3 | Inventory | $50*22 = 1100.00$ |
| 58 | 1 | Inven331 < Inven33 < Inven3 | Inventory | $20*25 = 500.00$ |
| 59 | 1 | Inven332 < Inven33 < Inven3 | Inventory | $45*40 = 1800.00$ |
| 60 | 1 | HGFCVB parts < QASXC parts < Inven3 | Inventory | $10*10 = 100.00$ |
| 61 | 1 | PPGHUP parts < ASDUP parts < Inven3 | Inventory | $20*30 = 600.00$ |
| 62 | 1 | Inven411 < Inven41 < Inven4 | Inventory | $5*102 = 510.00$ |
| 63 | 1 | Inven412 < Inven41 < Inven4 | Inventory | $18.5*20 = 370.00$ |
| 64 | 1 | TTTCU parts < TTT parts < Inven4 | Inventory | $20*115 = 2300.00$ |
| 65 | 1 | RRRHJK parts < Inven4 | Inventory | $20*70 = 1400.00$ |
| 66 | 1 | Truck1 part1 < Truck1 parts < Vehicle parts | Inventory | $8700.00*1 = 8700.00$ |
| 67 | 1 | Truck1 part2 < Truck1 parts < Vehicle parts | Inventory | $7600.00*1 = 7600.00$ |
| 68 | 1 | Truck1 part3 < Truck1 parts < Vehicle parts | Inventory | $5800.00*1 = 5800.00$ |
| 69 | 1 | Truck2 part1 < Truck2 parts < Vehicle parts | Inventory | $8500.00*1 = 8500.00$ |
| 70 | 1 | Truck2 part2 < Truck2 parts < Vehicle parts | Inventory | $7200.00*1 = 7200.00$ |
| 71 | 1 | Truck2 part3 < Truck2 parts < Vehicle parts | Inventory | $5400.00*1 = 5400.00$ |
| 72 | 1 | Car1 part1 < Car1 parts < Vehicle parts | Inventory | $8300.00*1 = 8300.00$ |
| 73 | 1 | Car1 part2 < Car1 parts < Vehicle parts | Inventory | $7200.00*1 = 7200.00$ |
| 74 | 1 | Car1 part3 < Car1 parts < Vehicle parts | Inventory | $5100.00*1 = 5100.00$ |
| 75 | 1 | Car2 part1 < Car2 parts < Vehicle parts | Inventory | $7900.00*1 = 7900.00$ |
| 76 | 1 | Car2 part2 < Car2 parts < Vehicle parts | Inventory | $6800.00*1 = 6800.00$ |
| 77 | 1 | Car2 part3 < Car2 parts < Vehicle parts | Inventory | $4900.00*1 = 4900.00$ |
| 78 | 1 | Car3 part1 < Car3 parts < Vehicle parts | Inventory | $7500.00*1 = 7500.00$ |
| 79 | 1 | Car3 part2 < Car3 parts < Vehicle parts | Inventory | $6400.00*1 = 6400.00$ |
| 80 | 1 | Car3 part3 < Car3 parts < Vehicle parts | Inventory | $4700.00*1 = 4700.00$ |
| 81 | 1 | Computer server1 part1 < Computer server parts < Computer parts | Inventory | $600.00*1 = 600.00$ |
| 82 | 1 | Computer server1 part2 < Computer server parts < Computer parts | Inventory | $400.00*1 = 400.00$ |
| 83 | 1 | Computer server2 part1 < Computer server parts < Computer parts | Inventory | $540.00*1 = 540.00$ |
| 84 | 1 | Computer server2 part2 < Computer server parts < Computer parts | Inventory | $380.00*1 = 380.00$ |
| 85 | 1 | Computer1 part1 < Computer parts | Inventory | $360.00*1 = 360.00$ |
| 86 | 1 | Computer1 part2 < Computer parts | Inventory | $310.00*1 = 310.00$ |
| 87 | 1 | Computer2 part1 < Computer parts | Inventory | $320.00*1 = 320.00$ |
| 88 | 1 | Computer2 part2 < Computer parts | Inventory | $290.00*1 = 290.00$ |
| 89 | 1 | Computer3 part1 < Computer parts | Inventory | $280.00*1 = 280.00$ |
| 90 | 1 | Computer3 part2 < Computer parts | Inventory | $260.00*1 = 260.00$ |

| 91 | 1 | Computer4 part1 < Computer parts | Inventory | 250.00*1 =250.00 |
|---|---|---|---|---|
| 92 | 1 | Computer4 part2 < Computer parts | Inventory | 240.00*1 = 240.00 |
| 93 | 1 | Truck1-inventory < Truck-inventory < Vehicle-inventory | Inventory | 33700.00*1 = 33700.00 |
| 94 | 1 | Truck2-inventory < Truck-inventory < Vehicle-inventory | Inventory | 30000.00*1 = 30000.00 |
| 95 | 1 | Car1-inventory < Car-inventory < Vehicle-inventory | Inventory | 28000.00*1 = 28000.00 |
| 96 | 1 | Car2-inventory < Car-inventory < Vehicle-inventory | Inventory | 27000.00*2 = 54000.00 |
| 97 | 1 | Car3-inventory < Car-inventory < Vehicle-inventory | Inventory | 26000.00*2 = 52000.00 |
| 98 | 1 | Computer server1-inventory < Computer server-inventory < Computer-inventory | Inventory | 1600.00*3 = 4800.00 |
| 99 | 1 | Computer server2-inventory < Computer server-inventory < Computer-inventory | Inventory | 1500.00*2 = 3000.00 |
| 100 | 1 | Computer1-inventory < Computer-inventory | Inventory | 1000.00*4 = 4000.00 |
| 101 | 1 | Computer2-inventory < Computer-inventory | Inventory | 920.00*4 = 3680.00 |
| 102 | 1 | Computer3-inventory < Computer-inventory | Inventory | 830.00*6 = 4980.00 |
| 103 | 1 | Computer4-inventory < Computer-inventory | Inventory | 770.00*10 = 7700.00 |
| 104 | 1 | Working-truck1 < Working-truck < Working-vehicle | Working-in-process inventory | 29572.91*2 = 59145.82 |
| 105 | 1 | Working-truck2 < Working-truck < Working-vehicle | Working-in-process inventory | 27863.74*3 = 83591.22 |
| 106 | 1 | Working-car1 < Working-car < Working-vehicle | Working-in-process inventory | 26987.33*2 = 53974.66 |
| 107 | 1 | Working-car2 < Working-car < Working-vehicle | Working-in-process inventory | 24549.81*2 = 49099.62 |
| 108 | 1 | Working-car3 < Working-car < Working-vehicle | Working-in-process inventory | 24412.17*3 = 73236.51 |
| 109 | 1 | Working-computer server1 < Working-computer server < Working-computer | Working-in-process inventory | 1556.45*4 = 6225.80 |
| 110 | 1 | Working-computer server2 < Working-computer server < Working-computer | Working-in-process inventory | 1476.29*4 = 5905.16 |
| 111 | 1 | Working-computer1 < Working-computer | Working-in-process inventory | 945.12*10 = 9451.20 |
| 112 | 1 | Working-computer2 < Working-computer | Working-in-process inventory | 817.12*10 = 8171.20 |
| 113 | 1 | Working-computer3 < Working-computer | Working-in-process inventory | 732.28*12 = 8787.36 |
| 114 | 1 | Working-computer4 < Working-computer | Working-in-process inventory | 680.54*15 = 10208.1 |
| 115 | 1 | Bond11 | Bonds | 10000.00 |
| 116 | 1 | Bond13 | Bonds | 3000.00 |
| 117 | 1 | Bond21 | Bonds | 9000.00 |
| 118 | 1 | Company2 share capital | Share | 36000.00 |
| 119 | 1 | Truck11 < Truck1 < Truck | Vehicle | 45000.00 |
| 120 | 1 | Truck21 < Truck2 < Truck | Vehicle | 40000.00 |
| 121 | 1 | Car31 < Car3 < Car | Vehicle | 36000.00 |
| 122 | 1 | Truck11-accumulated amortization < Truck1-accumulated amortization < Truck-accumulated amortization | Accumulated amortization: Vehicle | -19500.00 |
| 123 | 1 | Truck21-accumulated amortization < Truck2-accumulated amortization < Truck-accumulated amortization | Accumulated amortization: Vehicle | -17333.33 |
| 124 | 1 | Car31-accumulated amortization < Car3-accumulated amortization < Car-accumulated amortization | Accumulated amortization: Vehicle | -12000.00 |

| 125 | 1 | Computer server21 < Computer server2 < Computer server | Computer | 2700.00 |
|---|---|---|---|---|
| 126 | 1 | Computer31 < Computer3 | Computer | 1400.00 |
| 127 | 1 | Computer41 < Computer4 | Computer | 1300.00 |
| 128 | 1 | Computer server21-accumulated amortization < Computer server2-accumulated amortization < Computer server-accumulated amortization | Accumulated amortization: Computer | -2137.50 |
| 129 | 1 | Computer31-accumulated amortization < Computer3-accumulated amortization | Accumulated amortization: Computer | -1108.33 |
| 130 | 1 | Computer41-accumulated amortization < Computer4-accumulated amortization | Accumulated amortization: Computer | -1029.17 |
| 131 | 2 | 123456083 | Account payable | 13400.00 |
| 132 | 2 | 123456082 | Account payable | 10600.00 |
| 133 | 2 | 123456081 | Account payable | 2040.00 |
| 134 | 2 | 123456080 | Account payable | 1000.00 |
| 135 | 2 | Band31-interest payable < Bonds-interest payable | Accrued interest payable | 0 |
| 136 | 2 | Note11-interest payable < Notes-interest payable | Accrued interest payable | 0 |
| 137 | 2 | Note15-interest payable < Notes-interest payable | Accrued interest payable | 0 |
| 138 | 2 | Note21-interest payable < Notes-interest payable | Accrued interest payable | 0 |
| 139 | 2 | Bond31-88-654305 < Bond31 | Bonds payable | 5000.00 |
| 140 | 2 | Bond31-909876501 < Bond31 | Bonds payable | 3000.00 |
| 141 | 2 | Bond31-909876502 < Bond31 | Bonds payable | 6000.00 |
| 142 | 2 | Bond31-909876508 < Bond31 | Bonds payable | 5000.00 |
| 143 | 2 | Bond31-88-654311 < Bond31 | Bonds payable | 7000.00 |
| 144 | 2 | Bond31-88-654314 < Bond31 | Bonds payable | 2000.00 |
| 145 | 2 | Bond31-909876516 < Bond31 | Bonds payable | 4000.00 |
| 146 | 2 | Bond31-909876518 < Bond31 | Bonds payable | 2000.00 |
| 147 | 2 | Bond31-909876521 < Bond31 | Bonds payable | 3000.00 |
| 148 | 2 | Bond31-909876522 < Bond31 | Bonds payable | 5000.00 |
| 149 | 2 | Bond31-909876524 < Bond31 | Bonds payable | 3000.00 |
| 150 | 2 | Bond31-909876525 < Bond31 | Bonds payable | 5000.00 |
| 151 | 2 | Note11-88-654304 | Notes payable | 250000.00 |
| 152 | 2 | Note15-88-654304 | Notes payable | 170000.00 |
| 153 | 2 | Note21-88-654305 | Notes payable | 220000.00 |
| 154 | 3 | Capital-909876512 | Share capital | 80000.00 |
| 155 | 3 | Capital-909876515 | Share capital | 70000.00 |
| 156 | 3 | Capital-909876518 | Share capital | 50000.00 |
| 157 | 3 | n | Retained earnings (Conversion) | 13546.09 |
| 158 | 4 | Sales-909876513 | Sales | 0 |
| 159 | 5 | 909876513-travelling < Sales department-travelling | Travelling expenses | 0 |
| 160 | 5 | 909876514-travelling < Office department-travelling | Travelling expenses | 0 |

| 161 | 5 | 909876515-travelling < Product department-travelling | Travelling expenses | 0 |
| 162 | 5 | 909876513-other < Sales department-other | Other expenses | 0 |
| 163 | 5 | 909876514-other < Office department-other | Other expenses | 0 |
| 164 | 5 | 909876515-other < Product department-other | Other expenses | 0 |
| 165 | 5 | 909876514-salary < Office department-salary | Salary expenses | 0 |
| 166 | 5 | Supplies expenses | Cost of goods manufactured | 0 |
| 167 | 5 | 909876513-salary <  Sales department-salary < Salary expenses | Cost of goods manufactured | 0 |
| 168 | 5 | 909876515-salary < Product department-salary < Salary expenses | Cost of goods manufactured | 0 |
| 169 | 5 | General parts expenses | Cost of goods manufactured | 0 |
| 170 | 5 | Bond31-interest | Bond interest expenses | 0 |
| 171 | 5 | Note11-interest | Note interest expenses | 0 |
| 172 | 5 | Note15-interest | Note interest expenses | 0 |
| 173 | 5 | Note21-interest | Note interest expenses | 0 |
| 174 | 5 | Truck11-amortization < Truck1-amortization < Vehicle-truck-amortization | Amortization expenses | 0 |
| 175 | 5 | Truck21-amortization < Truck2-amortization < Vehicle-truck-amortization | Amortization expenses | 0 |
| 176 | 5 | Car31-amortization < Car3-amortization < Vehicle-car-amortization | Amortization expenses | 0 |
| 177 | 5 | Computer server21-amortization < Computer server2-amortization < Computer-amortization | Amortization expenses | 0 |
| 178 | 5 | Computer31-amortization < Computer3-amortization  < Computer-amortization | Amortization expenses | 0 |
| 179 | 5 | Computer41-amortization < Computer4-amortization  < Computer-amortization | Amortization expenses | 0 |
| 180 | 4 | Accrued interest income-bond11 < Bonds | Investment incomes | 0 |
| 181 | 4 | Accrued interest income-bond13 < Bonds | Investment incomes | 0 |
| 182 | 4 | Accrued interest income-bond21 < Bonds | Investment incomes | 0 |
| 183 | 4 | n | Deposits interest income | 0 |

Figure 2.4-23   Company1 Converting Multi-Subaccount Names Table

From the Figure 2.4-23, the Company1 has the balance of the Account receivable account and also the balance of the Account payable account for the same company. For example, for the Company2 (phone number: 123456783), the balances of the Account receivable account and the Account payable account are $600 and $13,400 respectively. The MathAccounting can deal with them correctly by the different phone numbers. If the Account receivable account of the Company2 has a phone number: 123456783, the Account payable account of the Company2 has another phone number: 123456083.

Before entering the dynamic accounting equation on December 31, 2015 into the database dcj06, I first enter two initialization sub-equations.

Account payable (2): 0 = Share capital (3): 0

0 = Sales (4): 0 – Cost of goods sold (5):0

From the Figure 2.4-18 and the Figure 2.4-23, the dynamic accounting equation on December 31, 2015 must be divided to the N transaction sub-equations because of the limitation of the MathAccounting software. Please pay attention here. Because the Inventory account and the Working-in-process inventory accounts need to enter unit number into the database, the two accounts cannot be divided. Every sub-equation has maximum twelve items. All converting transaction sub-equations can be designed and written as following.

- I build a transaction sub-equation for the Account receivable account and the Account payable account. The transaction sub-equation includes the part of the Cash account with the Order 1, the Account receivable account with the Order 41 to the Order 46, and the Account payable account with the Order 131 to the Order 134. The first transaction sub-equation is:

  Cash (1): 20640 + Account receivable (1): 1400 + Account receivable (1): 500 + Account receivable (1): 600 + Account receivable (1): 900 + Account receivable (1): 1000 + Account receivable (1): 2000 = Account payable (2): 13400 + Account payable (2): 10600 + Account payable (2): 2040 + Account payable (2): 1000

  After entering this transaction, the new balance of the Cash account with the Order 1 is $59,360 (= $80,000 - $20,640).

- The transaction sub-equation includes the rest ($59,360) of the Cash account with the Order 1, the Cash account with the Order 2 to the Order 6, the part of the Share capital account with the Order 154, the Share capital account with the Order 155 and the Order 156, and the Notes payable account with the Order 151 to the Order 153.

The second transaction sub-equation is:

Cash (1): 59360 + Cash (1): 70000 + Cash (1): 50000 + Cash (1): 250000 + Cash (1): 170000 + Cash (1): 220000 = Share capital (3): 59360 + Share capital (3): 70000 + Share capital (3): 50000 + Notes payable (2): 250000 + Notes payable (2): 170000 + Notes payable (2): 220000

After entering this transaction, the new balance of the Share capital account with the Order 154 is $20,640 (= $80,000 - $59,360).

- The transaction sub-equation includes the Cash account with the Order 7 to the Order 13 and the Bonds payable account with the Order 139 to the Order 144. Because the balance of the Cash with the Order 7 is zero, the third transaction sub-equation is:

  Cash (1): 5000 + Cash (1): 3000 + Cash (1): 6000 + Cash (1): 5000 + Cash (1): 7000 + Cash (1): 2000 = Bonds payable (2): 5000 + Bonds payable (2): 3000 + Bonds payable (2): 6000 + Bonds payable (?): 5000 + Bonds payable (2): 7000 + Bonds payable (2): 2000

- The transaction sub-equation includes the Cash account with the Order 14 to the Order 19 and the Bonds payable account with the Order 145 to the Order 150. The fourth transaction sub-equation is:

  Cash (1): 4000 + Cash (1): 2000 + Cash (1): 3000 + Cash (1): 5000 + Cash (1): 3000 + Cash (1): 5000 = Bonds payable (2): 4000 + Bonds payable (2): 2000 + Bonds payable (2): 3000 + Bonds payable (2): 5000 + Bonds payable (2): 3000 + Bonds payable (2): 5000

- The transaction sub-equation includes the Cash account with the Order 20 to the Order 22, the part of the Cash account with the Order 29, and the Inventory account with the Order 47 to the Order 54. The fifth transaction sub-equation is:

Cash (1): 766.67 + Cash (1): 45 + Cash (1): 615 + Cash (1): -16386.67 + Inventory (1): 740 + Inventory (1): 3800 + Inventory (1): 220 + Inventory (1): 1600 + Inventory (1): 2700 + Inventory (1): 900 + Inventory (1): 3000 + Inventory (1): 2000 = 0

After entering this transaction, the new balance of the Cash account with the Order 29 is -$169,334.66 (= -$185,721.33 + $16,386.67).

- The transaction sub-equation includes the Cash account with the Order 23 to the Order 28, the Vehicle account with the Order 119 to the Order 121, and the Computer account with the Order 125 to the Order 127. The sixth transaction sub-equation is:

Cash (1): -45000 + Cash (1): -40000 + Cash (1): -36000 + Cash (1): -2700 + Cash (1): -1400 + Cash (1): -1300 + Vehicle (1): 45000 + Vehicle (1): 40000 + Vehicle (1): 36000 + Computer (1): 2700 + Computer (1): 1400 + Computer (1): 1300 = 0

- The transaction sub-equation includes the part of the Cash account with the Order 29 and the Inventory account with the Order 55 to the Order 65. The seventh transaction sub-equation is:

Cash (1): -10080 + Inventory (1): 1000 + Inventory (1): 400 + Inventory (1): 1100 + Inventory (1): 500 + Inventory (1): 1800 + Inventory (1): 100 + Inventory (1): 60000 + Inventory (1): 510+ Inventory (1): 370 + Inventory (1): 2300 + Inventory (1): 1400 = 0

After entering this transaction, the new balance of the Cash account with the Order 29 is -$159,254.66 (= -$169,334.66 + $10,080).

- The transaction sub-equation includes the part of the Cash account with the Order 29, the Cash account with the Order 33 to the Order 35, and the Inventory account with the Order 66 to the Order 73. The eighth transaction sub-equation is:

Cash (1): -28700 + Cash (1): -1000 + Cash (1): -17000 + Cash (1): -12000 + Inventory (1): 8700 + Inventory (1): 7600 + Inventory (1): 5800 + Inventory (1): 8500 + Inventory (1): 7200 + Inventory (1): 5400 + Inventory (1): 8300 + Inventory (1): 7200 = 0

After entering this transaction, the new balance of the Cash account with the Order 29 is -$130,554.66 (= -$159,254.66 + $28,700).

- The transaction sub-equation includes the part of the Cash account with the Order 29, the Cash account with the Order 36 to the Order 38, and the Inventory account with the Order 74 to the Order 80. The ninth transaction sub-equation is:

Cash (1): -21300 + Cash (1): -10000 + Cash (1): -3000 + Cash (1): -9000 + Inventory (1): 5100 + Inventory (1): 7900 + Inventory (1): 6800 + Inventory (1): 4900 + Inventory (1): 7500 + Inventory (1): 6400 + Inventory (1): 4700 = 0

After entering this transaction, the new balance of the Cash account with the Order 29 is -$109,254.66 (= -$130,554.66 + $21,300).

- The transaction sub-equation includes the part of the Cash account with the Order 29 and the Inventory account with the Order 81 to the Order 91. The tenth transaction sub-equation is:

Cash (1): -3990 + Inventory (1): 600 + Inventory (1): 400 + Inventory (1): 540 + Inventory (1): 380 + Inventory (1): 360 + Inventory (1): 310 + Inventory (1): 320 + Inventory (1): 290 + Inventory (1): 280 + Inventory (1): 260 + Inventory (1): 250 = 0

After entering this transaction, the new balance of the Cash account with the Order 29 is -$105,264.66 (= -$109,254.66 + $3,990).

- The transaction sub-equation includes the rest of the Cash account with the Order 29, the part of the Cash account with the Order 30, the Cash account with the Order 32 and the Order 39, the Supplies account with the Order 40, and the Inventory account with the Order 92 to the Order 98. The eleventh transaction sub-equation is:

  Cash (1): -105264.66 + Cash (1): -8,894.75 + Cash (1): -52674.38 + Cash (1): -36000 + Supplies (1): 93.79 + Inventory (1): 240 + Inventory (1): 33700 + Inventory (1): 30000 + Inventory (1): 28000 + Inventory (1): 54000 + Inventory (1): 52000 + Inventory (1): 4800 = 0

  After entering this transaction, the new balance of the Cash account with the Order 30 is -$175,474.66 (= -$184369.41+ $8,894.75).

- The transaction sub-equation includes the part of the Cash account with the Order 30, the Cash account with the Order 31, the Inventory account with the Order 99 to the Order 103, and the Working-in-process inventory account with the Order 104 to the Order 108. The eleventh transaction sub-equation is:

  Cash (1): -156020.26 + Cash (1): -186387.57 + Inventory (1): 3000 + Inventory (1): 4000 + Inventory (1): 3680 + Inventory (1): 4980 + Inventory (1): 7700 + Working-in-process inventory (1): 59145.82 + Working-in-process inventory (1): 83591.22 + Working-in-process inventory (1): 53974.66 + Working-in-process inventory (1): 49099.62 + Working-in-process inventory (1): 73236.51 = 0

  After entering this transaction, the new balance of the Cash account with the Order 30 is -$19,454.4 (= -$175,474.66 + $156,020.26).

- The transaction sub-equation includes the part of the Cash account with the Order 30 (increase), the Working-in-process inventory account with the Order 109 to the Order 114, and the Accumulated amortization: Vehicle account with the Order 122 to the Order 124. The twelfth transaction sub-equation is:

Cash (1): 84.51 + Working-in-process inventory (1): 6225.8 + Working-in-process inventory (1): 5905.16 + Working-in-process inventory (1): 9451.2 + Working-in-process inventory (1): 8171.2 + Working-in-process inventory (1): 8787.36 + Working-in-process inventory (1): 10208.1 + Accumulated amortization: Vehicle (1): -19500 + Accumulated amortization: Vehicle (1): -17333.33 + Accumulated amortization: Vehicle (1): -12000 = 0

After entering this transaction, the new balance of the Cash account with the Order 30 is -$19,538.91 (= -$19,454.4 - $84.51).

- The transaction sub-equation includes rest (-$19,538.91) of the Cash account with the Order 30, the Bonds account with the Order 115 to the Order 117, the "Share" account with the Order 118, the Accumulated amortization: Computer account with the Order 128 and the Order 130, the rest ($20,640) of the Share capital account with the Order 154, and the Retained earnings (Conversion) account with the balance $13546.09. The thirteenth transaction sub-equation is:

  Cash (1): -19538.91 + Bonds (1): 10000 + Bonds (1): 3000 + Bonds (1): 9000 + Share (1): 36000 + Accumulated amortization: Computer (1): -2137.5 + Accumulated amortization: Computer (1): -1108.33 + Accumulated amortization: Computer (1): -1029.17 = Share capital (3): 20640 + Retained earnings (Conversion) (3): 13546.09

After completing this transaction, the dynamic accounting equation of the Company1 on December 31, 2015 has entered into the database dcj06.

## 2.4.3.2 Brief Summary of the Company1

The Figure 2.4-24 on the next page shows cash received or paid by other members table which is in the public database dcj100.

```
-use dcj100
 select sum(amount) as sum0 from CashByMembers where Recorder = '88-654306'
 select * from CashByMembers where Recorder = '88-654306'
```

100 %  ▾

☐ Results  ☐ Messages

| | sum0 |
|---|---|
| 1 | -67873.98 |

| | IDM | Amount | Symbol | MultiSubaccount | Recorder | TransDate |
|---|---|---|---|---|---|---|
| 1 | 909876512 | -20640.00 | i | 909876512-i-owners < Cash receipts from owners < Financial activities | 88-654306 | 2015-12-31 |
| 2 | 909876512 | -59360.00 | i | 909876512-i-owners < Cash receipts from owners < Financial activities | 88-654306 | 2015-12-31 |
| 3 | 909876515 | -70000.00 | i | 909876515-i-owners < Cash receipts from owners < Financial activities | 88-654306 | 2015-12-31 |
| 4 | 909876518 | -50000.00 | i | 909876518-i-owners < Cash receipts from owners < Financial activities | 88-654306 | 2015-12-31 |
| 5 | 88-654304 | -250000.00 | i | 88-654304-i-note11 < Cash receipts from banks < Financial activities | 88-654306 | 2015-12-31 |
| 6 | 88-654304 | -170000.00 | i | 88-654304-i-note15 < Cash receipts from banks < Financial activities | 88-654306 | 2015-12-31 |
| 7 | 88-654305 | -220000.00 | i | 88-654305-i-note21 < Cash receipts from banks < Financial activities | 88-654306 | 2015-12-31 |
| 8 | 88-654305 | -5000.00 | i | 88-654305-i-bond31 < Cash receipts from issued bonds < Financial activities | 88-654306 | 2015-12-21 |
| 9 | 909876501 | -3000.00 | i | 909876501-i-bond31 < Cash receipts from issued bonds < Financial activities | 88-654306 | 2015-12-21 |
| 10 | 909876502 | -6000.00 | i | 909876502-i-bond31 < Cash receipts from issued bonds < Financial activities | 88-654306 | 2015-12-21 |
| 11 | 909876508 | -5000.00 | i | 909876508-i-bond31 < Cash receipts from issued bonds < Financial activities | 88-654306 | 2015-12-21 |
| 12 | 909876511 | -7000.00 | i | 909876511-i-bond31 < Cash receipts from issued bonds < Financial activities | 88-654306 | 2015-12-21 |
| 13 | 909876514 | -2000.00 | i | 909876514-i-bond31 < Cash receipts from issued bonds < Financial activities | 88-654306 | 2015-12-21 |
| 14 | 909876516 | -4000.00 | i | 909876516-i-bond31 < Cash receipts from issued bonds < Financial activities | 88-654306 | 2015-12-31 |
| 15 | 909876518 | -2000.00 | i | 909876518-i-bond31 < Cash receipts from issued bonds < Financial activities | 88-654306 | 2015-12-31 |
| 16 | 909876521 | -3000.00 | i | 909876521-i-bond31 < Cash receipts from issued bonds < Financial activities | 88-654306 | 2015-12-31 |
| 17 | 909876522 | -5000.00 | i | 909876522-i-bond31 < Cash receipts from issued bonds < Financial activities | 88-654306 | 2015-12-31 |
| 18 | 909876524 | -3000.00 | i | 909876524-i-bond31 < Cash receipts from issued bonds < Financial activities | 88-654306 | 2015-12-31 |
| 19 | 909876525 | -5000.00 | i | 909876525-i-bond31 < Cash receipts from issued bonds < Financial activities | 88-654306 | 2015-12-31 |
| 20 | 88-654304 | -766.67 | c | 88-654304-c-interest of  investment bond11 < Cash receipts from investments < Investing activities | 88-654306 | 2015-12-31 |
| 21 | 88-654304 | -45.00 | c | 88-654304-c-interest of investment bond13 < Cash receipts from investments < Investing activities | 88-654306 | 2015-12-31 |
| 22 | 88-654305 | -615.00 | c | 88-654305-c-interest of investment bond21 < Cash receipts from investments < Investing activities | 88-654306 | 2015-12-31 |
| 23 | | 16386.67 | | Cash payments for operating expenses < Operating activities | 88-654306 | 2015-12-31 |
| 24 | 88-654306 | 45000.00 | t | 88-654306-t-truck1 < Cash payments for machinery < Operating activities | 88-654306 | 2015-12-31 |
| 25 | 88-654306 | 40000.00 | t | 88-654306-t-truck2 < Cash payments for machinery < Operating activities | 88-654306 | 2015-12-31 |

✅ Query executed successfully. LIU\SQLEXP

Figure 2.4-24   Company1 Cash Received or Paid by Other Members (Continue)

Figure 2.4-24   Company1 Cash Received or Paid by Other Members

The Figure 2.4-25 on the next page shows cash flows statement of the Company1 on December 31, 2015.

| Cash Flows Statement Year Ended 2015-12-31 | |
| --- | --- |
| **Operating activities** | |
| Cash payments for machinery | -$126,400.00 |
| Cash payments for operating expenses | -$609,152.69 |
| Cash payments to suppliers | -$30,000.00 |
| Net cash provided by Operating activities | -$765,552.69 |
| | |
| Investing activities | |
| Cash payments for investments | -$58,000.00 |
| Cash receipts from investments | $1,426.67 |
| Net cash provided by Investing activities | -$56,573.33 |
| | |
| Financial activities | |
| Cash receipts from banks | $640,000.00 |
| Cash receipts from issued bonds | $50,000.00 |
| Cash receipts from owners | $200,000.00 |
| Net cash provided by Financial activities | $890,000.00 |
| | |
| Net change in cash | $67,873.98 |
| Cash, Begining | $0.00 |
| Cash, Ending | $67,873.98 |

Figure 2.4-25   Company1 Cash Flows Statement

The Figure 2.4-26 on the next pages shows cash account table of the Company1 on December 31, 2015.

Cash

| ID | Multi-Name | Amount | Balance | General ID | Transaction Date |
|---|---|---|---|---|---|
| 1 | 909876512-i-owners < Cash receipts from owners < Financial activities | $20,640.00 | $20,640.00 | 3 | 2015-12-31 |
| 2 | 909876512-i-owners < Cash receipts from owners < Financial activities | $59,360.00 | $80,000.00 | 4 | 2015-12-31 |
| 3 | 909876515-i-owners < Cash receipts from owners < Financial activities | $70,000.00 | $150,000.00 | 4 | 2015-12-31 |
| 4 | 909876518-i-owners < Cash receipts from owners < Financial activities | $50,000.00 | $200,000.00 | 4 | 2015-12-31 |
| 5 | 88-654304-i-note11 < Cash receipts from banks < Financial activities | $250,000.00 | $450,000.00 | 4 | 2015-12-31 |
| 6 | 88-654304-i-note15 < Cash receipts from banks < Financial activities | $170,000.00 | $620,000.00 | 4 | 2015-12-31 |
| 7 | 88-654305-i-note21 < Cash receipts from banks < Financial activities | $220,000.00 | $840,000.00 | 4 | 2015-12-31 |
| 8 | 88-654305-i-bond31 < Cash receipts from issued bonds < Financial activ... | $5,000.00 | $845,000.00 | 5 | 2015-12-21 |
| 9 | 909876501-i-bond31 < Cash receipts from issued bonds < Financial acti... | $3,000.00 | $848,000.00 | 5 | 2015-12-21 |
| 10 | 909876502-i-bond31 < Cash receipts from issued bonds < Financial acti... | $6,000.00 | $854,000.00 | 5 | 2015-12-21 |
| 11 | 909876508-i-bond31 < Cash receipts from issued bonds < Financial acti... | $5,000.00 | $859,000.00 | 5 | 2015-12-21 |
| 12 | 909876511-i-bond31 < Cash receipts from issued bonds < Financial acti... | $7,000.00 | $866,000.00 | 5 | 2015-12-21 |
| 13 | 909876514-i-bond31 < Cash receipts from issued bonds < Financial acti... | $2,000.00 | $868,000.00 | 5 | 2015-12-21 |
| 14 | 909876516-i-bond31 < Cash receipts from issued bonds < Financial acti... | $4,000.00 | $872,000.00 | 6 | 2015-12-31 |
| 15 | 909876518-i-bond31 < Cash receipts from issued bonds < Financial acti... | $2,000.00 | $874,000.00 | 6 | 2015-12-31 |
| 16 | 909876521-i-bond31 < Cash receipts from issued bonds < Financial acti... | $3,000.00 | $877,000.00 | 6 | 2015-12-31 |
| 17 | 909876522-i-bond31 < Cash receipts from issued bonds < Financial acti... | $5,000.00 | $882,000.00 | 6 | 2015-12-31 |
| 18 | 909876524-i-bond31 < Cash receipts from issued bonds < Financial acti... | $3,000.00 | $885,000.00 | 6 | 2015-12-31 |
| 19 | 909876525-i-bond31 < Cash receipts from issued bonds < Financial acti... | $5,000.00 | $890,000.00 | 6 | 2015-12-31 |
| 20 | 88-654304-c-interest of investment bond11 < Cash receipts from invest... | $766.67 | $890,766.67 | 7 | 2015-12-31 |
| 21 | 88-654304-c-interest of investment bond13 < Cash receipts from investm... | $45.00 | $890,811.67 | 7 | 2015-12-31 |
| 22 | 88-654305-c-interest of investment bond21 < Cash receipts from investm... | $615.00 | $891,426.67 | 7 | 2015-12-31 |
| 23 | Cash payments for operating expenses < Operating activities | -$16,386.67 | $875,040.00 | 7 | 2015-12-31 |
| 24 | 88-654306-t-truck1 < Cash payments for machinery < Operating activities | -$45,000.00 | $830,040.00 | 8 | 2015-12-31 |

Figure 2.4-26   Company1 Cash Account Table (Continue)

Cash

| ID | Multi-Name | Amount | Balance | General ID | Transaction Date |
|---|---|---|---|---|---|
| 25 | 88-654306-t-truck2 < Cash payments for machinery < Operating activities | -$40,000.00 | $790,040.00 | 8 | 2015-12-31 |
| 26 | 88-654306-t-car3 < Cash payments for machinery < Operating activities | -$36,000.00 | $754,040.00 | 8 | 2015-12-31 |
| 27 | 88-654306-t-computer server2 < Cash payments for machinery < Operati... | -$2,700.00 | $751,340.00 | 8 | 2015-12-31 |
| 28 | 88-654306-t-computer3 < Cash payments for machinery < Operating acti... | -$1,400.00 | $749,940.00 | 8 | 2015-12-31 |
| 29 | 88-654306-t-computer4 < Cash payments for machinery < Operating acti... | -$1,300.00 | $748,640.00 | 8 | 2015-12-31 |
| 30 | Cash payments for operating expenses < Operating activities | -$10,080.00 | $738,560.00 | 9 | 2015-12-31 |
| 31 | Cash payments for operating expenses < Operating activities | -$28,700.00 | $709,860.00 | 10 | 2015-12-31 |
| 32 | 88-654308-t-operating < Cash payments to suppliers<Operating activities | -$1,000.00 | $708,860.00 | 10 | 2015-12-31 |
| 33 | 88-654309-t-operating < Cash payments to suppliers<Operating activities | -$17,000.00 | $691,860.00 | 10 | 2015-12-31 |
| 34 | 88-654310-t-operating < Cash payments to suppliers<Operating activities | -$12,000.00 | $679,860.00 | 10 | 2015-12-31 |
| 35 | Cash payments for operating expenses < Operating activities | -$21,300.00 | $658,560.00 | 11 | 2015-12-31 |
| 36 | 88-654304-n-investment bond11 < Cash payments for investments < Inv... | -$10,000.00 | $648,560.00 | 11 | 2015-12-31 |
| 37 | 88-654304-n-investment bond13 < Cash payments for investments < Inv... | -$3,000.00 | $645,560.00 | 11 | 2015-12-31 |
| 38 | 88-654305-n-investment bond21 < Cash payments for investments < Inv... | -$9,000.00 | $636,560.00 | 11 | 2015-12-31 |
| 39 | Cash payments for operating expenses < Operating activities | -$3,990.00 | $632,570.00 | 12 | 2015-12-31 |
| 40 | Cash payments for operating expenses < Operating activities | -$105,264.66 | $527,305.34 | 13 | 2015-12-31 |
| 41 | Cash payments for operating expenses < Operating activities | -$8,894.75 | $518,410.59 | 13 | 2015-12-31 |
| 42 | 88-654303-n-tax < Cash payments for operating expenses < Operating a... | -$52,674.38 | $465,736.21 | 13 | 2015-12-31 |
| 43 | 88-654307-n-company2 share capital < Cash payments for investments ... | -$36,000.00 | $429,736.21 | 13 | 2015-12-31 |
| 44 | Cash payments for operating expenses < Operating activities | -$156,020.26 | $274,915.95 | 14 | 2015-12-31 |
| 45 | Cash payments for operating expenses < Operating activities | -$186,387.57 | $88,528.38 | 14 | 2015-12-31 |
| 46 | Cash payments for operating expenses < Operating activities | $84.51 | $87,412.89 | 15 | 2015-12-31 |
| 47 | Cash payments for operating expenses < Operating activities | -$19,538.91 | $67,873.98 | 16 | 2015-12-31 |

Figure 2.4-26   Company1 Cash Account Table

The Figure 2.4-27 on the next page shows balance sheet table of the Company1 on December 31, 2015.

Balance Sheet

| | As at 12/31/2015 |
|---|---|
| **ASSETS** | |
| Current assets | |
| Cash | $67,873.98 |
| Supplies | $93.79 |
| Account receivable | $6,400.00 |
| Inventory | $357,130.00 |
| Working-in-process inventory | $367,796.65 |
| | $799,294.42 |
| Long term investments | |
| Bonds | $22,000.00 |
| Share | $36,000.00 |
| | $58,000.00 |
| Equipment | |
| Vehicle | $121,000.00 |
| Accumulated amortization: Vehicle | -$48,833.33 |
| Computer | $5,400.00 |
| Accumulated amortization: Computer | -$4,275.00 |
| | $73,291.67 |
| Total Assets | $930,586.09 |
| | |
| LIABILITIES | |
| Current liabilities | |
| Account payable | $27,040.00 |
| Long term liabilities | |
| Bonds payable | $50,000.00 |
| Notes payable | $640,000.00 |
| | $690,000.00 |
| Total Liability | $717,040.00 |
| | |
| SHAREHOLDERS' EQUITY | |
| Owners capital | |
| Share capital | $200,000.00 |
| Retained earnings (conversion) | $13,546.09 |
| | $213,546.09 |
| Retined earnings | $0.00 |
| Accumulated other comprehensive income | $0.00 |
| Total Shareholders' Equity | $213,546.09 |
| | |
| Total Liabilities and Shareholders' Equity | $930,586.09 |

Figure 2.4-27   Company1 Balance Sheet

## 2.4.4 Sample of the Company2

The Company2 has total share capital $180,000 and three shareholders of the individual A13, the individual A14, and the Company1. Their percentages of the share capital are 50%, 30%, and 20% respectively. The Company2 produces the parts of vehicles and the computers. The Figure 2.4-28 shows its product names, costs, and sale prices.

| Order | Product (the Lowest-level Subaccount) Names | Multi-subaccount Names | Costs | Sale Prices |
|---|---|---|---|---|
| 1 | Truck1 part1 | Truck1 part1 < Truck1 parts < Vehicle parts | 5600.00 | 8700.00 |
| 2 | Truck1 part2 | Truck1 part2 < Truck1 parts < Vehicle parts | 4950.00 | 7600.00 |
| 3 | Truck1 part3 | Truck1 part3 < Truck1 parts < Vehicle parts | 3750.00 | 5800.00 |
| 4 | Truck2 part1 | Truck2 part1 < Truck2 parts < Vehicle parts | 5500.00 | 8500.00 |
| 5 | Truck2 part2 | Truck2 part2 < Truck2 parts < Vehicle parts | 4660.00 | 7200.00 |
| 6 | Truck2 part3 | Truck2 part3 < Truck2 parts < Vehicle parts | 3500.00 | 5400.00 |
| 7 | Car1 part1 | Car1 part1 < Car1 parts < Vehicle parts | 5380.00 | 8300.00 |
| 8 | Car1 part2 | Car1 part2 < Car1 parts < Vehicle parts | 4650.00 | 7200.00 |
| 9 | Car1 part3 | Car1 part3 < Car1 parts < Vehicle parts | 3300.00 | 5100.00 |
| 10 | Car2 part1 | Car2 part1 < Car2 parts < Vehicle parts | 5100.00 | 7900.00 |
| 11 | Car2 part2 | Car2 part2 < Car2 parts < Vehicle parts | 4400.00 | 6800.00 |
| 12 | Car2 part3 | Car2 part3 < Car2 parts < Vehicle parts | 3170.00 | 4900.00 |
| 13 | Car3 part1 | Car3 part1 < Car3 parts < Vehicle parts | 4850.00 | 7500.00 |
| 14 | Car3 part2 | Car3 part2 < Car3 parts < Vehicle parts | 4150.00 | 6400.00 |
| 15 | Car3 part3 | Car3 part3 < Car3 parts < Vehicle parts | 3050.00 | 4700.00 |
| 16 | Computer server1 part1 | Computer server1 part1 < Computer server parts < Computer parts | 390.00 | 600.00 |
| 17 | Computer server1 part2 | Computer server1 part2 < Computer server parts < Computer parts | 260.00 | 400.00 |
| 18 | Computer server2 part1 | Computer server2 part1 < Computer server parts < Computer parts | 350.00 | 540.00 |
| 19 | Computer server2 part2 | Computer server2 part2 < Computer server parts < Computer parts | 250.00 | 380.00 |
| 20 | Computer1 part1 | Computer1 part1 < Computer parts | 235.00 | 360.00 |
| 21 | Computer1 part2 | Computer1 part2 < Computer parts | 202.00 | 310.00 |
| 22 | Computer2 part1 | Computer2 part1 < Computer parts | 208.00 | 320.00 |
| 23 | Computer2 part2 | Computer2 part2 < Computer parts | 189.00 | 290.00 |
| 24 | Computer3 part1 | Computer3 part1 < Computer parts | 182.00 | 280.00 |
| 25 | Computer3 part2 | Computer3 part2 < Computer parts | 169.00 | 260.00 |
| 26 | Computer4 part1 | Computer4 part1 < Computer parts | 162.00 | 250.00 |
| 27 | Computer4 part2 | Computer4 part2 < Computer parts | 156.00 | 240.00 |

Figure 2.4-28   Company2 Products and Sale Prices Table

For a manufacturing company, the Company2 is similar to the Company1. When the Company2 uses the MathAccounting software, the Working-in-process inventory account is treated as a parent account of the class 1 and the Cost of goods manufactured account is treated as the parent accounts of the class 5. For simplification, the Cost of goods manufactured account has only three one-level subaccounts of the "Supplies expenses", the "Salary expenses" for employees of A16 and A18, and the "Other general parts" in this book.

## 2.4.4.1 Conversion of the Company2

The Company2 will convert to the MathAccounting software on January 1, 2016, so I design a converting reference table, seeing the Figure 2.4-29 on this page and the next page, in order to enter its dynamic accounting equation on December 31, 2015 into the database dcj08.

| Order | Class | Account Name (Subtotal Name) | Balance | Row |
|-------|-------|------------------------------|---------|-----|
| 1 | 1 | (Current assets) | - | 103 |
| 2 | 1 | Cash | 47393.19 | 104 |
| 3 | 1 | Supplies | 192.45 | 106 |
| 4 | 1 | Account receivable | 15150.00 | 108 |
| 5 | 1 | Inventory | 406970.00 | 110 |
| 6 | 1 | Working-in-process inventory | 309085.02 | 112 |
| 7 | 1 | (Long term investments) | - | 141 |
| 8 | 1 | Bonds | 14000.00 | 142 |
| 9 | 1 | (Equipment) | - | 171 |
| 10 | 1 | Vehicle | 125000.00 | 172 |
| 11 | 1 | Accumulated amortization: Vehicle | -44083.33 | 173 |
| 12 | 1 | Computer | 5900.00 | 174 |
| 13 | 1 | Accumulated amortization: Computer | -4179.16 | 175 |
| 14 | 2 | (Current liabilities) | - | 203 |
| 15 | 2 | Account payable | 7400.00 | 204 |
| 16 | 2 | Accrued interest payable | 0 | 206 |
| 17 | 2 | Tax payable | 0 | 208 |
| 18 | 2 | (Long term liabilities) | - | 251 |
| 19 | 2 | Bonds payable | 40000.00 | 252 |
| 20 | 2 | Note payable | 630000.00 | 254 |
| 21 | 3 | (Owners' capital) | - | 303 |
| 22 | 3 | Share capital | 180000.00 | 304 |
| 23 | 3 | Retained earnings (Conversion) | 18028.17 | 306 |
| 24 | 4 | (Revenues) | - | 403 |

| 25 | 4 | Sales | | 404 |
|---|---|---|---|---|
| **26** | **5** | **(Cost)** | - | **431** |
| 27 | 5 | Cost of goods sold | | 432 |
| **28** | **5** | **(Operating and administrative expenses)** | - | **453** |
| 29 | 5 | Travelling expenses | 0 | 454 |
| 30 | 5 | Other expenses | 0 | 455 |
| 31 | 5 | Salary expenses | 0 | 456 |
| 32 | 5 | Cost of goods manufactured | 0 | 457 |
| 33 | 5 | Bond interest expenses | 0 | 458 |
| 34 | 5 | Note interest expenses | 0 | 460 |
| 35 | 5 | Amortization expenses | 0 | 462 |
| **36** | **4** | **(Other income)** | - | **475** |
| 37 | 4 | Investment incomes | | 476 |
| 38 | 4 | Deposits interest incomes | 0 | 478 |
| **39** | **5** | **(Tax)** | - | **600** |
| 40 | 5 | Tax expenses | 0 | 602 |

Figure 2.4-29   Company2 Converting Reference Table

From the Figure 2.4-29, there are total 29 accounts among which the balances of the Sales account, the Cost of goods sold account, and all expenses accounts are zero. In addition, the balance of the Retained earnings should be added to the balance of the Share capital, and its balance should be zero prior to conversion. However, for knowing the original share capital and the distinguishing the Retained earnings after conversion, I keep the Retained earnings prior to conversion and give it a different name of the Retained earnings (Conversion).

The Bonds account has two one-level subaccounts of the "Bond12 (issued by the Business Bank1 and purchased $8,000, beginning on July 1, 2014, five years, and annual interest rate 4.2%) and the "Bond22" (issued by the Business Bank2 and purchased $6,000, beginning on February 1, 2015, five years, and annual interest rate 4.4%).

The Company2 has one truck1 (five years, straight line, 25 months), one truck2 (five years, straight line, 20 months), and one car1 (five years, straight line, 18 months), so the multi-subaccount names of the Vehicle parent account are the "Truck11 < Truck1 < Truck", the "Truck21 < Truck2 < Truck", and the "Car11 < Car1 < Car" respectively. Their balances are $45,000, $40,000 and $40,000 respectively. Accordingly, the multi-subaccount names of the Accumulated amortization: Vehicle account are the "Truck11-accumulated amortization < Truck1-accumulated amortization < Truck-accumulated amortization", the "Truck2-accumulated amortization < Truck2-accumulated amortization < Truck-accumulated amortization", and the "Car11-accumulated amortization < Car1-accumulated amortization < Car-accumulated amortization". Their balances are -$18,750, -$13,333.33 and -$12,000 respectively.

The Company2 has one computer server1 (two years, straight line, 17 months), one computer1" (the same as above), and one computer2" (the same as above), so the multi-subaccount names of the Computer parent account are the "Computer server11 < Computer server1 < Computer server", the "Computer11 < Computer1", and the "Computer21 < Computer2" respectively. Their balances are $2,800, $1,600, and $1,500 respectively. Accordingly, the multi-subaccount names of the Accumulated amortization: Computer account are the "Computer server11-accumulated amortization < Computer server1-accumulated amortization < Computer server-accumulated amortization", the "Computer11-accumulated amortization < Computer1-accumulated amortization", and the "Computer21-accumulated amortization < Computer2-accumulated amortization". Their balances are respectively -$1,983.33, $1,133.33, and -$1,062.50.

The Company2 issued one bond, seeing the Figure 2.4-30 on the next page. The Figure 2.4-30 shows the detail information of the issued bond ($40,000, beginning on March 1, 2015, five years, and annual interest rate 4.7%). The Bonds payable account has one one-level subaccount of the "Bond41-payable". Of course, the Bonds payable has also many two-level subaccounts, The Notes payable account has three one-level subaccounts of the "Note12" ($140,000 from the Business Bank1, beginning on March 1, 2014, four years, and annual interest rate 9%), the "Note14" ($250,000 from the Business Bank1, beginning on June 1, 2014, four years, and annual interest rate 9.2%), and the "Note22" ($240,000 from the Business Bank2, beginning on May 1, 2014, Five years, and annual interest rate 9%). Therefore, the Accrued interest payable account has two one-level subaccounts of the "Bonds-interest payable" and the "Notes-interest payable". Accordingly, the balance of the Accrued interest payable account is zero prior to the conversion.

| Order | Bond | Amount | Term | Purchaser Name | Identity |
|---|---|---|---|---|---|
| 1 | Bond41 | 8000 | March 1, 2015, Five years, 4.7% annually | Business Bank2 | 88-654305 |
| 2 | Bond41 | 4000 | March 1, 2015, Five years, 4.7% annually | A4 | 909876504 |
| 3 | Bond41 | 2000 | March 1, 2015, Five years, 4.7% annually | A5 | 909876505 |
| 4 | Bond41 | 1000 | March 1, 2015, Five years, 4.7% annually | A6 | 909876506 |
| 5 | Bond41 | 3000 | March 1, 2015, Five years, 4.7% annually | A10 | 909876510 |
| 6 | Bond41 | 5000 | March 1, 2015, Five years, 4.7% annually | A13 | 909876513 |
| 7 | Bond41 | 2000 | March 1, 2015, Five years, 4.7% annually | A15 | 909876515 |
| 8 | Bond41 | 3000 | March 1, 2015, Five years, 4.7% annually | A19 | 909876519 |
| 9 | Bond41 | 2000 | March 1, 2015, Five years, 4.7% annually | A20 | 909876520 |
| 10 | Bond41 | 3000 | March 1, 2015, Five years, 4.7% annually | A23 | 909876523 |
| 11 | Bond41 | 5000 | March 1, 2015, Five years, 4.7% annually | A24 | 909876524 |
| 12 | Bond41 | 2000 | March 1, 2015, Five years, 4.7% annually | A25 | 909876525 |
| 13 | **Total** | **40000** | | | |

Figure 2.4-30  Company2 Issued Bond Information Table

The Account receivable account and the Account payable account need transaction dates during the conversion, so I assume that their transaction dates are also on December 31, 2015 for simplification.

For the Company2, the balances of the "Cash receipts from customers<Operating activities" and the "Cash payments to suppliers<Operating activities" are respectively zero and -$15,000. The reason is as same as the Company1. The balance -$15,000 of the "Cash payments to suppliers<Operating activities" is only to pay to the Company3.

Following above information, I can build a table of the multi-subaccount names, seeing the Figure 2.4-31 on this page and the next pages.

| Order | Class | Multi-subaccount Name | Parent Name | Lowest Subaccount Balance |
|---|---|---|---|---|
| 1 | 1 | 909876513-i-owners < Cash receipts from owners < Financial activities | Cash | 90000.00 |
| 2 | 1 | 909876514-i-owners < Cash receipts from owners < Financial activities | Cash | 54000.00 |
| 3 | 1 | 88-654306-i-owners < Cash receipts from owners < Financial activities | Cash | 36000.00 |
| 4 | 1 | 88-654304-i-note12 < Cash receipts from banks < Financial activities | Cash | 140000.00 |

| 5 | 1 | 88-654304-i-note14 < Cash receipts from banks < Financial activities | Cash | 250000.00 |
|---|---|---|---|---|
| 6 | 1 | 88-654305-i-note22 < Cash receipts from banks < Financial activities | Cash | 240000.00 |
| 7 | 1 | Cash receipts from customers < Operating activities | Cash | 0 |
| 8 | 1 | 88-654305-i-bond41 < Cash receipts from issued bonds < Financial activities | Cash | 8000.00 |
| 9 | 1 | 909876504-i-bond41 < Cash receipts from issued bonds < Financial activities | Cash | 4000.00 |
| 10 | 1 | 909876505-i-bond41 < Cash receipts from issued bonds < Financial activities | Cash | 2000.00 |
| 11 | 1 | 909876506-i-bond41 < Cash receipts from issued bonds < Financial activities | Cash | 1000.00 |
| 12 | 1 | 909876510-i-bond41 < Cash receipts from issued bonds < Financial activities | Cash | 3000.00 |
| 13 | 1 | 909876513-i-bond41 < Cash receipts from issued bonds < Financial activities | Cash | 5000.00 |
| 14 | 1 | 909876515-i-bond41 < Cash receipts from issued bonds < Financial activities | Cash | 2000.00 |
| 15 | 1 | 909876519-i-bond41 < Cash receipts from issued bonds < Financial activities | Cash | 3000.00 |
| 16 | 1 | 909876520-i-bond41 < Cash receipts from issued bonds < Financial activities | Cash | 2000.00 |
| 17 | 1 | 909876523-i-bond41 < Cash receipts from issued bonds < Financial activities | Cash | 3000.00 |
| 18 | 1 | 909876524-i-bond41 < Cash receipts from issued bonds < Financial activities | Cash | 5000.00 |
| 19 | 1 | 909876525-i-bond41 < Cash receipts from issued bonds < Financial activities | Cash | 2000.00 |
| 20 | 1 | 88-654304-c-interest of investment bond12 < Cash receipts from investments < Investing activities | Cash | 504.00 |
| 21 | 1 | 88-654305-c-interest of investment bond22 < Cash receipts from investments < Investing activities | Cash | 242.00 |
| 22 | 1 | 88-654306-t-truck1 < Cash payments for machinery < Operating activities | Cash | -45000.00 |
| 23 | 1 | 88-654306-t-truck2 < Cash payments for machinery < Operating activities | Cash | -40000.00 |
| 24 | 1 | 88-654306-t-car1 < Cash payments for machinery < Operating activities | Cash | -40000.00 |
| 25 | 1 | 88-654306-t-computer server1 < Cash payments for machinery < Operating activities | Cash | -2800.00 |
| 26 | 1 | 88-654306-t-computer1 < Cash payments for machinery < Operating activities | Cash | -1600.00 |
| 27 | 1 | 88-654306-t-computer2 < Cash payments for machinery < Operating activities | Cash | -1500.00 |
| 28 | 1 | Cash payments for operating expenses < Operating activities | Cash | -191371.25 |
| 29 | 1 | Cash payments for operating expenses < Operating activities | Cash | -190789.41 |
| 30 | 1 | Cash payments for operating expenses < Operating activities | Cash | -189973.52 |
| 31 | 1 | 88-654303-n-tax < Cash payments for operating expenses < Operating activities | Cash | -71318.63 |
| 32 | 1 | 88-654308-t-operating < Cash payments to suppliers<Operating activities | Cash | -15000.00 |
| 33 | 1 | 88-654304-n-investment bond12 < Cash payments for investments < Investing activities | Cash | -8000.00 |
| 34 | 1 | 88-654305-n-investment bond22 < Cash payments for investments < Investing activities | Cash | -6000.00 |
| 35 | 1 | n | Supplies | 192.45 |
| 36 | 1 | 123456788 | Account receivable | 500.00 |
| 37 | 1 | 123456787 | Account receivable | 400.00 |

| 38 | 1 | 123456784 | Account receivable | 13400.00 |
|---|---|---|---|---|
| 39 | 1 | 123456782 | Account receivable | 600.00 |
| 40 | 1 | 123456781 | Account receivable | 250.00 |
| 41 | 1 | 123456780 | Account receivable | 0 |
| 42 | 1 | Inven111 < Inven11 < Inven1 | Inventory | 10*100 = 1000.00 |
| 43 | 1 | Inven112 < Inven11 < Inven1 | Inventory | 40*80 = 3200.00 |
| 44 | 1 | Inven121 < Inven12 < Inven1 | Inventory | 0.8*200 = 160.00 |
| 45 | 1 | Inven122 < Inven12 < Inven1 | Inventory | 50*60 = 3000.00 |
| 46 | 1 | Inven21 < Inven2 | Inventory | 30*50 = 1500.00 |
| 47 | 1 | Inven221 < Inven22 < Inven2 | Inventory | 30*100 = 3000.00 |
| 48 | 1 | Inven222 < Inven22 < Inven2 | Inventory | 50*40 = 2000.00 |
| 49 | 1 | PPUK parts < ASD parts < Inven2 | Inventory | 40*60 = 2400.00 |
| 50 | 1 | PPGH parts < ASD parts < Inven2 | Inventory | 2*200 = 400.00 |
| 51 | 1 | Inven51 < Inven5 | Inventory | 10*150 = 1500.00 |
| 52 | 1 | Inven52 < Inven5 | Inventory | 50*50 = 2500.00 |
| 53 | 1 | Inven531 < Inven53 < Inven5 | Inventory | 25*100 = 2500.00 |
| 54 | 1 | Inven532 < Inven53 < Inven5 | Inventory | 35*100 = 3500.00 |
| 55 | 1 | Inven541 < Inven54 < Inven5 | Inventory | 12*100 = 1200.00 |
| 56 | 1 | Inven542 < Inven54 < Inven5 | Inventory | 15*80 = 1200.00 |
| 57 | 1 | Inven611 < Inven61 < Inven6 | Inventory | 6.5*100 = 650.00 |
| 58 | 1 | Inven612 < Inven61 < Inven6 | Inventory | 12.5*100 = 1250.00 |
| 59 | 1 | Inven621 < Inven62 < Inven6 | Inventory | 18*100 = 1800.00 |
| 60 | 1 | Inven63 < Inven6 | Inventory | 16*100 = 1600.00 |
| 61 | 1 | Truck1 part1 < Truck1 parts < Vehicle parts | Inventory | 5600.00*5 = 28000.00 |
| 62 | 1 | Truck1 part2 < Truck1 parts < Vehicle parts | Inventory | 4950.00*5 = 24750.00 |
| 63 | 1 | Truck1 part3 < Truck1 parts < Vehicle parts | Inventory | 3750.00*5 = 18750.00 |
| 64 | 1 | Truck2 part1 < Truck2 parts < Vehicle parts | Inventory | 5500.00*5 = 27500.00 |
| 65 | 1 | Truck2 part2 < Truck2 parts < Vehicle parts | Inventory | 4660.00*5 = 23300.00 |
| 66 | 1 | Truck2 part3 < Truck2 parts < Vehicle parts | Inventory | 3500.00*5 = 17500.00 |
| 67 | 1 | Car1 part1 < Car1 parts < Vehicle parts | Inventory | 5380.00*5 = 26900.00 |
| 68 | 1 | Car1 part2 < Car1 parts < Vehicle parts | Inventory | 4650.00*5 = 23250.00 |
| 69 | 1 | Car1 part3 < Car1 parts < Vehicle parts | Inventory | 3300.00*5 = 16500.00 |
| 70 | 1 | Car2 part1 < Car2 parts < Vehicle parts | Inventory | 5100.00*5 = 25500.00 |
| 71 | 1 | Car2 part2 < Car2 parts < Vehicle parts | Inventory | 4400.00*5 = 22000.00 |
| 72 | 1 | Car2 part3 < Car2 parts < Vehicle parts | Inventory | 3170.00*5 = 15850.00 |
| 73 | 1 | Car3 part1 < Car3 parts < Vehicle parts | Inventory | 4850.00*5 = 24250.00 |
| 74 | 1 | Car3 part2 < Car3 parts < Vehicle parts | Inventory | 4150.00*5 = 20750.00 |
| 75 | 1 | Car3 part3 < Car3 parts < Vehicle parts | Inventory | 3050.00*5 = 15250.00 |
| 76 | 1 | Computer server1 part1 < Computer server parts < Computer parts | Inventory | 390.00*10 = 3900.00 |
| 77 | 1 | Computer server1 part2 < Computer server parts < Computer parts | Inventory | 260.00*10 = 2600.00 |
| 78 | 1 | Computer server2 part1 < Computer server parts < Computer parts | Inventory | 350.00*10 = 3500.00 |

| 79 | 1 | Computer server2 part2 < Computer server parts < Computer parts | Inventory | 250.00*10 = 2500.00 |
|---|---|---|---|---|
| 80 | 1 | Computer1 part1 < Computer parts | Inventory | 235.00*20 = 4700.00 |
| 81 | 1 | Computer1 part2 < Computer parts | Inventory | 202.00*20 = 4040.00 |
| 82 | 1 | Computer2 part1 < Computer parts | Inventory | 208.00*20 = 4160.00 |
| 83 | 1 | Computer2 part2 < Computer parts | Inventory | 189.00*20 = 3780.00 |
| 84 | 1 | Computer3 part1 < Computer parts | Inventory | 182.00*20 = 3640.00 |
| 85 | 1 | Computer3 part2 < Computer parts | Inventory | 169.00*20 = 3380.00 |
| 86 | 1 | Computer4 part1 < Computer parts | Inventory | 162.00*20 = 3240.00 |
| 87 | 1 | Computer4 part2 < Computer parts | Inventory | 156.00*20 = 3120.00 |
| 88 | 1 | Working-truck1 part1 < Working-truck1 parts < Working-vehicle parts | Working-in-process inventory | 4709.33*5 = 23546.65 |
| 89 | 1 | Working-truck1 part2 < Working-truck1 parts < Working-vehicle parts | Working-in-process inventory | 4236.78*5 = 21183.90 |
| 90 | 1 | Working-truck1 part3 < Working-truck1 parts < Working-vehicle parts | Working-in-process inventory | 3012.51*5 = 15062.55 |
| 91 | 1 | Working-truck2 part1 < Working-truck2 parts < Working-vehicle parts | Working-in-process inventory | 4684.25*5 = 23421.25 |
| 92 | 1 | Working-truck2 part2 < Working-truck2 parts < Working-vehicle parts | Working-in-process inventory | 2967.59*5 = 14837.95 |
| 93 | 1 | Working-truck2 part3 < Working-truck2 parts < Working-vehicle parts | Working-in-process inventory | 2787.26*5 = 13936.30 |
| 94 | 1 | Working-car1 part1 < Working-car1 parts < Working-vehicle parts | Working-in-process inventory | 4594.23*5 = 22971.15 |
| 95 | 1 | Working-car1 part2 < Working-car1 parts < Working-vehicle parts | Working-in-process inventory | 3758.87*5 = 18794.35 |
| 96 | 1 | Working-car1 part3 < Working-car1 parts < Working-vehicle parts | Working-in-process inventory | 2564.77*5 = 12823.85 |
| 97 | 1 | Working-car2 part1 < Working-car2 parts < Working-vehicle parts | Working-in-process inventory | 4482.66*5 = 22413.30 |
| 98 | 1 | Working-car2 part2 < Working-car2 parts < Working-vehicle parts | Working-in-process inventory | 3577.41*5 = 17887.05 |
| 99 | 1 | Working-car2 part3 < Working-car2 parts < Working-vehicle parts | Working-in-process inventory | 2469.88*5 = 12349.40 |
| 100 | 1 | Working-car3 part1 < Working-car3 parts < Working-vehicle parts | Working-in-process inventory | 4177.56*6 = 25065.36 |
| 101 | 1 | Working-car3 part2 < Working-car3 parts < Working-vehicle parts | Working-in-process inventory | 3327.45*6 = 19964.70 |
| 102 | 1 | Working-car3 part3 < Working-car3 parts < Working-vehicle parts | Working-in-process inventory | 2285.21*6 = 13711.26 |
| 103 | 1 | Working-computer server1 part1 < Working-computer server1 < Working-computer parts | Working-in-process inventory | 329.00*6 = 1974.00 |
| 104 | 1 | Working-computer server1 part2 < Working-computer server1 < Working-computer parts | Working-in-process inventory | 186.00*6 = 1116.00 |
| 105 | 1 | Working-computer server2 part1 < Working-computer server2 < Working-computer parts | Working-in-process inventory | 285.00*6 = 1710.00 |
| 106 | 1 | Working-computer server2 part2 < Working-computer server2 < Working-computer parts | Working-in-process inventory | 175.00*6 = 1050.00 |
| 107 | 1 | Working-computer1 part1< Working-computer parts | Working-in-process inventory | 208.50*20 = 4170.00 |
| 108 | 1 | Working-computer1 part2< Working-computer parts | Working-in-process inventory | 182.20*20 = 3644.00 |
| 109 | 1 | Working-computer2 part1< Working-computer parts | Working-in-process inventory | 178.80*20 = 3576.00 |
| 110 | 1 | Working-computer2 part2< Working-computer parts | Working-in-process inventory | 157.90*20 = 3158.00 |
| 111 | 1 | Working-computer3 part1< Working-computer parts | Working-in-process inventory | 150.20*20 = 3004.00 |

| 112 | 1 | Working-computer3 part2< Working-computer parts | Working-in-process inventory | 135.90*20 = 2718.00 |
|---|---|---|---|---|
| 113 | 1 | Working-computer4 part1< Working-computer parts | Working-in-process inventory | 128.20*20 = 2564.00 |
| 114 | 1 | Working-computer4 part2< Working-computer parts | Working-in-process inventory | 121.60*20 = 2432.00 |
| 115 | 1 | Bond12 | Bonds | 8000.00 |
| 116 | 1 | Bond22 | Bonds | 6000.00 |
| 117 | 1 | Truck11 < Truck1 < Truck | Vehicle | 45000.00 |
| 118 | 1 | Truck21 < Truck2 < Truck | Vehicle | 40000.00 |
| 119 | 1 | Car11 < Car1 < Car | Vehicle | 40000.00 |
| 120 | 1 | Truck11-accumulated amortization < Truck1-accumulated amortization < Truck-accumulated amortization | Accumulated amortization: Vehicle | -18750.00 |
| 121 | 1 | Truck21-accumulated amortization < Truck2-accumulated amortization < Truck-accumulated amortization | Accumulated amortization: Vehicle | -13333.33 |
| 122 | 1 | Car11-accumulated amortization < Car1-accumulated amortization < Car-accumulated amortization | Accumulated amortization: Vehicle | -12000.00 |
| 123 | 1 | Computer server11 < Computer server1 < Computer server | Computer | 2800.00 |
| 124 | 1 | Computer11 < Computer1 | Computer | 1600.00 |
| 125 | 1 | Computer21 < Computer2 | Computer | 1500.00 |
| 126 | 1 | Computer server11-accumulated amortization < Computer server1-accumulated amortization < Computer server-accumulated amortization | Accumulated amortization: Computer | -1983.33 |
| 127 | 1 | Computer11-accumulated amortization < Computer1-accumulated amortization | Accumulated amortization: Computer | -1133.33 |
| 128 | 1 | Computer21-accumulated amortization < Computer2-accumulated amortization | Accumulated amortization: Computer | -1062.50 |
| 129 | 2 | 123456084 | Account payable | 600.00 |
| 130 | 2 | 123456082 | Account payable | 6000.00 |
| 131 | 2 | 123456081 | Account payable | 500.00 |
| 132 | 2 | 123456080 | Account payable | 300.00 |
| 133 | 2 | Band41-interest payable < Bonds-interest payable | Accrued interest payable | 0 |
| 134 | 2 | Note12-interest payable < Notes-interest payable | Accrued interest payable | 0 |
| 135 | 2 | Note14-interest payable < Notes-interest payable | Accrued interest payable | 0 |
| 136 | 2 | Note22-interest payable < Notes-interest payable | Accrued interest payable | 0 |
| 137 | 2 | Bond41-88-654305 < Bond41 | Bonds payable | 8000.00 |
| 138 | 2 | Bond41-909876504 < Bond41 | Bonds payable | 4000.00 |
| 139 | 2 | Bond41-909876505 < Bond41 | Bonds payable | 2000.00 |
| 140 | 2 | Bond41-909876506 < Bond41 | Bonds payable | 1000.00 |
| 141 | 2 | Bond41-909876510 < Bond41 | Bonds payable | 3000.00 |
| 142 | 2 | Bond41-909876513 < Bond41 | Bonds payable | 5000.00 |
| 143 | 2 | Bond41-909876515 < Bond41 | Bonds payable | 2000.00 |
| 144 | 2 | Bond41-909876519 < Bond41 | Bonds payable | 3000.00 |
| 145 | 2 | Bond41-909876520 < Bond41 | Bonds payable | 2000.00 |
| 146 | 2 | Bond41-909876523 < Bond41 | Bonds payable | 3000.00 |

| 147 | 2 | Bond41-909876524 < Bond41 | Bonds payable | 5000.00 |
|---|---|---|---|---|
| 148 | 2 | Bond41-909876525 < Bond41 | Bonds payable | 2000.00 |
| 149 | 2 | Note12-88-654304 | Notes payable | 140000.00 |
| 150 | 2 | Note14-88-654304 | Notes payable | 250000.00 |
| 151 | 2 | Note22-88-654305 | Notes payable | 240000.00 |
| 152 | 3 | Capital-909876513 | Share capital | 90000.00 |
| 153 | 3 | Capital-909876514 | Share capital | 54000.00 |
| 154 | 3 | Capital-88-654306 | Share capital | 36000.00 |
| 155 | 3 | n | Retained earnings (Conversion) | 18028.17 |
| 156 | 4 | Sales-909876516 | Sales | 0 |
| 157 | 5 | 909876516-travelling < Sales department-travelling | Travelling expenses | 0 |
| 158 | 5 | 909876517-travelling < Office department-travelling | Travelling expenses | 0 |
| 159 | 5 | 909876518-travelling < Product department-travelling | Travelling expenses | 0 |
| 160 | 5 | 909876516-other < Sales department-other | Other expenses | 0 |
| 161 | 5 | 909876517-other < Office department-other | Other expenses | 0 |
| 162 | 5 | 909876518-other < Product department-other | Other expenses | 0 |
| 163 | 5 | 909876517-salary < Office department-salary | Salary expenses | 0 |
| 164 | 5 | Supplies expenses | Cost of goods manufactured | 0 |
| 165 | 5 | 909876516-salary < Sales department-salary < Salary expenses | Cost of goods manufactured | 0 |
| 166 | 5 | 909876518-salary < Product department-salary < Salary expenses | Cost of goods manufactured | 0 |
| 167 | 5 | General parts expenses | Cost of goods manufactured | 0 |
| 168 | 5 | Bond41-interest | Bond interest expenses | 0 |
| 169 | 5 | Note12-interest | Note interest expenses | 0 |
| 170 | 5 | Note14-interest | Note interest expenses | 0 |
| 171 | 5 | Note22-interest | Note interest expenses | 0 |
| 172 | 5 | Truck11-amortization < Truck1-amortization < Vehicle-truck-amortization | Amortization expenses | 0 |
| 173 | 5 | Truck21-amortization < Truck2-amortization < Vehicle-truck-amortization | Amortization expenses | 0 |
| 174 | 5 | Car11-amortization < Car1-amortization < Vehicle-car-amortization | Amortization expenses | 0 |
| 175 | 5 | Computer server11-amortization < Computer server1-amortization < Computer-amortization | Amortization expenses | 0 |
| 176 | 5 | Computer11-amortization < Computer1-amortization < Computer-amortization | Amortization expenses | 0 |
| 177 | 5 | Computer21-amortization < Computer2-amortization < Computer-amortization | Amortization expenses | 0 |
| 178 | 4 | Accrued interest income-bond12 < Bonds | Investment incomes | 0 |
| 179 | 4 | Accrued interest income-bond22 < Bonds | Investment incomes | 0 |
| 180 | 4 | n | Deposits interest income | 0 |

Figure 2.4-31   Company2 Converting Multi-Subaccount Names Table

Before entering the dynamic accounting equation on December 31, 2015 into the database dcj06, I first enter two initialization sub-equations.

Account payable (2): 0 = Share capital (3): 0

0 = Sales (4): 0 – Cost of goods sold (5):0

From the Figure 2.4-29 and the Figure 2.4-31, the dynamic accounting equation on December 31, 2015 must be divided to the N transaction sub-equations because of the limitation of the MathAccounting software. Every sub-equation has maximum twelve items. All converting transaction sub-equations can be designed and written as the followings

- I build a transaction sub-equation for the Account receivable and the Account payable accounts. The transaction sub-equation includes the Account receivable account with the Order 36 to the Order 41, the Account payable account with the Order 129 to the Order 132, and the part of the Share capital account with the Order 152. Because the balances of the Account receivable with the Order 41 is zero, the first transaction sub-equation is:

  Account receivable (1): 500 + Account receivable (1): 400 + Account receivable (1): 13400 + Account receivable (1): 600 + Account receivable (1): 250 = Account payable (2): 600 + Account payable (2): 6000 + Account payable (2): 500 + Account payable (2): 300 + Share capital (3): 7750

  After entering this transaction, the new balance of the Share capital account with the Order 152 is $82,250 (= $90,000 - $7,750).

- The transaction sub-equation includes the part of the Cash account with the Order 1, the Cash account with the Order 2 to the Order 6, the rest ($82,250) of the Share capital account with the Order 152, the Share capital account with the Order 153 and the Order 154, and the Notes payable account with the Order 149 to the Order 151.

The second transaction sub-equation is:

Cash (1): 82250 + Cash (1): 54000 + Cash (1): 36000 + Cash (1): 140000 + Cash (1): 250000 + Cash (1): 240000 = Share capital (3): 82250 + Share capital (3): 54000 + Share capital (3): 36000 + Notes payable (2): 140000 + Notes payable (2): 250000 + Notes payable (2): 240000

After entering this transaction, the new balance of the Cash account with the Order 1 is $7,750 (= $90,000 - $82,250).

- The transaction sub-equation includes the Cash account with the Order 7 to the Order 13 and the Bonds payable account with the Order 137 to the Order 142. Because the balance of the Cash account with the Order 7 is zero, the third transaction sub-equation is:

Cash (1): 8000 + Cash (1): 4000 + Cash (1): 2000 + Cash (1): 1000 + Cash (1): 3000 + Cash (1): 5000 = Bonds payable (2): 8000 + Bonds payable (2): 4000 + Bonds payable (2): 2000 + Bonds payable (2): 1000 + Bonds payable (2): 3000 + Bonds payable (2): 5000

- The transaction sub-equation includes the Cash account with the Order 14 to the Order 19 and the Bonds payable account with the Order 143 to the Order 148. The fourth transaction sub-equation is:

Cash (1): 2000 + Cash (1): 3000 + Cash (1): 2000 + Cash (1): 3000 + Cash (1): 5000 + Cash (1): 2000 = Bonds payable (2): 2000 + Bonds payable (2): 3000 + Bonds payable (2): 2000 + Bonds payable (2): 3000 + Bonds payable (2): 5000 + Bonds payable (2): 2000

- The transaction sub-equation includes the rest ($7,750) of the Cash account with the Order 1, the Cash account with the Order 20 and the Order 21, the part of the Cash account with the Order 28, and the Inventory account with the Order 42 to the Order 49. The fifth transaction sub-equation is:

Cash (1): 7750 + Cash (1): 504 + Cash (1): 242 + Cash (1): -24756 + Inventory (1): 1000 + Inventory (1): 3200 + Inventory (1): 160 + Inventory (1): 3000 + Inventory (1): 1500 + Inventory (1): 3000 + Inventory (1): 2000 + Inventory (1): 2400 = 0

After entering this transaction, the new balance of the Cash account with the Order 28 is -$166,615.25 (= -$191,371.25 + $24,756).

- The transaction sub-equation includes the Cash account with the Order 22 to the Order 27, the Vehicle account with the Order 117 to the Order 119, and the Computer account with the Order 123 to the Order 125. The sixth transaction sub-equation is:

Cash (1): -45000 + Cash (1): -40000 + Cash (1): -40000 + Cash (1): -2800 + Cash (1): -1600 + Cash (1): -1500 + Vehicle (1): 45000 + Vehicle (1): 40000 + Vehicle (1): 40000 + Computer (1): 2800 + Computer (1): 1600 + Computer (1): 1500 = 0

- The transaction sub-equation includes the part of the Cash account with the Order 28 and the Inventory account with the Order 50 to the Order 60. The seventh transaction sub-equation is:

Cash (1): -18100 + Inventory (1): 400 + Inventory (1): 1500 + Inventory (1): 2500 + Inventory (1): 2500 + Inventory (1): 3500 + Inventory (1): 1200 + Inventory (1): 1200 + Inventory (1): 650+ Inventory (1): 1250 + Inventory (1): 1800 + Inventory (1): 1600 = 0

After entering this transaction, the new balance of the Cash account with the Order 28 is -$148,515.25 (= -$166,615.25 + $18,100).

- The transaction sub-equation includes the part of the Cash account with the Order

29, the Cash account with the Order 32 to the Order 34, and the Inventory account with the Order 61 to the Order 68. The eighth transaction sub-equation is:

Cash (1): -160,950 + Cash (1): -15000 + Cash (1): -8000 + Cash (1): -6000 + Inventory (1): 28000 + Inventory (1): 24750 + Inventory (1): 18750 + Inventory (1): 27500 + Inventory (1): 23300 + Inventory (1): 17500 + Inventory (1): 26900 + Inventory (1): 23250 = 0

After entering this transaction, the new balance of the Cash account with the Order 29 is -$29,839.41 (= -$190,789.41 + $160,950).

- The transaction sub-equation includes the part of the Cash account with the Order 28, the rest (-$29,839.41) of the Cash account with the Order 29, and the Inventory account with the Order 69 to the Order 75. The ninth transaction sub-equation is:

Cash (1): -110260.59+ Cash (1): -29839.41 + Inventory (1): 16500 + Inventory (1): 25500 + Inventory (1): 22000 + Inventory (1): 15850 + Inventory (1): 24250 + Inventory (1): 20750 + Inventory (1): 15250 = 0

After entering this transaction, the new balance of the Cash account with the Order 28 is -$38,254.66 (= -$148,515.25 + $110,260.59).

- The transaction sub-equation includes the part of the Cash account with the Order 28 and the Inventory account with the Order 76 to the Order 85. The tenth transaction sub-equation is:

Cash (1): -36200 + Inventory (1): 3900 + Inventory (1): 2600 + Inventory (1): 3500 + Inventory (1): 2500 + Inventory (1): 4700 + Inventory (1): 4040 + Inventory (1): 4160 + Inventory (1): 3780 + Inventory (1): 3640 + Inventory (1): 3380 = 0

After entering this transaction, the new balance of the Cash account with the Order

28 is -$2,054.66 (= -$38,254.66 + $36,200).

- The transaction sub-equation includes the rest (-$2,054.66) of the Cash account with the Order 28, the part of the Cash account with the Order 30, the Inventory account with the Order 86 and the Order 87, and the Working-in-process inventory account with the Order 88 to the Order 95. The eleventh transaction sub-equation is:

Cash (1): -2054.66 + Cash (1): -158059.44 + Inventory (1): 3240 + Inventory (1): 3120 + Working-in-process inventory (1): 23546.65 + Working-in-process inventory (1): 21183.90 + Working-in-process inventory (1): 15062.55 + Working-in-process inventory (1): 23421.25 + Working-in-process inventory (1): 14837.95 + Working-in-process inventory (1): 13936.30 + Working-in-process inventory (1): 22971.15 + Working-in-process inventory (1): 18794.35 = 0

After entering this transaction, the new balance of the Cash account with the Order 30 is -$31,914.08 (= -$189,973.52 + $158,059.44).

- The transaction sub-equation includes the rest (-$31,914.08) of the Cash account with the Order 30, the Cash account with the Order 31, the Supplies account with the Order 35, the Working-in-process inventory account with the Order 96 to the Order 102, the Accumulated amortization: Vehicle account with the Order 120, and the part of the Accumulated amortization: Vehicle account with the Order 121. The twelfth transaction sub-equation is:

Cash (1): -31914.08 + Cash (1): -71318.63 + Supplies (1): 192.45 + Working-in-process inventory (1): 12823.85 + Working-in-process inventory (1): 22413.30 + Working-in-process inventory (1): 17887.05 + Working-in-process inventory (1): 12349.40 + Working-in-process inventory (1): 25065.36 + Working-in-process inventory (1): 19964.70 + Working-in-process inventory (1): 13711.26 + Accumulated amortization: Vehicle (1): -18750 + Accumulated amortization: Vehicle (1): -2424.66 = 0

After entering this transaction, the new balance of the Accumulated amortization: Vehicle account with the Order 121 is -$10,908.67 (= -$13,333.33 + $2,424.66).

- The transaction sub-equation includes the rest (-$10,908.67) of the Accumulated amortization: Vehicle account with the Order 121, the Accumulated amortization: Vehicle account with the Order 122, the Working-in-process inventory account with the Order 103 to the Order 110, the part of the Bonds account with the Order 115. The thirteenth transaction sub-equation is:

Accumulated amortization: Vehicle (1): -10908.67 + Accumulated amortization: Vehicle (1): -12000 + Working-in-process inventory (1): 1974 + Working-in-process inventory (1): 1116 + Working-in-process inventory (1): 1710 + Working-in-process inventory (1): 1050 + Working-in-process inventory (1): 4170 + Working-in-process inventory (1): 3644 + Working-in-process inventory (1): 3576 + Working-in-process inventory (1): 3158 + Bonds (1): 2510.67 = 0

After entering this transaction, the new balance of the Bonds account with the Order 115 is $5,489.33 (= $8,000 - $2,510.67).

- The transaction sub-equation includes the Working-in-process inventory account with the Order 111, the part of the Bonds account with the Order 115, and the Accumulated amortization: Computer account with the Order 126 and the Order 128. The fourteenth transaction sub-equation is:

Working-in-process inventory (1): $3004 + Bonds (1): 1175.16 + Accumulated amortization: Computer (1): -1983.33 + Accumulated amortization: Computer (1): -1133.33 + Accumulated amortization: Computer (1): -1062.50 = 0

After entering this transaction, the new balance of the Bonds account with the Order 115 is $4,314.17 (= $5,489.33 - $1,175.16).

- The transaction sub-equation includes the rest ($4,314.17) of the Bonds account with the Order 115, the Bonds account with the Order 116, the Working-in-process inventory account with the Order 112 to the Order 114, and the Retained earnings account with the balance $18028.17. The fifteenth transaction sub-equation is:

Bonds (1): 4314.17 + Bonds (1): 6000 + Working-in-process inventory (1): 2718 + Working-in-process inventory (1): 2564 + Working-in-process inventory (1): 2432 = Retained earnings (3): 18,028.17

After completing this transaction, the dynamic accounting equation of the Company2 on December 31, 2015 has entered into the database dcj08.

## 2.4.4.2 Brief Summary of the Company2

The Figure 2.4-32 on the next pages shows cash received or paid by other members table which is in the public database dcj100.

```
SQLQuery2.sql - LIU...SS.dcj100 (sa (52))*  ×

 use dcj100
  select sum(amount) as sum0 from CashByMembers where Recorder = '88-654307'
  select * from CashByMembers where Recorder = '88-654307'
```

100 %  ▾

☐ Results  ☐ Messages

|   | sum0 |
|---|------|
| 1 | -47393.19 |

|    | IDM | Amount | Symbol | MultiSubaccount | Recorder | TransDate |
|----|-----|--------|--------|-----------------|----------|-----------|
| 1  | 909876513 | -82250.00 | i | 909876513-i-owners < Cash receipts from owners < Financial activities | 88-654307 | 2015-12-31 |
| 2  | 909876514 | -54000.00 | i | 909876514-i-owners < Cash receipts from owners < Financial activities | 88-654307 | 2015-12-31 |
| 3  | 88-654306 | -36000.00 | i | 88-654306-i-owners < Cash receipts from owners < Financial activities | 88-654307 | 2015-12-31 |
| 4  | 88-654304 | -140000.00 | i | 88-654304-i-note12 < Cash receipts from banks < Financial activities | 88-654307 | 2015-12-31 |
| 5  | 88-654304 | -250000.00 | i | 88-654304-i-note14 < Cash receipts from banks < Financial activities | 88-654307 | 2015-12-31 |
| 6  | 88-654305 | -240000.00 | i | 88-654305-i-note22 < Cash receipts from banks < Financial activities | 88-654307 | 2015-12-31 |
| 7  | 88-654305 | -8000.00 | i | 88-654305-i-bond41 < Cash receipts from issued bonds < Financial activities | 88-654307 | 2015-12-31 |
| 8  | 909876504 | -4000.00 | i | 909876504-i-bond41 < Cash receipts from issued bonds < Financial activities | 88-654307 | 2015-12-31 |
| 9  | 909876505 | -2000.00 | i | 909876505-i-bond41 < Cash receipts from issued bonds < Financial activities | 88-654307 | 2015-12-31 |
| 10 | 909876506 | -1000.00 | i | 909876506-i-bond41 < Cash receipts from issued bonds < Financial activities | 88-654307 | 2015-12-31 |
| 11 | 909876510 | -3000.00 | i | 909876510-i-bond41 < Cash receipts from issued bonds < Financial activities | 88-654307 | 2015-12-31 |
| 12 | 909876513 | -5000.00 | i | 909876513-i-bond41 < Cash receipts from issued bonds < Financial activities | 88-654307 | 2015-12-31 |
| 13 | 909876515 | -2000.00 | i | 909876515-i-bond41 < Cash receipts from issued bonds < Financial activities | 88-654307 | 2015-12-31 |
| 14 | 909876519 | -3000.00 | i | 909876519-i-bond41 < Cash receipts from issued bonds < Financial activities | 88-654307 | 2015-12-31 |
| 15 | 909876520 | -2000.00 | i | 909876520-i-bond41 < Cash receipts from issued bonds < Financial activities | 88-654307 | 2015-12-31 |
| 16 | 909876523 | -3000.00 | i | 909876523-i-bond41 < Cash receipts from issued bonds < Financial activities | 88-654307 | 2015-12-31 |
| 17 | 909876524 | -5000.00 | i | 909876524-i-bond41 < Cash receipts from issued bonds < Financial activities | 88-654307 | 2015-12-31 |
| 18 | 909876525 | -2000.00 | i | 909876525-i-bond41 < Cash receipts from issued bonds < Financial activities | 88-654307 | 2015-12-31 |
| 19 | 909876513 | -7750.00 | i | 909876513-i-owners < Cash receipts from owners < Financial activities | 88-654307 | 2015-12-31 |
| 20 | 88-654304 | -504.00 | c | 88-654304-c-interest of investment bond12 < Cash receipts from investments < Investing activities | 88-654307 | 2015-12-31 |
| 21 | 88-654305 | -242.00 | c | 88-654305-c-interest of investment bond22 < Cash receipts from investments < Investing activities | 88-654307 | 2015-12-31 |
| 22 |  | 24756.00 |  | Cash payments for operating expenses < Operating activities | 88-654307 | 2015-12-31 |
| 23 | 88-654306 | 45000.00 | t | 88-654306-t-truck1 < Cash payments for machinery < Operating activities | 88-654307 | 2015-12-31 |
| 24 | 88-654306 | 40000.00 | t | 88-654306-t-truck2 < Cash payments for machinery < Operating activities | 88-654307 | 2015-12-31 |
| 25 | 88-654306 | 40000.00 | t | 88-654306-t-car1 < Cash payments for machinery < Operating activities | 88-654307 | 2015-12-31 |

☑ Query executed successfully.                                                                                          LIU\SQLEX

Figure 2.4-32   Company2 Cash Received or Paid by Other Members (Continue)

```
SQLQuery2.sql - LIU...SS.dcj100 (sa (52))*   ×

  -use dcj100
   select sum(amount) as sum0 from CashByMembers where Recorder = '88-654307'
   select * from CashByMembers where Recorder = '88-654307'

100 %   ▾
☐ Results  ┊ Messages
     sum0
1    -47393.19
```

| | IDM | Amount | Symbol | MultiSubaccount | Recorder | TransDate |
|---|---|---|---|---|---|---|
| 17 | 909876524 | -5000.00 | i | 909876524-i-bond41 < Cash receipts from issued bonds < Financial activities | 88-654307 | 2015-12-31 |
| 18 | 909876525 | -2000.00 | i | 909876525-i-bond41 < Cash receipts from issued bonds < Financial activities | 88-654307 | 2015-12-31 |
| 19 | 909876513 | -7750.00 | i | 909876513-i-owners < Cash receipts from owners < Financial activities | 88-654307 | 2015-12-31 |
| 20 | 88-654304 | -504.00 | c | 88-654304-c-interest of investment bond12 < Cash receipts from investments < Investing activities | 88-654307 | 2015-12-31 |
| 21 | 88-654305 | -242.00 | c | 88-654305-c-interest of investment bond22 < Cash receipts from investments < Investing activities | 88-654307 | 2015-12-31 |
| 22 | | 24756.00 | | Cash payments for operating expenses < Operating activities | 88-654307 | 2015-12-31 |
| 23 | 88-654306 | 45000.00 | t | 88-654306-t-truck1 < Cash payments for machinery < Operating activities | 88-654307 | 2015-12-31 |
| 24 | 88-654306 | 40000.00 | t | 88-654306-t-truck2 < Cash payments for machinery < Operating activities | 88-654307 | 2015-12-31 |
| 25 | 88-654306 | 40000.00 | t | 88-654306-t-car1 < Cash payments for machinery < Operating activities | 88-654307 | 2015-12-31 |
| 26 | 88-654306 | 2800.00 | t | 88-654306-t-computer server1 < Cash payments for machinery < Operating activities | 88-654307 | 2015-12-31 |
| 27 | 88-654306 | 1600.00 | t | 88-654306-t-computer1 < Cash payments for machinery < Operating activities | 88-654307 | 2015-12-31 |
| 28 | 88-654306 | 1500.00 | t | 88-654306-t-computer2 < Cash payments for machinery < Operating activities | 88-654307 | 2015-12-31 |
| 29 | | 18100.00 | | Cash payments for operating expenses < Operating activities | 88-654307 | 2015-12-31 |
| 30 | | 160950.00 | | Cash payments for operating expenses < Operating activities | 88-654307 | 2015-12-31 |
| 31 | 88-654308 | 15000.00 | t | 88-654308-t-operating < Cash payments to suppliers<Operating activities | 88-654307 | 2015-12-31 |
| 32 | 88-654304 | 8000.00 | n | 88-654304-n-investment bond12 < Cash payments for investments < Investing activities | 88-654307 | 2015-12-31 |
| 33 | 88-654305 | 6000.00 | n | 88-654305-n-investment bond22 < Cash payments for investments < Investing activities | 88-654307 | 2015-12-31 |
| 34 | | 109760.59 | | Cash payments for operating expenses < Operating activities | 88-654307 | 2015-12-31 |
| 35 | | 29839.41 | | Cash payments for operating expenses < Operating activities | 88-654307 | 2015-12-31 |
| 36 | | 500.00 | | Cash payments for operating expenses < Operating activities | 88-654307 | 2015-12-31 |
| 37 | | 36200.00 | | Cash payments for operating expenses < Operating activities | 88-654307 | 2015-12-31 |
| 38 | | 2054.66 | | Cash payments for operating expenses < Operating activities | 88-654307 | 2015-12-31 |
| 39 | | 158059.44 | | Cash payments for operating expenses < Operating activities | 88-654307 | 2015-12-31 |
| 40 | | 31914.08 | | Cash payments for operating expenses < Operating activities | 88-654307 | 2015-12-31 |
| 41 | 88-654303 | 71318.63 | n | 88-654303-n-tax < Cash payments for operating expenses < Operating activities | 88-654307 | 2015-12-31 |

```
◎ Query executed successfully.                                                    LIU\SQLEX
```

Figure 2.4-32   Company2 Cash Received or Paid by Other Members

The Figure 2.4-33 on the next page shows cash flows statement of the Company2 on December 31, 2015.

| Cash Flows Statement Year Ended 2015-12-31 | |
|---|---:|
| **Operating activities** | |
| Cash payments for machinery | -$130,900.00 |
| Cash payments for operating expenses | -$643,452.81 |
| Cash payments to suppliers | -$15,000.00 |
| Net cash provided by Operating activities | -$789,352.81 |
| | |
| Investing activities | |
| Cash payments for investments | -$14,000.00 |
| Cash receipts from investments | $746.00 |
| Net cash provided by Investing activities | -$13,254.00 |
| | |
| Financial activities | |
| Cash receipts from banks | $630,000.00 |
| Cash receipts from issued bonds | $40,000.00 |
| Cash receipts from owners | $180,000.00 |
| Net cash provided by Financial activities | $850,000.00 |
| | |
| Net change in cash | $47,393.19 |
| Cash, Begining | $0.00 |
| Cash, Ending | $47,393.19 |

Figure 2.4-33   Company2 Cash Flows Statement

The Figure 2.4-34 on the next pages shows cash account table of the Company2 on December 31, 2015.

Cash

| ID | Multi-Name | Amount | Balance | General ID | Transaction Date |
|----|-----------|--------|---------|-----------|------------------|
| 1 | 909876513-i-owners < Cash receipts from owners < Financial activities | $82,250.00 | $82,250.00 | 4 | 2015-12-31 |
| 2 | 909876514-i-owners < Cash receipts from owners < Financial activities | $54,000.00 | $136,250.00 | 4 | 2015-12-31 |
| 3 | 88-654306-i-owners < Cash receipts from owners < Financial activities | $36,000.00 | $172,250.00 | 4 | 2015-12-31 |
| 4 | 88-654304-i-note12 < Cash receipts from banks < Financial activities | $140,000.00 | $312,250.00 | 4 | 2015-12-31 |
| 5 | 88-654304-i-note14 < Cash receipts from banks < Financial activities | $250,000.00 | $562,250.00 | 4 | 2015-12-31 |
| 6 | 88-654305-i-note22 < Cash receipts from banks < Financial activities | $240,000.00 | $802,250.00 | 4 | 2015-12-31 |
| 7 | 88-654305-i-bond4 1 < Cash receipts from issued bonds < Financial activi... | $8,000.00 | $810,250.00 | 5 | 2015-12-31 |
| 8 | 909876504-i-bond41 < Cash receipts from issued bonds < Financial activ... | $4,000.00 | $814,250.00 | 5 | 2015-12-31 |
| 9 | 909876505-i-bond41 < Cash receipts from issued bonds < Financial activ... | $2,000.00 | $816,250.00 | 5 | 2015-12-31 |
| 10 | 909876506-i-bond41 < Cash receipts from issued bonds < Financial activ... | $1,000.00 | $817,250.00 | 5 | 2015-12-31 |
| 11 | 909876510-i-bond41 < Cash receipts from issued bonds < Financial activ... | $3,000.00 | $820,250.00 | 5 | 2015-12-31 |
| 12 | 909876513-i-bond41 < Cash receipts from issued bonds < Financial activ... | $5,000.00 | $825,250.00 | 5 | 2015-12-31 |
| 13 | 909876515-i-bond41 < Cash receipts from issued bonds < Financial activ... | $2,000.00 | $827,250.00 | 6 | 2015-12-31 |
| 14 | 909876519-i-bond41 < Cash receipts from issued bonds < Financial activ... | $3,000.00 | $830,250.00 | 6 | 2015-12-31 |
| 15 | 909876520-i-bond41 < Cash receipts from issued bonds < Financial activ... | $2,000.00 | $832,250.00 | 6 | 2015-12-31 |
| 16 | 909876523-i-bond41 < Cash receipts from issued bonds < Financial activ... | $3,000.00 | $835,250.00 | 6 | 2015-12-31 |
| 17 | 909876524-i-bond41 < Cash receipts from issued bonds < Financial activ... | $5,000.00 | $840,250.00 | 6 | 2015-12-31 |
| 18 | 909876525-i-bond41 < Cash receipts from issued bonds < Financial activ... | $2,000.00 | $842,250.00 | 6 | 2015-12-31 |
| 19 | 909876513-i-owners < Cash receipts from owners < Financial activities | $7,750.00 | $850,000.00 | 7 | 2015-12-31 |
| 20 | 88-654304-c-interest of investment bond12 < Cash receipts from investm... | $504.00 | $850,504.00 | 7 | 2015-12-31 |
| 21 | 88-654305-c-interest of investment bond22 < Cash receipts from investm... | $242.00 | $850,746.00 | 7 | 2015-12-31 |
| 22 | Cash payments for operating expenses < Operating activities | -$24,756.00 | $825,990.00 | 7 | 2015-12-31 |
| 23 | 88-654306-t-truck1 < Cash payments for machinery < Operating activities | -$45,000.00 | $780,990.00 | 8 | 2015-12-31 |
| 24 | 88-654306-t-truck2 < Cash payments for machinery < Operating activities | -$40,000.00 | $740,990.00 | 8 | 2015-12-31 |

Figure 2.4-34   Company2 Cash Account Table (Continue)

Cash

| ID | Multi-Name | Amount | Balance | General ID | Transaction Date |
|---|---|---|---|---|---|
| 20 | 88-654304-c-interest of investment bond12 < Cash receipts from investm... | $504.00 | $850,504.00 | 7 | 2015-12-31 |
| 21 | 88-654305-c-interest of investment bond22 < Cash receipts from investm... | $242.00 | $850,746.00 | 7 | 2015-12-31 |
| 22 | Cash payments for operating expenses < Operating activities | -$24,756.00 | $825,990.00 | 7 | 2015-12-31 |
| 23 | 88-654306-t-truck1 < Cash payments for machinery < Operating activities | -$45,000.00 | $780,990.00 | 8 | 2015-12-31 |
| 24 | 88-654306-t-truck2 < Cash payments for machinery < Operating activities | -$40,000.00 | $740,990.00 | 8 | 2015-12-31 |
| 25 | 88-654306-t-car1 < Cash payments for machinery < Operating activities | -$40,000.00 | $700,990.00 | 8 | 2015-12-31 |
| 26 | 88-654306-t-computer server1 < Cash payments for machinery < Operati... | -$2,800.00 | $698,190.00 | 8 | 2015-12-31 |
| 27 | 88-654306-t-computer1 < Cash payments for machinery < Operating activ... | -$1,600.00 | $696,590.00 | 8 | 2015-12-31 |
| 28 | 88-654306-t-computer2 < Cash payments for machinery < Operating activ... | -$1,500.00 | $695,090.00 | 8 | 2015-12-31 |
| 29 | Cash payments for operating expenses < Operating activities | -$18,100.00 | $676,990.00 | 9 | 2015-12-31 |
| 30 | Cash payments for operating expenses < Operating activities | -$160,950.00 | $516,040.00 | 10 | 2015-12-31 |
| 31 | 88-654308-t-operating < Cash payments to suppliers<Operating activities | -$15,000.00 | $501,040.00 | 10 | 2015-12-31 |
| 32 | 88-654304-n-investment bond12 < Cash payments for investments < Inve... | -$8,000.00 | $493,040.00 | 10 | 2015-12-31 |
| 33 | 88-654305-n-investment bond22 < Cash payments for investments < Inve... | -$6,000.00 | $487,040.00 | 10 | 2015-12-31 |
| 34 | Cash payments for operating expenses < Operating activities | -$109,760.59 | $377,279.41 | 11 | 2015-12-31 |
| 35 | Cash payments for operating expenses < Operating activities | -$29,839.41 | $347,440.00 | 11 | 2015-12-31 |
| 36 | Cash payments for operating expenses < Operating activities | -$500.00 | $346,940.00 | 11 | 2015-12-31 |
| 37 | Cash payments for operating expenses < Operating activities | -$36,200.00 | $310,740.00 | 12 | 2015-12-31 |
| 38 | Cash payments for operating expenses < Operating activities | -$2,054.66 | $308,685.34 | 13 | 2015-12-31 |
| 39 | Cash payments for operating expenses < Operating activities | -$158,059.44 | $150,625.90 | 13 | 2015-12-31 |
| 40 | Cash payments for operating expenses < Operating activities | -$31,914.08 | $118,711.82 | 14 | 2015-12-31 |
| 41 | 88-654303-n-tax < Cash payments for operating expenses < Operating ac... | -$71,318.63 | $47,393.19 | 14 | 2015-12-31 |

Figure 2.4-34   Company2 Cash Account Table

The Figure 2.4-35 on the next page shows balance sheet table of the Company2 on December 31, 2015.

| | As at 12/31/2015 |
|---|---:|
| **ASSETS** | |
| Current assets | |
| Cash | $47,393.19 |
| Supplies | $192.45 |
| Account receivable | $15,150.00 |
| Inventory | $406,970.00 |
| Working-in-process inventory | $309,085.02 |
| | $778,790.66 |
| Long term investments | |
| Bonds | $14,000.00 |
| Equipment | |
| Vehicle | $125,000.00 |
| Accumulated amortization Vehicle | -$44,083.33 |
| Computer | $5,900.00 |
| Accumulated amortization Computer | -$4,179.16 |
| | $82,637.51 |
| Total Assets | $875,428.17 |
| | |
| LIABILITIES | |
| Current liabilities | |
| Account payable | $7,400.00 |
| Long term liabilities | |
| Bonds payable | $40,000.00 |
| Notes payable | $630,000.00 |
| | $670,000.00 |
| Total Liability | $677,400.00 |
| | |
| SHAREHOLDERS' EQUITY | |
| Owners capital | |
| Share capital | $180,000.00 |
| Retained earnings (conversion) | $18,028.17 |
| | $198,028.17 |
| Retined earnings | $0.00 |
| Accumulated other comprehensive income | $0.00 |
| Total Shareholders' Equity | $198,028.17 |
| | |
| Total Liabilities and Shareholders' Equity | $875,428.17 |

Figure 2.4-35   Company2 Balance Sheet

## 2.4.5 Sample of the Company3

The Company3 has total share capital $220,000 and three shareholders of the individual A7, the individual A17, and the individual A19. Their percentages of the share capital are 30%, 30%, and 40% respectively. The Company3 extracts ore materials and produces the general parts. The Figure 2.4-36 shows its product names, costs, and sale prices.

| Order | Product (the Lowest-level Subaccount) Names | Multi-subaccount Names | Costs | Sale Prices |
|---|---|---|---|---|
| 1 | Inven111 | Inven111 < Inven11 < Inven1 | 6.00 | 10.00 |
| 2 | Inven112 | Inven112 < Inven11 < Inven1 | 25.00 | 40.00 |
| 3 | Inven121 | Inven121 < Inven12 < Inven1 | 0.40 | 0.80 |
| 4 | Inven122 | Inven122 < Inven12 < Inven1 | 30.00 | 50.00 |
| 5 | Inven21 | Inven21 < Inven2 | 20.00 | 30.00 |
| 6 | Inven221 | Inven221 < Inven22 < Inven2 | 20.00 | 30.00 |
| 7 | Inven222 | Inven222 < Inven22 < Inven2 | 27.00 | 50.00 |
| 8 | PPUK parts | PPUK parts < ASD parts < Inven2 | 22.40 | 40.00 |
| 9 | PPGH parts | PPGH parts < ASD parts < Inven2 | 1.00 | 2.00 |
| 10 | Inven51 | Inven51 < Inven5 | 6.00 | 10.00 |
| 11 | Inven52 | Inven52 < Inven5 | 30.00 | 50.00 |
| 12 | Inven531 | Inven531 < Inven53 < Inven5 | 15.00 | 25.00 |
| 13 | Inven532 | Inven532 < Inven53 < Inven5 | 21.00 | 35.00 |
| 14 | Inven541 | Inven541 < Inven54 < Inven5 | 7.20 | 12.00 |
| 15 | Inven542 | Inven542 < Inven54 < Inven5 | 7.50 | 15.00 |
| 16 | Inven611 | Inven611 < Inven61 < Inven6 | 4.00 | 6.50 |
| 17 | Inven612 | Inven612 < Inven61 < Inven6 | 7.50 | 12.50 |
| 18 | Inven621 | Inven621 < Inven62 < Inven6 | 10.00 | 18.00 |
| 19 | Inven63 | Inven63 < Inven6 | 8.00 | 16.00 |
| 20 | Inven711 | Inven711 < Inven71 < Inven7 | 21.60 | 36.00 |
| 21 | Inven712 | Inven712 < Inven71 < Inven7 | 18.60 | 31.00 |
| 22 | Inven721 | Inven721 < Inven72 < Inven7 | 12.50 | 22.00 |
| 23 | Inven722 | Inven722 < Inven72 < Inven7 | 12.00 | 20.00 |
| 24 | Inven731 | Inven731 < Inven73 < Inven7 | 10.80 | 18.00 |
| 25 | Inven732 | Inven732 < Inven73 < Inven7 | 9.60 | 16.00 |
| 26 | Inven811 | Inven811 < Inven81 < Inven8 | 15.00 | 25.00 |
| 27 | Inven812 | Inven812 < Inven81 < Inven8 | 14.40 | 24.00 |
| 28 | Inven813 | Inven813 < Inven81 < Inven8 | 13.80 | 23.00 |
| 29 | Inven82 | Inven82 < Inven8 | 12.00 | 20.00 |
| 30 | Inven831 | Inven831 < Inven83 < Inven8 | 10.80 | 18.00 |
| 31 | Inven832 | Inven832 < Inven83 < Inven8 | 9.60 | 16.00 |

Figure 2.4-36   Company3 Products and Sale Prices Table

For a manufacturing company of the Company3, the costs of its products are mainly the labor and inventory costs. When the Company3 uses the MathAccounting software, the Working-in-process inventory account is treated as a parent account of the class 1 and the Cost of goods manufactured account is treated as the parent accounts of the class 5. For simplification, the Cost of goods manufactured account has only three one-level subaccounts of the "Supplies expenses", the "Salary expenses" for employees of A19 and A21, and the "Other general parts" in this book.

### 2.4.5.1 Conversion of the Company3

The Company3 will convert to the MathAccounting software on January 1, 2016, so I design a converting reference table, seeing the Figure 2.4-37 on this page and the next page, in order to enter its dynamic accounting equation on December 31, 2015 into the database dcj09.

| Order | Class | Account Name (**Subtotal Name**) | Balance | Row |
|---|---|---|---|---|
| **1** | **1** | **(Current assets)** | - | **103** |
| 2 | 1 | Cash | 10660.36 | 104 |
| 3 | 1 | Supplies | 209.88 | 106 |
| 4 | 1 | Account receivable | 17450.00 | 108 |
| 5 | 1 | Inventory | 343370.00 | 110 |
| 6 | 1 | Working-in-process inventory | 365110.00 | 112 |
| **7** | **1** | **(Long term investments)** | - | **141** |
| 8 | 1 | Bonds | 20000.00 | 142 |
| **9** | **1** | **(Equipment)** | - | **171** |
| 10 | 1 | Vehicle | 246000.00 | 172 |
| 11 | 1 | Accumulated amortization: Vehicle | -103466.67 | 173 |
| 12 | 1 | Computer | 5400.00 | 174 |
| 13 | 1 | Accumulated amortization: Computer | -4275.00 | 175 |
| **14** | **2** | **(Current liabilities)** | - | **203** |
| 15 | 2 | Account payable | 3900.00 | 204 |
| 16 | 2 | Accrued interest payable | 0 | 206 |
| 17 | 2 | Tax payable | 0 | 208 |
| **18** | **2** | **(Long term liabilities)** | - | **251** |
| 19 | 2 | Bonds payable | 80000.00 | 252 |
| 20 | 2 | Note payable | 580000.00 | 254 |
| **21** | **3** | **(Owners' capital)** | - | **303** |
| 22 | 3 | Share capital | 220000.00 | 304 |

| 23 | 3 | Retained earnings (Conversion) | 16558.57 | 306 |
|---|---|---|---|---|
| **24** | **4** | **(Revenues)** | - | **403** |
| 25 | 4 | Sales | | 404 |
| **26** | **5** | **(Cost)** | - | **431** |
| 27 | 5 | Cost of goods sold | | 432 |
| **28** | **5** | **(Operating and administrative expenses)** | - | **453** |
| 29 | 5 | Travelling expenses | 0 | 454 |
| 30 | 5 | Other expenses | 0 | 455 |
| 31 | 5 | Salary expenses | 0 | 456 |
| 32 | 5 | Cost of goods sold | 0 | 457 |
| 33 | 5 | Bond interest expenses | 0 | 458 |
| 34 | 5 | Note interest expenses | 0 | 460 |
| 35 | 5 | Amortization expenses | 0 | 462 |
| **36** | **4** | **(Other income)** | - | **475** |
| 37 | 4 | Investment incomes | | 476 |
| 38 | 4 | Deposits interest incomes | 0 | 478 |
| **39** | **5** | **(Tax)** | - | **600** |
| 40 | 5 | Tax expenses | 0 | 602 |

Figure 2.4-37   Company3 Converting Reference Table

From the Figure 2.4-37, there are total 29 accounts among which the balances of the Sales account, the Cost of goods sold account, and all expenses accounts are zero. In addition, the balance of the Retained earnings should be added to the balance of the Share capital, and its balance should be zero prior to conversion. However, for knowing the original share capital and the distinguishing Retained earnings account after conversion, I keep the Retained earnings prior to conversion and give it a different name Retained earnings (Conversion).

The Bonds account has two one-level subaccounts of the "Bond11 (issued by the Business Bank1 and purchased $8,000, beginning on February 1, 2014, five years, and annual interest rate 4%) and the "Bond21" (issued by the Business Bank2 and purchased $12,000, beginning on May 1, 2015, five years, and annual interest rate 4.1%).

The Company3 has four trucks and two cars (purchased them from the "Company1" in market price, five years, straight line), so the Vehicle account has six three-level subaccounts. The Figure 2.4-38 on the next page shows detail information of the Vehicle parent account and the balance of the Vehicle parent account.

| Order | Product (the Lowest-level Subaccount) Names | Multi-subaccount Names | Costs | Amortization Months |
|---|---|---|---|---|
| 1 | Truck11 | Truck11 < Truck1 < Truck | 45000.00 | 28 |
| 2 | Truck12 | Truck12 < Truck1 < Truck | 45000.00 | 28 |
| 3 | Truck21 | Truck21 < Truck2 < Truck | 40000.00 | 27 |
| 4 | Truck22 | Truck22 < Truck2 < Truck | 40000.00 | 22 |
| 5 | Car31 | Car31 < Car3 < Car | 36000.00 | 28 |
| 6 | Car32 | Car32 < Car3 < Car | 36000.00 | 20 |
| 7 | **Total** | | **242000.00** | |

Figure 2.4-38   Vehicle Detail Information Table

Accordingly, the multi-subaccount names of the Accumulated amortization: Vehicle account and their balances are showed in the following Figure 2.4-39.

| Order | One-level Subaccount Names | Multi-subaccounts Names | Accumulated amortization | Amortization Months |
|---|---|---|---|---|
| 1 | Truck-accumulated amortization | Truck11-accumulated amortization < Truck1-accumulated amortization < Truck-accumulated amortization | -21000.00 | 28 |
| 2 | Truck-accumulated amortization | Truck12-accumulated amortization < Truck1-accumulated amortization < Truck-accumulated amortization | -21000.00 | 28 |
| 3 | Truck-accumulated amortization | Truck21-accumulated amortization < Truck2-accumulated amortization < Truck-accumulated amortization | -18000.00 | 27 |
| 4 | Truck-accumulated amortization | Truck22-accumulated amortization < Truck2-accumulated amortization < Truck-accumulated amortization | -14666.67 | 22 |
| 5 | Car-accumulated amortization | Car31-accumulated amortization < Car3-accumulated amortization < Car-accumulated amortization | -16800.00 | 28 |
| 6 | Car-accumulated amortization | Car32-accumulated amortization < Car3-accumulated amortization < Car-accumulated amortization | -12000.00 | 20 |
| 7 | **Total** | - | **-103466.67** | - |

Figure 2.4-39   Accumulated amortization: vehicle Detail Information Table

The Company3 has one computer server2 (two years, straight line, 19 months), one computer3" (two years, straight line, 19 months), and one computer4" (two years, straight line, 19 months), so the multi-subaccount names of the Computer parent account are the "Computer server21 < Computer server2 < Computer server", the "Computer31 < Computer3", and the "Computer41 < Computer4" respectively. Their balances are $2,700,

$1,400, and $1,300 respectively. Accordingly, the multi-subaccount names of the Accumulated amortization: Computer account are the "Computer server21-accumulated amortization < Computer server2-accumulated amortization < Computer server-accumulated amortization", the "Computer31-accumulated amortization < Computer3-accumulated amortization", and the "Computer41-accumulated amortization < Computer4-accumulated amortization". Their balances are respectively -$2,137.50, -$1,108.33, and -$1,029.17.

The Company3 issued one bond, seeing the Figure 2.4-40 on this page and the next page, which shows the detail information of the issued bond ($80,000, beginning on June 1, 2015, five years, and annual interest rate 4.8%). The Bonds payable account has one one-level subaccount of the "Bond51-payable". Of course, the Bonds payable has also many two-level subaccounts, The Notes payable has three one-level subaccounts of the "Note13" ($200,000 from the Business Bank1, beginning on May 1, 2014, four years, and annual interest rate 9%), the "Note23" ($180,000 from the Business Bank2, beginning on June 1, 2014, four years, and annual interest rate 9%), and the "Note24" ($200,000 from the Business Bank2, beginning on July 1, 2014, four years, and annual interest rate 9.1%). Therefore, the Accrued interest payable account has two one-level subaccounts of the "Bonds-interest payable" and the "Notes-interest payable". Accordingly, the balances of the Accrued interest payable account are zero prior to the conversion.

| Order | Bond | Amount | Term | Purchaser Name | Identity |
|---|---|---|---|---|---|
| 1 | Bond51 | 6000 | June 1, 2015, Five years, 4.8% annually | A1 | 909876501 |
| 2 | Bond51 | 4000 | June 1, 2015, Five years, 4.8% annually | A2 | 909876502 |
| 3 | Bond51 | 7000 | June 1, 2015, Five years, 4.8% annually | A3 | 909876503 |
| 4 | Bond51 | 6000 | June 1, 2015, Five years, 4.8% annually | A7 | 909876507 |
| 5 | Bond51 | 7000 | June 1, 2015, Five years, 4.8% annually | A8 | 909876508 |
| 6 | Bond51 | 5000 | June 1, 2015, Five years, 4.8% annually | A9 | 909876509 |
| 7 | Bond51 | 4000 | June 1, 2015, Five years, 4.8% annually | A11 | 909876511 |
| 8 | Bond51 | 8000 | June 1, 2015, Five years, 4.8% annually | A12 | 909876512 |
| 9 | Bond51 | 5000 | June 1, 2015, Five years, 4.8% annually | A14 | 909876514 |

| | | | | | |
|---|---|---|---|---|---|
| 10 | Bond51 | 7000 | June 1, 2015, Five years, 4.8% annually | A16 | 909876516 |
| 11 | Bond51 | 5000 | June 1, 2015, Five years, 4.8% annually | A17 | 909876517 |
| 12 | Bond51 | 6000 | June 1, 2015, Five years, 4.8% annually | A18 | 909876518 |
| 13 | Bond51 | 4000 | June 1, 2015, Five years, 4.8% annually | A21 | 909876521 |
| 14 | Bond51 | 6000 | June 1, 2015, Five years, 4.8% annually | A22 | 909876522 |
| **15** | **Total** | **80000** | | | |

Figure 2.4-40   Company3 Issued Bond Information Table

The Account receivable account and the Account payable account need transaction dates during the conversion, so I assume that their transaction dates are also on December 31, 2015 for simplification.

For the Company3, the balances of the "Cash receipts from customers<Operating activities" and the "Cash payments to suppliers<Operating activities" are respectively $16,000 and zero. The reason is as same as the Company1. The following Figure 2.4-41 shows the difference detail information of the Company3.

| Order | Customer Company Name | Cash Receipts From Customers | Twin Cash Paid by Customers | Balance (Difference) |
|---|---|---|---|---|
| 1 | Company1 | 1000 | 0 | 1000 |
| 2 | Company2 | 15000 | 0 | 15000 |
| **4** | **Total** | **16000** | **0** | **16000** |

Figure 2.4-41   Difference Information Table

Following above information, I can build a table of the multi-subaccount names, seeing the Figure 2.4-42 on this page and the next pages.

| Order | Class | Multi-subaccount Name | Parent Name | Lowest Subaccount Balance |
|---|---|---|---|---|
| 1 | 1 | 909876507-i-owners < Cash receipts from owners < Financial activities | Cash | 66000.00 |
| 2 | 1 | 909876517-i-owners < Cash receipts from owners < Financial activities | Cash | 66000.00 |
| 3 | 1 | 909876519-i-owners < Cash receipts from owners < Financial activities | Cash | 88000.00 |
| 4 | 1 | 88-654304-i-note13 < Cash receipts from banks < Financial activities | Cash | 200000.00 |

| 5 | 1 | 88-654305-i-note23 < Cash receipts from banks < Financial activities | Cash | 180000.00 |
|---|---|---|---|---|
| 6 | 1 | 88-654305-i-note24 < Cash receipts from banks < Financial activities | Cash | 200000.00 |
| 7 | 1 | 88-654306-c-operating < Cash receipts from customers < Operating activities | Cash | 1000.00 |
| 8 | 1 | 88-654307-c-operating < Cash receipts from customers < Operating activities | Cash | 15000.00 |
| 9 | 1 | 909876501-i-bond51 < Cash receipts from issued bonds < Financial activities | Cash | 6000.00 |
| 10 | 1 | 909876502-i-bond51 < Cash receipts from issued bonds < Financial activities | Cash | 4000.00 |
| 11 | 1 | 909876503-i-bond51 < Cash receipts from issued bonds < Financial activities | Cash | 7000.00 |
| 12 | 1 | 909876507-i-bond51 < Cash receipts from issued bonds < Financial activities | Cash | 6000.00 |
| 13 | 1 | 909876508-i-bond51 < Cash receipts from issued bonds < Financial activities | Cash | 7000.00 |
| 14 | 1 | 909876509-i-bond51 < Cash receipts from issued bonds < Financial activities | Cash | 5000.00 |
| 15 | 1 | 909876511-i-bond51 < Cash receipts from issued bonds < Financial activities | Cash | 4000.00 |
| 16 | 1 | 909876512-i-bond51 < Cash receipts from issued bonds < Financial activities | Cash | 8000.00 |
| 17 | 1 | 909876514-i-bond51 < Cash receipts from issued bonds < Financial activities | Cash | 5000.00 |
| 18 | 1 | 909876516-i-bond51 < Cash receipts from issued bonds < Financial activities | Cash | 7000.00 |
| 19 | 1 | 909876517-i-bond51 < Cash receipts from issued bonds < Financial activities | Cash | 5000.00 |
| 20 | 1 | 909876518-i-bond51 < Cash receipts from issued bonds < Financial activities | Cash | 6000.00 |
| 21 | 1 | 909876521-i-bond51 < Cash receipts from issued bonds < Financial activities | Cash | 4000.00 |
| 22 | 1 | 909876522-i-bond51 < Cash receipts from issued bonds < Financial activities | Cash | 6000.00 |
| 23 | 1 | 88-654304-c-interest of investment bond11 < Cash receipts from investments < Investing activities | Cash | 613.33 |
| 24 | 1 | 88-654305-c-interest of investment bond21 < Cash receipts from investments < Investing activities | Cash | 820.00 |
| 25 | 1 | 88-654306-t-truck1 < Cash payments for machinery < Operating activities | Cash | -90000.00 |
| 26 | 1 | 88-654306-t-truck2 < Cash payments for machinery < Operating activities | Cash | -80000.00 |
| 27 | 1 | 88-654306-t-car2 < Cash payments for machinery < Operating activities | Cash | -76000.00 |
| 28 | 1 | 88-654306-t-computer server2 < Cash payments for machinery < Operating activities | Cash | -2700.00 |
| 29 | 1 | 88-654306-t-computer3 < Cash payments for machinery < Operating activities | Cash | -1400.00 |
| 30 | 1 | 88-654306-t-computer4 < Cash payments for machinery < Operating activities | Cash | -1300.00 |
| 31 | 1 | Cash payments for operating expenses < Operating activities | Cash | -190377.25 |
| 32 | 1 | Cash payments for operating expenses < Operating activities | Cash | -189189.46 |
| 33 | 1 | Cash payments for operating expenses < Operating activities | Cash | -184352.55 |
| 34 | 1 | 88-654303-n-tax < Cash payments for operating expenses < Operating activities | Cash | -51453.71 |
| 35 | 1 | Cash payments to suppliers<Operating activities | Cash | 0 |
| 36 | 1 | 88-654304-n-investment bond11 < Cash payments for investments < Investing activities | Cash | -8000.00 |

| 37 | 1 | 88-654305-n-investment bond21 < Cash payments for investments < Investing activities | Cash | -12000.00 |
|---|---|---|---|---|
| 38 | 1 | n | Supplies | 209.88 |
| 39 | 1 | 123456789 | Account receivable | 200.00 |
| 40 | 1 | 123456787 | Account receivable | 300.00 |
| 41 | 1 | 123456784 | Account receivable | 10600.00 |
| 42 | 1 | 123456783 | Account receivable | 6000.00 |
| 43 | 1 | 123456781 | Account receivable | 150.00 |
| 44 | 1 | 123456780 | Account receivable | 200.00 |
| 45 | 1 | Inven111 < Inven11 < Inven1 | Inventory | $6*1000 = 6000.00$ |
| 46 | 1 | Inven112 < Inven11 < Inven1 | Inventory | $25*800 = 20000.00$ |
| 47 | 1 | Inven121 < Inven12 < Inven1 | Inventory | $0.40*20000 = 8000.00$ |
| 48 | 1 | Inven122 < Inven12 < Inven1 | Inventory | $30*1000 = 30000.00$ |
| 49 | 1 | Inven21 < Inven2 | Inventory | $20*1250= 25000.00$ |
| 50 | 1 | Inven221 < Inven22 < Inven2 | Inventory | $20*750 = 15000.00$ |
| 51 | 1 | Inven222 < Inven22 < Inven2 | Inventory | $27*400 = 10800.00$ |
| 52 | 1 | PPUK parts < ASD parts < Inven2 | Inventory | $22.4*500 = 11200.00$ |
| 53 | 1 | PPGH parts < ASD parts < Inven2 | Inventory | $1.00*1600 = 1600.00$ |
| 54 | 1 | Inven51 < Inven5 | Inventory | $6*1000 = 6000.00$ |
| 55 | 1 | Inven52 < Inven5 | Inventory | $30*500 = 15000.00$ |
| 56 | 1 | Inven531 < Inven53 < Inven5 | Inventory | $15*1000 = 15000.00$ |
| 57 | 1 | Inven532 < Inven53 < Inven5 | Inventory | $21*1000 = 21000.00$ |
| 58 | 1 | Inven541 < Inven54 < Inven5 | Inventory | $7.2*1000 = 7200.00$ |
| 59 | 1 | Inven542 < Inven54 < Inven5 | Inventory | $7.5*1000 = 7500.00$ |
| 60 | 1 | Inven611 < Inven61 < Inven6 | Inventory | $4*1300 = 5200.00$ |
| 61 | 1 | Inven612 < Inven61 < Inven6 | Inventory | $7.5*1000 = 7500.00$ |
| 62 | 1 | Inven621 < Inven62 < Inven6 | Inventory | $10*900 = 9000.00$ |
| 63 | 1 | Inven63 < Inven6 | Inventory | $8*1000 = 8000.00$ |
| 64 | 1 | Inven711 < Inven71 < Inven7 | Inventory | $21.60*500 = 10800.00$ |
| 65 | 1 | Inven712 < Inven71 < Inven7 | Inventory | $18.60*100 = 1860.00$ |
| 66 | 1 | Inven721 < Inven72 < Inven7 | Inventory | $12.50*744 = 9300.00$ |
| 67 | 1 | Inven722 < Inven72 < Inven7 | Inventory | $12.00*600 = 7200.00$ |
| 68 | 1 | Inven731 < Inven73 < Inven7 | Inventory | $10.80*600 = 6480.00$ |
| 69 | 1 | Inven732 < Inven73 < Inven7 | Inventory | $9.60*1000 = 9600.00$ |
| 70 | 1 | Inven811 < Inven81 < Inven8 | Inventory | $15.00*600 = 9000.00$ |
| 71 | 1 | Inven812 < Inven81 < Inven8 | Inventory | $14.40*600 = 8640.00$ |
| 72 | 1 | Inven813 < Inven81 < Inven8 | Inventory | $13.80*600 = 8280.00$ |
| 73 | 1 | Inven82 < Inven8 | Inventory | $12.00*600 = 7200.00$ |
| 74 | 1 | Inven831 < Inven83 < Inven8 | Inventory | $10.80*600 = 6480.00$ |
| 75 | 1 | Inven832 < Inven83 < Inven8 | Inventory | $9.60*800 = 7680.00$ |
| 76 | 1 | Inven31 < Inven3 | Inventory | $10*100 = 1000.00$ |
| 77 | 1 | Inven32 < Inven3 | Inventory | $50*100 = 5000.00$ |
| 78 | 1 | Inven331 < Inven33 < Inven3 | Inventory | $20*100 = 2000.00$ |

| 79 | 1 | Inven332 < Inven33 < Inven3 | Inventory | 45*100 = 4500.00 |
|---|---|---|---|---|
| 80 | 1 | HGFCVB parts < QASXC parts < Inven3 | Inventory | 10*100 = 1000.00 |
| 81 | 1 | PPGHUP parts < ASDUP parts < Inven3 | Inventory | 20*100 = 2000.00 |
| 82 | 1 | Inven411 < Inven41 < Inven4 | Inventory | 5*100 = 500.00 |
| 83 | 1 | Inven412 < Inven41 < Inven4 | Inventory | 18.5*100 = 1850.00 |
| 84 | 1 | TTTCU parts < TTT parts < Inven4 | Inventory | 20*100 = 2000.00 |
| 85 | 1 | RRRHJK parts < Inven4 | Inventory | 20*100 = 2000.00 |
| 86 | 1 | Working-Inven111 < Working-Inven11 < Working-Inven1 | Working-in-process inventory | 4.78*1000 = 4780.00 |
| 87 | 1 | Working-Inven112 < Working-Inven11 < Working-Inven1 | Working-in-process inventory | 20.12*1000 = 20120.00 |
| 88 | 1 | Working-Inven121 < Working-Inven12 < Working-Inven1 | Working-in-process inventory | 0.20*10000 = 2000.00 |
| 89 | 1 | Working-Inven122 < Working-Inven12 < Working-Inven1 | Working-in-process inventory | 25.78*1000 = 25780.00 |
| 90 | 1 | Working-Inven21 < Working-Inven2 | Working-in-process inventory | 14.36*1000 = 14360.00 |
| 91 | 1 | Working-Inven221 < Working-Inven22 < Working-Inven2 | Working-in-process inventory | 14.77*1000 = 14770.00 |
| 92 | 1 | Working-Inven222 < Working-Inven22 < Working-Inven2 | Working-in-process inventory | 25.33*1000 = 25330.00 |
| 93 | 1 | Working-PPUK parts < Working-ASD parts < Working-Inven2 | Working-in-process inventory | 19.84*1000 = 19840.00 |
| 94 | 1 | Working-PPGH parts < Working-ASD parts < Working-Inven2 | Working-in-process inventory | 0.85*6000 = 5100.00 |
| 95 | 1 | Working-Inven51 < Working-Inven5 | Working-in-process inventory | 5.25*5000 = 26250.00 |
| 96 | 1 | Working-Inven52 < Working-Inven5 | Working-in-process inventory | 24.47*1000 = 24470.00 |
| 97 | 1 | Working-Inven531 < Working-Inven53 < Working-Inven5 | Working-in-process inventory | 12.83*1000 = 12830.00 |
| 98 | 1 | Working-Inven532 < Working-Inven53 < Working-Inven5 | Working-in-process inventory | 17.37*1000 = 17370.00 |
| 99 | 1 | Working-Inven541 < Working-Inven54 < Working-Inven5 | Working-in-process inventory | 6.22*1000 = 6220.00 |
| 100 | 1 | Working-Inven542 < Working-Inven54 < Working-Inven5 | Working-in-process inventory | 7.11*1000 = 7110.00 |
| 101 | 1 | Working-Inven611 < Working-Inven61 < Working-Inven6 | Working-in-process inventory | 3.39*5000 = 16950.00 |
| 102 | 1 | Working-Inven612 < Working-Inven61 < Working-Inven6 | Working-in-process inventory | 6.49*1000 = 6490.00 |
| 103 | 1 | Working-Inven621 < Working-Inven62 < Working-Inven6 | Working-in-process inventory | 8.87*1000 = 8870.00 |
| 104 | 1 | Working-Inven63 < Working-Inven6 | Working-in-process inventory | 7.95*1000 = 7950.00 |
| 105 | 1 | Working-Inven711 < Working-Inven71 < Working-Inven7 | Working-in-process inventory | 10.60*1000 = 10600.00 |
| 106 | 1 | Working-Inven712 < Working-Inven71 < Working-Inven7 | Working-in-process inventory | 9.43*1000 = 9430.00 |
| 107 | 1 | Working-Inven721 < Working-Inven72 < Working-Inven7 | Working-in-process inventory | 6.81*1000 = 6810.00 |
| 108 | 1 | Working-Inven722 < Working-Inven72 < Working-Inven7 | Working-in-process inventory | 6.13*1000 = 6130.00 |
| 109 | 1 | Working-Inven731 < Working-Inven73 < Working-Inven7 | Working-in-process inventory | 5.38*1000 = 5380.00 |
| 110 | 1 | Working-Inven732 < Working-Inven73 < Working-Inven7 | Working-in-process inventory | 5.04*1000 = 5040.00 |
| 111 | 1 | Working-Inven811 < Working-Inven81 < Working-Inven8 | Working-in-process inventory | 7.29*1000 = 7290.00 |

| 112 | 1 | Working-Inven812 < Working-Inven81 < Working-Inven8 | Working-in-process inventory | 7.17*1000 = 7170.00 |
|---|---|---|---|---|
| 113 | 1 | Working-Inven813 < Working-Inven81 < Working-Inven8 | Working-in-process inventory | 6.94*1000 = 6940.00 |
| 114 | 1 | Working-Inven82 < Working-Inven8 | Working-in-process inventory | 5.68*1000 = 5680.00 |
| 115 | 1 | Working-Inve831 < Working-Inven83 < Working-Inven8 | Working-in-process inventory | 4.76*3000 = 14280.00 |
| 116 | 1 | Working-Inven832 < Working-Inven83 < Working-Inven8 | Working-in-process inventory | 4.59*3000 = 13770.00 |
| 117 | 1 | Bond11 | Bonds | 8000.00 |
| 118 | 1 | Bond21 | Bonds | 12000.00 |
| 119 | 1 | Truck11 < Truck1 < Truck | Vehicle | 45000.00 |
| 120 | 1 | Truck12 < Truck1 < Truck | Vehicle | 45000.00 |
| 121 | 1 | Truck21 < Truck2 < Truck | Vehicle | 40000.00 |
| 122 | 1 | Truck22 < Truck2 < Truck | Vehicle | 40000.00 |
| 123 | 1 | Car31 < Car3 < Car | Vehicle | 38000.00 |
| 124 | 1 | Car32 < Car3 < Car | Vehicle | 38000.00 |
| 125 | 1 | Truck11-accumulated amortization < Truck1-accumulated amortization < Truck-accumulated amortization | Accumulated amortization: Vehicle | -21000.00 |
| 126 | 1 | Truck12-accumulated amortization < Truck1-accumulated amortization < Truck-accumulated amortization | Accumulated amortization: Vehicle | -21000.00 |
| 127 | 1 | Truck21-accumulated amortization < Truck2-accumulated amortization < Truck-accumulated amortization | Accumulated amortization: Vehicle | -18000.00 |
| 128 | 1 | Truck22-accumulated amortization < Truck2-accumulated amortization < Truck-accumulated amortization | Accumulated amortization: Vehicle | -14666.67 |
| 129 | 1 | Car31-accumulated amortization < Car3-accumulated amortization < Car-accumulated amortization | Accumulated amortization: Vehicle | -16800.00 |
| 130 | 1 | Car32-accumulated amortization < Car3-accumulated amortization < Car-accumulated amortization | Accumulated amortization: Vehicle | -12000.00 |
| 131 | 1 | Computer server21 < Computer server2 < Computer server | Computer | 2700.00 |
| 132 | 1 | Computer31 < Computer3 | Computer | 1400.00 |
| 133 | 1 | Computer41 < Computer4 | Computer | 1300.00 |
| 134 | 1 | Computer server21-accumulated amortization < Computer server2-accumulated amortization < Computer server-accumulated amortization | Accumulated amortization: Computer | -2137.50 |
| 135 | 1 | Computer31-accumulated amortization < Computer3-accumulated amortization | Accumulated amortization: Computer | -1108.33 |
| 136 | 1 | Computer41-accumulated amortization < Computer4-accumulated amortization | Accumulated amortization: Computer | -1029.17 |
| 137 | 2 | 123456084 | Account payable | 900.00 |
| 138 | 2 | 123456083 | Account payable | 600.00 |
| 139 | 2 | 123456081 | Account payable | 1600.00 |
| 140 | 2 | 123456080 | Account payable | 800.00 |
| 141 | 2 | Bond51-interest payable < Bonds-interest payable | Accrued interest payable | 0 |
| 142 | 2 | Note13-interest payable < Notes-interest payable | Accrued interest payable | 0 |
| 143 | 2 | Note23-interest payable < Notes-interest payable | Accrued interest payable | 0 |

| 144 | 2 | Note24-interest payable < Notes-interest payable | Accrued interest payable | 0 |
|---|---|---|---|---|
| 145 | 2 | Bond51-909876501 < Bond51 | Bonds payable | 6000.00 |
| 146 | 2 | Bond51-909876502 < Bond51 | Bonds payable | 4000.00 |
| 147 | 2 | Bond51-909876503 < Bond51 | Bonds payable | 7000.00 |
| 148 | 2 | Bond51-909876507 < Bond51 | Bonds payable | 6000.00 |
| 149 | 2 | Bond51-909876508 < Bond51 | Bonds payable | 7000.00 |
| 150 | 2 | Bond51-909876509 < Bond51 | Bonds payable | 5000.00 |
| 151 | 2 | Bond51-909876511 < Bond51 | Bonds payable | 4000.00 |
| 152 | 2 | Bond51-909876512 < Bond51 | Bonds payable | 8000.00 |
| 153 | 2 | Bond51-909876514 < Bond51 | Bonds payable | 5000.00 |
| 154 | 2 | Bond51-909876516 < Bond51 | Bonds payable | 7000.00 |
| 155 | 2 | Bond51-909876517 < Bond51 | Bonds payable | 5000.00 |
| 156 | 2 | Bond51-909876518 < Bond51 | Bonds payable | 6000.00 |
| 157 | 2 | Bond51-909876521 < Bond51 | Bonds payable | 4000.00 |
| 158 | 2 | Bond51-909876522 < Bond51 | Bonds payable | 6000.00 |
| 159 | 2 | Note13-88-654304 | Notes payable | 200000.00 |
| 160 | 2 | Note23-88-654305 | Notes payable | 180000.00 |
| 161 | 2 | Note24-88-654305 | Notes payable | 200000.00 |
| 162 | 3 | Capital-909876507 | Share capital | 66000.00 |
| 163 | 3 | Capital-909876517 | Share capital | 66000.00 |
| 164 | 3 | Capital-909876519 | Share capital | 88000.00 |
| 165 | 3 | n | Retained earnings (Conversion) | 16558.57 |
| 166 | 4 | Sales-909876519 | Sales | 0 |
| 167 | 5 | 909876519-travelling < Sales department-travelling | Travelling expenses | 0 |
| 168 | 5 | 909876520-travelling < Office department-travelling | Travelling expenses | 0 |
| 169 | 5 | 909876521-travelling < Product department-travelling | Travelling expenses | 0 |
| 170 | 5 | 909876519-other < Sales department-other | Other expenses | 0 |
| 171 | 5 | 909876520-other < Office department-other | Other expenses | 0 |
| 172 | 5 | 909876521-other < Product department-other | Other expenses | 0 |
| 173 | 5 | 909876520-salary < Office department-salary | Salary expenses | 0 |
| 174 | 5 | Supplies expenses | Cost of goods manufactured | 0 |
| 175 | 5 | 909876519-salary < Sales department-salary < Salary expenses | Cost of goods manufactured | 0 |
| 176 | 5 | 909876521-salary < Product department-salary < Salary expenses | Cost of goods manufactured | 0 |
| 177 | 5 | General parts expenses | Cost of goods manufactured | 0 |
| 178 | 5 | Bond51-interest | Bond interest expenses | 0 |
| 179 | 5 | Note13-interest | Note interest expenses | 0 |
| 180 | 5 | Note23-interest | Note interest expenses | 0 |
| 181 | 5 | Note24-interest | Note interest expenses | 0 |

| 182 | 5 | Truck1-1-amortization < Truck1-amortization < Vehicle-truck-amortization | Amortization expenses | 0 |
|-----|---|---|---|---|
| 183 | 5 | Truck1-2-amortization < Truck1-amortization < Vehicle-truck-amortization | Amortization expenses | 0 |
| 184 | 5 | Truck2-1-amortization < Truck2-amortization < Vehicle-truck-amortization | Amortization expenses | 0 |
| 185 | 5 | Truck2-2-amortization < Truck2-amortization < Vehicle-truck-amortization | Amortization expenses | 0 |
| 186 | 5 | Car31-amortization < Car3-amortization < Vehicle-car-amortization | Amortization expenses | 0 |
| 187 | 5 | Car32-amortization < Car3-amortization < Vehicle-car-amortization | Amortization expenses | 0 |
| 188 | 5 | Computer server21-amortization < Computer server2-amortization < Computer-amortization | Amortization expenses | 0 |
| 189 | 5 | Computer31-amortization < Computer3-amortization < Computer-amortization | Amortization expenses | 0 |
| 190 | 5 | Computer41-amortization < Computer4-amortization < Computer-amortization | Amortization expenses | 0 |
| 191 | 4 | Accrued interest income-bond11 < Bonds | Investment incomes | 0 |
| 192 | 4 | Accrued interest income-bond21 < Bonds | Investment incomes | 0 |
| 193 | 4 | n | Deposits interest income | 0 |

Figure 2.4-42   Company3 Converting Multi-Subaccount Names Table

Before entering the dynamic accounting equation on December 31, 2015 into the database dcj06, I first enter three initialization sub-equations.

Account payable (2): 0 = Share capital (3): 0

0 = Sales (4): 0 – Cost of goods sold (5):0

Cash (1): 0 = Retained earnings (Conversion) (3): 0

From the Figure 2.4-37 and the Figure 2.4-42, the dynamic accounting equation on December 31, 2015 must be divided to the N transaction sub-equations because of the restriction of the MathAccounting software. Every sub-equation has maximum twelve items. All converting transaction sub-equations can be designed and written as following.

- I build a transaction sub-equation for the Account receivable account and the Account payable account. The transaction sub-equation includes the Account receivable account with the Order 39 to the Order 44, the Account payable account with the Order 137 to the Order 140, and the part of the Cash account with the Order 31, The first transaction sub-equation is:

Account receivable (1): 200 + Account receivable (1): 300 + Account receivable (1): 10600 + Account receivable (1): 600 + Account receivable (1): 150 + Account receivable (1): 200 + Cash (1): -13550 = Account payable (2): 900 + Account payable (2): 600 + Account payable (2): 1600 + Account payable (2): 800

After entering this transaction, the new balance of the Cash account with the Order 31 is -$176,827.25 (= -$190377.25 + $13,550).

- The transaction sub-equation includes the Cash account with the Order 1 to the Order 6, the Share capital account with the Order 162 to the Order 164, and the Notes payable account with the Order 159 to the Order 161. The second transaction sub-equation is:

Cash (1): 66000 + Cash (1): 66000 + Cash (1): 88000 + Cash (1): 200000 + Cash (1): 180000 + Cash (1): 200000 = Share capital (3): 66000 + Share capital (3): 66000 + Share capital (3): 88000 + Notes payable (2): 200000 + Notes payable (2): 180000 + Notes payable (2): 200000

- The transaction sub-equation includes the Cash account with the Order 9 to the Order 14 and the Bonds payable account with the Order 145 to the Order 150. The third transaction sub-equation is:

Cash (1): 6000 + Cash (1): 4000 + Cash (1): 7000 + Cash (1): 6000 + Cash (1): 7000 + Cash (1): 5000 = Bonds payable (2): 6000 + Bonds payable (2): 4000 + Bonds payable (2): 7000 + Bonds payable (2): 6000 + Bonds payable (2): 7000 + Bonds payable (2): 5000

- The transaction sub-equation includes the Cash account with the Order 15 to the

Order 20 and the Bonds payable account with the Order 151 to the Order 156. The fourth transaction sub-equation is:

Cash (1): 4000 + Cash (1): 8000 + Cash (1): 5000 + Cash (1): 7000 + Cash (1): 5000 + Cash (1): 6000 = Bonds payable (2): 4000 + Bonds payable (2): 8000 + Bonds payable (2): 5000 + Bonds payable (2): 7000 + Bonds payable (2): 5000 + Bonds payable (2): 6000

- The transaction sub-equation includes the part of the Cash account with the Order 31, the Cash account with the Order 21 to the Order 24, the Inventory account with the Order 45 to the Order 48, and the Bonds payable account with the Order 157 and the Order 158. The fifth transaction sub-equation is:

Cash (1): -65433.33 + Cash (1): 4000 + Cash (1): 6000 + Cash (1): 613.33 + Cash (1): 820 + Inventory (1): 6000 + Inventory (1): 20000 + Inventory (1): 8000 + Inventory (1): 30000 = Bonds payable (2): 4000 + Bonds payable (2): 6000

After entering this transaction, the new balance of the Cash account with the Order 31 is -$111,393.92 (= -$176,827.25 + $65,433.33).

- The transaction sub-equation includes the Cash account with the Order 25 to the Order 27 and the Vehicle account with the Order 119 to the Order 124. The sixth transaction sub-equation is:

Cash (1): -90000 + Cash (1): -80000 + Cash (1): -76000 + Vehicle (1): 45000 + Vehicle (1): 45000 + Vehicle (1): 40000 + Vehicle (1): 40000 + Vehicle (1): 38000 + Vehicle (1): 38000 = 0

- The transaction sub-equation includes the part of the Cash account with the Order 31, the Cash account with the Order 28 to the Order 30, the Computer account with the Order 131 to the Order 133, and the Inventory account with the Order 49 to the

Order 53. The seventh transaction sub-equation is:

Cash (1): -63600 + Cash (1): -2700 + Cash (1): -1400 + Cash (1): -1300 + Computer (1): 2700 + Computer (1): 1400 + Computer (1): 1300 + Inventory (1): 25000 + Inventory (1): 15000 + Inventory (1): 10800 + Inventory (1): 11200 + Inventory (1): 1600 = 0

After entering this transaction, the new balance of the Cash account with the Order 31 is -$47,793.92 (= -$111,393.92+ $63,600).

- The transaction sub-equation includes the part of the Cash account with the Order 32 and the Inventory account with the Order 54 to the Order 64. The eighth transaction sub-equation is:

Cash (1): -112200 + Inventory (1): 6000 + Inventory (1): 15000 + Inventory (1): 15000 + Inventory (1): 21000 + Inventory (1): 7200 + Inventory (1): 7500 + Inventory (1): 5200 + Inventory (1): 7500+ Inventory (1): 9000 + Inventory (1): 8000 + Inventory (1): 10800 = 0

After entering this transaction, the new balance of the Cash account with the Order 32 is -$76,989.46 (= -$189,189.46 + $112,200).

- The transaction sub-equation includes the part of the Cash account with the Order 31, the Cash account with the Order 35 to the Order 37, and the Inventory account with the Order 65 to the Order 72. Because the balances of the Cash with the Order 35 is zero, the ninth transaction sub-equation is:

Cash (1): -40360 + Cash (1): -8000 + Cash (1): -12000 + Inventory (1): 1860 + Inventory (1): 9300 + Inventory (1): 7200 + Inventory (1): 6480 + Inventory (1): 9600 + Inventory (1): 9000 + Inventory (1): 8640 + Inventory (1): 8280 = 0

After entering this transaction, the new balance of the Cash account with the Order 31 is -$7,433.92 (= -$47,793.92 + $40,360).

- The transaction sub-equation includes the rest (-$7,433.92) of the Cash account with the Order 31, the part of the Cash account with the Order 32, and the Inventory account with the Order 73 to the Order 82. The tenth transaction sub-equation is:

Cash (1): -7433.92 + Cash (1): -29926.08 + Inventory (1): 7200 + Inventory (1): 6480 + Inventory (1): 7680 + Inventory (1): 1000 + Inventory (1): 5000 + Inventory (1): 2000 + Inventory (1): 4500 + Inventory (1): 1000 + Inventory (1): 2000 + Inventory (1): 500 = 0

After entering this transaction, the new balance of the Cash account with the Order 32 is -$47,063.38 (= -$76,989.46 + $29,926.08).

- The transaction sub-equation includes the rest (-$47,063.38) of the Cash account with the Order 32, the part of the Cash account with the Order 33, the Inventory account with the Order 83 to the Order 85, and the Working-in-process inventory account with the Order 86 to the Order 92. The eleventh transaction sub-equation is:

Cash (1): -47063.38 + Cash (1): -65926.62 + Inventory (1): 1850 + Inventory (1): 2000 + Inventory (1): 2000 + Working-in-process inventory (1): 4780 + Working-in-process inventory (1): 20120 + Working-in-process inventory (1): 2000 + Working-in-process inventory (1): 25780 + Working-in-process inventory (1): 14360 + Working-in-process inventory (1): 14770 + Working-in-process inventory (1): 25330 = 0

After entering this transaction, the new balance of the Cash account with the Order 33 is -$118,425.93 (= -$184,352.55 + $65,926.62).

- The transaction sub-equation includes the rest (-$118,425.93) of the Cash account with the Order 33, the part of the Cash account with the Order 34, and the Working-in-process inventory account with the Order 93 to the Order 102. The twelfth transaction sub-equation is:

Cash (1): -118425.93 + Cash (1): -24204.07 + Working-in-process inventory (1): 19840 + Working-in-process inventory (1): 5100 + Working-in-process inventory (1): 26250 + Working-in-process inventory (1): 24470 + Working-in-process inventory (1): 12830 + Working-in-process inventory (1): 17370 + Working-in-process inventory (1): 6220 + Working-in-process inventory (1): 7110 + Working-in-process inventory (1): 16950 + Working-in-process inventory (1): 6490 = 0

After entering this transaction, the new balance of the Cash account with the Order 34 is -$27,249.64 (= -$51,453.71+ $24,204.07).

- The transaction sub-equation includes the part of the Cash account with the Order 34, the Supplies account with the Order 35, the Working-in-process inventory account with the Order 103 to the Order 108, the Accumulated amortization: Vehicle account with the Order 125 and the Order 126. The thirteenth transaction sub-equation is:

Cash (1): -7999.88 + Supplies (1): 209.88 + Working-in-process inventory (1): 8870 + Working-in-process inventory (1): 7950 + Working-in-process inventory (1): 10600 + Working-in-process inventory (1): 9430 + Working-in-process inventory (1): 6810 + Working-in-process inventory (1): 6130 + Accumulated amortization: Vehicle (1): -21000 + Accumulated amortization: Vehicle (1): -21000 = 0

After entering this transaction, the new balance of the Cash account with the Order 34 is -$19,249.76 (= -$27,249.64 + $7,999.88).

- The transaction sub-equation includes the part of the Cash account with the Order

34, the Working-in-process inventory account with the Order 109 to the Order 113, and the Accumulated amortization: Vehicle account with the Order 127. The fourteenth transaction sub-equation is:

Cash (1): -13820 + Working-in-process inventory (1): 5380 + Working-in-process inventory (1): 5040 + Working-in-process inventory (1): 7290 + Working-in-process inventory (1): 7170 + Working-in-process inventory (1): 6940 + Accumulated amortization: Vehicle (1): -18000 = 0

After entering this transaction, the new balance of the Cash account with the Order 34 is -$5,429.76 (= -$19,249.76 + $13820).

- The transaction sub-equation includes the part of the Cash account with the Order 34, the Cash account with the Order 8, the Working-in-process inventory account with the Order 114 to the Order 116, and the Accumulated amortization: Vehicle account with the Order 128 to the Order 130. The fifteenth sub-equation is:

Cash (1): -5263.33 + Cash (1): 15000 + Working-in-process inventory (1): 5680 + Working-in-process inventory (1): 14280 + Working-in-process inventory (1): 13770 + Accumulated amortization: Vehicle (1): -14666.67 + Accumulated amortization: Vehicle (1): -16800 + Accumulated amortization: Vehicle (1): -12000 = 0

After entering this transaction, the new balance of the Cash account with the Order 34 is -$166.43 (= -$5,429.76 + $5,263.33).

- The transaction sub-equation includes the rest (-$166.43) of the Cash account with the Order 34, the Cash account with the Order 7, the Accumulated amortization: Computer account with the Order 134 to the Order 136, the Bonds account with the Order 117 and the Order 118, and the Retained earnings (Conversion) account with the balance $28,302.19. The sixteenth transaction sub-equation is:

Cash (1): -166.43 + Cash (1): 1000 + Accumulated amortization: Computer (1): -2137.5 + Accumulated amortization: Computer (1): -1108.33 + Accumulated amortization: Computer (1): -1029.17 + Bonds (1): 8000 + Bonds (1): 12000 = Retained earnings (Conversion) (3): 16558.57

After completing this transaction, the dynamic accounting equation of the Company3 on December 31, 2015 has entered into the database dcj09.

### 2.4.5.2 Brief Summary of the Company3

The Figure 2.4-43 on this and the next page shows cash received or paid by other members table which is in the public database dcj100.

| | IDM | Amount | Symbol | MultiSubaccount | Recorder | TransDate |
|---|---|---|---|---|---|---|
| 1 | | 0.00 | | Cash payments for operating expenses < Operating activities | 88-654308 | 2015-12-31 |
| 2 | | 13550.00 | | Cash payments for operating expenses < Operating activities | 88-654308 | 2015-12-31 |
| 3 | 909876507 | -66000.00 | i | 909876507-i-owners < Cash receipts from owners < Financial activities | 88-654308 | 2015-12-31 |
| 4 | 909876517 | -66000.00 | i | 909876517-i-owners < Cash receipts from owners < Financial activities | 88-654308 | 2015-12-31 |
| 5 | 909876519 | -88000.00 | i | 909876519-i-owners < Cash receipts from owners < Financial activities | 88-654308 | 2015-12-31 |
| 6 | 88-654304 | -200000.00 | i | 88-654304-i-note13 < Cash receipts from banks < Financial activities | 88-654308 | 2015-12-31 |
| 7 | 88-654305 | -180000.00 | i | 88-654305-i-note23 < Cash receipts from banks < Financial activities | 88-654308 | 2015-12-31 |
| 8 | 88-654305 | -200000.00 | i | 88-654305-i-note24 < Cash receipts from banks < Financial activities | 88-654308 | 2015-12-31 |
| 9 | 909876501 | -6000.00 | i | 909876501-i-bond51 < Cash receipts from issued bonds < Financial activities | 88-654308 | 2015-12-31 |
| 10 | 909876502 | -4000.00 | i | 909876502-i-bond51 < Cash receipts from issued bonds < Financial activities | 88-654308 | 2015-12-31 |
| 11 | 909876503 | -7000.00 | i | 909876503-i-bond51 < Cash receipts from issued bonds < Financial activities | 88-654308 | 2015-12-31 |
| 12 | 909876507 | -6000.00 | i | 909876507-i-bond51 < Cash receipts from issued bonds < Financial activities | 88-654308 | 2015-12-31 |
| 13 | 909876508 | -7000.00 | i | 909876508-i-bond51 < Cash receipts from issued bonds < Financial activities | 88-654308 | 2015-12-31 |
| 14 | 909876509 | -5000.00 | i | 909876509-i-bond51 < Cash receipts from issued bonds < Financial activities | 88-654308 | 2015-12-31 |
| 15 | 909876511 | -4000.00 | i | 909876511-i-bond51 < Cash receipts from issued bonds < Financial activities | 88-654308 | 2015-12-31 |
| 16 | 909876512 | -8000.00 | i | 909876512-i-bond51 < Cash receipts from issued bonds < Financial activities | 88-654308 | 2015-12-31 |
| 17 | 909876514 | -5000.00 | i | 909876514-i-bond51 < Cash receipts from issued bonds < Financial activities | 88-654308 | 2015-12-31 |
| 18 | 909876516 | -7000.00 | i | 909876516-i-bond51 < Cash receipts from issued bonds < Financial activities | 88-654308 | 2015-12-31 |
| 19 | 909876517 | -5000.00 | i | 909876517-i-bond51 < Cash receipts from issued bonds < Financial activities | 88-654308 | 2015-12-31 |
| 20 | 909876518 | -6000.00 | i | 909876518-i-bond51 < Cash receipts from issued bonds < Financial activities | 88-654308 | 2015-12-31 |
| 21 | | 65433.33 | | Cash payments for operating expenses < Operating activities | 88-654308 | 2015-12-31 |
| 22 | 909876521 | -4000.00 | i | 909876521-i-bond51 < Cash receipts from issued bonds < Financial activities | 88-654308 | 2015-12-31 |
| 23 | 909876522 | -6000.00 | i | 909876522-i-bond51 < Cash receipts from issued bonds < Financial activities | 88-654308 | 2015-12-31 |
| 24 | 88-654304 | -613.33 | c | 88-654304-c-interest of investment bond11 < Cash receipts from investments < Investing activities | 88-654308 | 2015-12-31 |
| 25 | 88-654305 | -820.00 | c | 88-654305-c-interest of investment bond21 < Cash receipts from investments < Investing activities | 88-654308 | 2015-12-31 |

Figure 2.4-43   Company3 Cash Received or Paid by Other Members (Continue)

```
SQLQuery2.sql - LIU...SS.dcj100 (sa (52))*  ×
    -use dcj100
    select sum(amount) as sum0 from CashByMembers where Recorder = '88-654308'
    select * from CashByMembers where Recorder = '88-654308'
```

100 %  ▾

Results  Messages

| | sum0 |
|---|---|
| 1 | -10660.36 |

| | IDM | Amount | Symbol | MultiSubaccount | Recorder | TransDate |
|---|---|---|---|---|---|---|
| 24 | 88-654304 | -613.33 | c | 88-654304-c-interest of investment bond11 < Cash receipts from investments < Investing activities | 88-654308 | 2015-12-31 |
| 25 | 88-654305 | -820.00 | c | 88-654305-c-interest of investment bond21 < Cash receipts from investments < Investing activities | 88-654308 | 2015-12-31 |
| 26 | 88-654306 | 90000.00 | t | 88-654306-t-truck1 < Cash payments for machinery < Operating activities | 88-654308 | 2015-12-31 |
| 27 | 88-654306 | 80000.00 | t | 88-654306-t-truck2 < Cash payments for machinery < Operating activities | 88-654308 | 2015-12-31 |
| 28 | 88-654306 | 76000.00 | t | 88-654306-t-car2 < Cash payments for machinery < Operating activities | 88-654308 | 2015-12-31 |
| 29 | | 63600.00 | | Cash payments for operating expenses < Operating activities | 88-654308 | 2015-12-31 |
| 30 | 88-654306 | 2700.00 | t | 88-654306-t-computer server2 < Cash payments for machinery < Operating activities | 88-654308 | 2015-12-31 |
| 31 | 88-654306 | 1400.00 | t | 88-654306-t-computer3 < Cash payments for machinery < Operating activities | 88-654308 | 2015-12-31 |
| 32 | 88-654306 | 1300.00 | t | 88-654306-t-computer4 < Cash payments for machinery < Operating activities | 88-654308 | 2015-12-31 |
| 33 | | 112200.00 | | Cash payments for operating expenses < Operating activities | 88-654308 | 2015-12-31 |
| 34 | | 40360.00 | | Cash payments for operating expenses < Operating activities | 88-654308 | 2015-12-31 |
| 35 | 88-654304 | 8000.00 | n | 88-654304-n-investment bond11 < Cash payments for investments < Investing activities | 88-654308 | 2015-12-31 |
| 36 | 88-654305 | 12000.00 | n | 88-654305-n-investment bond21 < Cash payments for investments < Investing activities | 88-654308 | 2015-12-31 |
| 37 | | 7433.92 | | Cash payments for operating expenses < Operating activities | 88-654308 | 2015-12-31 |
| 38 | | 29926.08 | | Cash payments for operating expenses < Operating activities | 88-654308 | 2015-12-31 |
| 39 | | 47063.38 | | Cash payments for operating expenses < Operating activities | 88-654308 | 2015-12-31 |
| 40 | | 65926.62 | | Cash payments for operating expenses < Operating activities | 88-654308 | 2015-12-31 |
| 41 | | 118425.93 | | Cash payments for operating expenses < Operating activities | 88-654308 | 2015-12-31 |
| 42 | 88-654303 | 24204.07 | n | 88-654303-n-tax < Cash payments for operating expenses < Operating activities | 88-654308 | 2015-12-31 |
| 43 | 88-654303 | 7999.88 | n | 88-654303-n-tax < Cash payments for operating expenses < Operating activities | 88-654308 | 2015-12-31 |
| 44 | 88-654303 | 13820.00 | n | 88-654303-n-tax < Cash payments for operating expenses < Operating activities | 88-654308 | 2015-12-31 |
| 45 | 88-654303 | 5263.33 | n | 88-654303-n-tax < Cash payments for operating expenses < Operating activities | 88-654308 | 2015-12-31 |
| 46 | 88-654307 | -15000.00 | c | 88-654307-c-operating < Cash receipts from customers < Operating activities | 88-654308 | 2015-12-31 |
| 47 | 88-654303 | 166.43 | n | 88-654303-n-tax < Cash payments for operating expenses < Operating activities | 88-654308 | 2015-12-31 |
| 48 | 88-654306 | -1000.00 | c | 88-654306-c-operating < Cash receipts from customers < Operating activities | 88-654308 | 2015-12-31 |

Query executed successfully.                                                    LIU\SQLEXI

Figure 2.4-43   Company3 Cash Received or Paid by Other Members

The Figure 2.4-44 on the next page shows cash flows statement of the Company3 on December 31, 2015. The Figure 2.4-45 on the next page shows the entering process of the cash with the Order 34.

Cash Flow Statement

| Cash Flows Statement Year Ended 2015-12-31 | |
|---|---|
| **Operating activities** | |
| Cash payments for machinery | -$251,400.00 |
| Cash payments for operating expenses | -$615,372.97 |
| Cash receipts from customers | $16,000.00 |
| Net cash provided by Operating activities | -$850,772.97 |
| | |
| Investing activities | |
| Cash payments for investments | -$20,000.00 |
| Cash receipts from investments | $1,433.33 |
| Net cash provided by Investing activities | -$18,566.67 |
| | |
| Financial activities | |
| Cash receipts from banks | $580,000.00 |
| Cash receipts from issued bonds | $80,000.00 |
| Cash receipts from owners | $220,000.00 |
| Net cash provided by Financial activities | $880,000.00 |
| | |
| Net change in cash | $10,660.36 |
| Cash, Begining | $0.00 |
| Cash, Ending | $10,660.36 |

Figure 2.4-44   Company3 Cash Flows Statement

Cash: 88-654303-n-tax

| ID | Multi-Name | Amount | Unit | General ID | Transaction Data |
|---|---|---|---|---|---|
| 42 | 88-654303-n-tax < Cash payments for operating expenses < Operating activit... | -$24,204.07 | 1 | 15 | 2015-12-31 |
| 43 | 88-654303-n-tax < Cash payments for operating expenses < Operating activit... | -$7,999.88 | 1 | 16 | 2015-12-31 |
| 44 | 88-654303-n-tax < Cash payments for operating expenses < Operating activit... | -$13,820.00 | 1 | 17 | 2015-12-31 |
| 45 | 88-654303-n-tax < Cash payments for operating expenses < Operating activit... | -$5,263.33 | 1 | 18 | 2015-12-31 |
| 47 | 88-654303-n-tax < Cash payments for operating expenses < Operating activit... | -$166.43 | 1 | 19 | 2015-12-31 |
| | | -$51,453.71 | 5 | | |

Figure 2.4-45   Entering Process of Cash (Order 34)

The Figure 2.4-46 on the next pages shows Cash account table of the Company3 on December 31, 2015.

Cash

| ID | Multi-Name | Amount | Balance | General ID | Transaction Date |
|---|---|---|---|---|---|
| 1 | Cash payments for operating expenses < Operating activities | $0.00 | $0.00 | 3 | 2015-12-31 |
| 2 | Cash payments for operating expenses < Operating activities | -$13,550.00 | -$13,550.00 | 4 | 2015-12-31 |
| 3 | 909876507-i-owners < Cash receipts from owners < Financial activities | $66,000.00 | $52,450.00 | 5 | 2015-12-31 |
| 4 | 909876517-i-owners < Cash receipts from owners < Financial activities | $66,000.00 | $118,450.00 | 5 | 2015-12-31 |
| 5 | 909876519-i-owners < Cash receipts from owners < Financial activities | $88,000.00 | $206,450.00 | 5 | 2015-12-31 |
| 6 | 88-654304-i-note13 < Cash receipts from banks < Financial activities | $200,000.00 | $406,450.00 | 5 | 2015-12-31 |
| 7 | 88-654305-i-note23 < Cash receipts from banks < Financial activities | $180,000.00 | $586,450.00 | 5 | 2015-12-31 |
| 8 | 88-654305-i-note24 < Cash receipts from banks < Financial activities | $200,000.00 | $786,450.00 | 5 | 2015-12-31 |
| 9 | 909876501-i-bond51 < Cash receipts from issued bonds < Financial activiti... | $6,000.00 | $792,450.00 | 6 | 2015-12-31 |
| 10 | 909876502-i-bond51 < Cash receipts from issued bonds < Financial activiti... | $4,000.00 | $796,450.00 | 6 | 2015-12-31 |
| 11 | 909876503-i-bond51 < Cash receipts from issued bonds < Financial activiti... | $7,000.00 | $803,450.00 | 6 | 2015-12-31 |
| 12 | 909876507-i-bond51 < Cash receipts from issued bonds < Financial activiti... | $6,000.00 | $809,450.00 | 6 | 2015-12-31 |
| 13 | 909876508-i-bond51 < Cash receipts from issued bonds < Financial activiti... | $7,000.00 | $816,450.00 | 6 | 2015-12-31 |
| 14 | 909876509-i-bond51 < Cash receipts from issued bonds < Financial activiti... | $5,000.00 | $821,450.00 | 6 | 2015-12-31 |
| 15 | 909876511-i-bond51 < Cash receipts from issued bonds < Financial activiti... | $4,000.00 | $825,450.00 | 7 | 2015-12-31 |
| 16 | 909876512-i-bond51 < Cash receipts from issued bonds < Financial activiti... | $8,000.00 | $833,450.00 | 7 | 2015-12-31 |
| 17 | 909876514-i-bond51 < Cash receipts from issued bonds < Financial activiti... | $5,000.00 | $838,450.00 | 7 | 2015-12-31 |
| 18 | 909876516-i-bond51 < Cash receipts from issued bonds < Financial activiti... | $7,000.00 | $845,450.00 | 7 | 2015-12-31 |
| 19 | 909876517-i-bond51 < Cash receipts from issued bonds < Financial activiti... | $5,000.00 | $850,450.00 | 7 | 2015-12-31 |
| 20 | 909876518-i-bond51 < Cash receipts from issued bonds < Financial activiti... | $6,000.00 | $856,450.00 | 7 | 2015-12-31 |
| 21 | Cash payments for operating expenses < Operating activities | -$65,433.33 | $791,016.67 | 8 | 2015-12-31 |
| 22 | 909876521-i-bond51 < Cash receipts from issued bonds < Financial activiti... | $4,000.00 | $795,016.67 | 8 | 2015-12-31 |
| 23 | 909876522-i-bond51 < Cash receipts from issued bonds < Financial activiti... | $6,000.00 | $801,016.67 | 8 | 2015-12-31 |
| 24 | 88-654304-c-interest of investment bond11 < Cash receipts from investme... | $613.33 | $801,630.00 | 8 | 2015-12-31 |

Figure 2.4-46   Company3 Cash Account Table (Continue)

Cash

| ID | Multi-Name | Amount | Balance | General ID | Transaction Date |
|---|---|---|---|---|---|
| 25 | 88-654305-c-interest of investment bond21 < Cash receipts from investme... | $820.00 | $802,450.00 | 8 | 2015-12-31 |
| 26 | 88-654306-t-truck1 < Cash payments for machinery < Operating activities | -$90,000.00 | $712,450.00 | 9 | 2015-12-31 |
| 27 | 88-654306-t-truck2 < Cash payments for machinery < Operating activities | -$80,000.00 | $632,450.00 | 9 | 2015-12-31 |
| 28 | 88-654306-t-car2 < Cash payments for machinery < Operating activities | -$76,000.00 | $556,450.00 | 9 | 2015-12-31 |
| 29 | Cash payments for operating expenses < Operating activities | -$63,600.00 | $492,850.00 | 10 | 2015-12-31 |
| 30 | 88-654306-t-computer server2 < Cash payments for machinery < Operating... | -$2,700.00 | $490,150.00 | 10 | 2015-12-31 |
| 31 | 88-654306-t-computer3 < Cash payments for machinery < Operating activiti... | -$1,400.00 | $488,750.00 | 10 | 2015-12-31 |
| 32 | 88-654306-t-computer4 < Cash payments for machinery < Operating activiti... | -$1,300.00 | $487,450.00 | 10 | 2015-12-31 |
| 33 | Cash payments for operating expenses < Operating activities | -$112,200.00 | $375,250.00 | 11 | 2015-12-31 |
| 34 | Cash payments for operating expenses < Operating activities | -$40,360.00 | $334,890.00 | 12 | 2015-12-31 |
| 35 | 88-654304-n-investment bond11 < Cash payments for investments < Invest... | -$8,000.00 | $326,890.00 | 12 | 2015-12-31 |
| 36 | 88-654305-n-investment bond21 < Cash payments for investments < Invest... | -$12,000.00 | $314,890.00 | 12 | 2015-12-31 |
| 37 | Cash payments for operating expenses < Operating activities | -$7,433.92 | $307,456.08 | 13 | 2015-12-31 |
| 38 | Cash payments for operating expenses < Operating activities | -$29,926.08 | $277,530.00 | 13 | 2015-12-31 |
| 39 | Cash payments for operating expenses < Operating activities | -$47,063.38 | $230,466.62 | 14 | 2015-12-31 |
| 40 | Cash payments for operating expenses < Operating activities | -$65,926.62 | $164,540.00 | 14 | 2015-12-31 |
| 41 | Cash payments for operating expenses < Operating activities | -$118,425.93 | $46,114.07 | 15 | 2015-12-31 |
| 42 | 88-654303-n-tax < Cash payments for operating expenses < Operating acti... | -$24,204.07 | $21,910.00 | 15 | 2015-12-31 |
| 43 | 88-654303-n-tax < Cash payments for operating expenses < Operating acti... | -$7,999.88 | $13,910.12 | 16 | 2015-12-31 |
| 44 | 88-654303-n-tax < Cash payments for operating expenses < Operating acti... | -$13,820.00 | $90.12 | 17 | 2015-12-31 |
| 45 | 88-654303-n-tax < Cash payments for operating expenses < Operating acti... | -$5,263.33 | -$5,173.21 | 18 | 2015-12-31 |
| 46 | 88-654307-c-operating < Cash receipts from customers < Operating activiti... | $15,000.00 | $9,826.79 | 18 | 2015-12-31 |
| 47 | 88-654303-n-tax < Cash payments for operating expenses < Operating acti... | -$166.43 | $9,660.36 | 19 | 2015-12-31 |
| 48 | 88-654306-c-operating < Cash receipts from customers < Operating activiti... | $1,000.00 | $10,660.36 | 19 | 2015-12-31 |

Figure 2.4-46   Company3 Cash Account Table

The Figure 2.4-47 on the next page shows balance sheet table of the Company3 on December 31, 2015.

Balance Sheet

| | As at 12/31/2015 |
|---|---|
| **ASSETS** | |
| Current assets | |
| Cash | $10,660.36 |
| Supplies | $209.88 |
| Account receivable | $17,450.00 |
| Inventory | $343,370.00 |
| Working-in-process inventory | $365,110.00 |
| | $736,800.24 |
| Long term investments | |
| Bonds | $20,000.00 |
| Equipment | |
| Vehicle | $246,000.00 |
| Accumulated amortization: Vehicle | -$103,466.67 |
| Computer | $5,400.00 |
| Accumulated amortization: Computer | -$4,275.00 |
| | $143,658.33 |
| Total Assets | $900,458.57 |
| | |
| LIABILITIES | |
| Current liabilities | |
| Account payable | $3,900.00 |
| Long term liabilities | |
| Bonds payable | $80,000.00 |
| Notes payable | $580,000.00 |
| | $660,000.00 |
| Total Liability | $663,900.00 |
| | |
| SHAREHOLDERS' EQUITY | |
| Owners capital | |
| Share capital | $220,000.00 |
| Retained earnings (Conversion) | $16,558.57 |
| | $236,558.57 |
| Retined earnings | $0.00 |
| Accumulated other comprehensive income | $0.00 |
| Total Shareholders' Equity | $236,558.57 |
| | |
| Total Liabilities and Shareholders' Equity | $900,458.57 |

Figure 2.4-47   Company3 Balance Sheet

## 2.4.6 Sample of the Proprietorship1

The Proprietorship1 is owned by the individual A23 completely and has total share capital $160,000. The Proprietorship1 produces the general parts and the foods. The Figure 2.4-48 shows its product names, costs, and sale prices.

| Order | Product (the Lowest-level Subaccount) Names | Multi-subaccount Names | Costs | Sale Prices |
|---|---|---|---|---|
| 1 | Inven31 | Inven31 < Inven3 | 6.00 | 10.00 |
| 2 | Inven32 | Inven32 < Inven3 | 30.00 | 50.00 |
| 3 | Inven331 | Inven331 < Inven33 < Inven3 | 10.00 | 20.00 |
| 4 | Inven332 | Inven332 < Inven33 < Inven3 | 27.00 | 45.00 |
| 5 | HGFCVB parts | HGFCVB parts < QASXC parts < Inven3 | 6.00 | 10.00 |
| 6 | PPGHUP parts | PPGHUP parts < ASDUP parts < Inven3 | 12.00 | 20.00 |
| 7 | Food111 | Food111 < Food11 < Food1 | 5.00 | 10.00 |
| 8 | Food112 | Food112 < Food11 < Food1 | 5.50 | 11.00 |
| 9 | Food113 | Food113 < Food11 < Food1 | 6.00 | 12.00 |
| 10 | Food121 | Food121 < Food12 < Food1 | 6.50 | 13.00 |
| 11 | Food122 | Food122 < Food12 < Food1 | 7.00 | 14.00 |
| 12 | Food123 | Food123 < Food12 < Food1 | 7.50 | 15.00 |
| 13 | Food211 | Food211 < Food21 < Food2 | 4.00 | 8.00 |
| 14 | Food212 | Food212 < Food21 < Food2 | 4.50 | 9.00 |
| 15 | Food213 | Food213 < Food21 < Food2 | 5.00 | 10.00 |
| 16 | Food214 | Food214 < Food21 < Food2 | 5.50 | 11.00 |
| 17 | Food221 | Food221 < Food22 < Food2 | 6.00 | 12.00 |
| 18 | Food222 | Food222 < Food22 < Food2 | 6.50 | 13.00 |
| 19 | Food23 | Food23 < Food2 | 7.50 | 16.00 |
| 20 | Food311 | Food311 < Food31 < Food3 | 8.50 | 20.00 |
| 21 | Food312 | Food312 < Food31 < Food3 | 11.00 | 24.00 |
| 22 | Food321 | Food321 < Food32 < Food3 | 12.00 | 27.00 |
| 23 | Food322 | Food322 < Food32 < Food3 | 13.00 | 30.00 |

Figure 2.4-48   Proprietorship1 Products and Sale Prices Table

For a producing foods company of the Proprietorship1, the costs of its food products are most the labor and inventory costs. When the Proprietorship1 uses the MathAccounting software, the Working-in-process inventory account is treated as a parent account of the class 1 and the Cost of goods sold account is treated as the parent accounts of the class 5. For simplification, the Cost of goods sold account has only three one-level subaccounts of the "Supplies expenses", the "Salary expenses" for employee A22, and the "Other general parts" in this book.

## 2.4.6.1 Conversion of the Proprietorship1

The Proprietorship1 will convert to the MathAccounting software on January 1, 2016, so I design a converting reference table, seeing the Figure 2.4-49 on this page and the next page, in order to enter its dynamic accounting equation on December 31, 2015 into the database dcj10.

| Order | Class | Account Name (**Subtotal Name**) | Balance | Row |
|---|---|---|---|---|
| **1** | **1** | **(Current assets)** | - | **103** |
| 2 | 1 | Cash | 18783.78 | 104 |
| 3 | 1 | Supplies | 155.45 | 106 |
| 4 | 1 | Account receivable | 4540.00 | 108 |
| 5 | 1 | Inventory | 218350.00 | 110 |
| 6 | 1 | Working-in-process inventory | 60420.00 | 112 |
| **7** | **1** | **(Long term investments)** | - | **141** |
| 8 | 1 | Bonds | 18000.00 | 142 |
| **9** | **1** | **(Equipment)** | - | **171** |
| 10 | 1 | Vehicle | 40000.00 | 172 |
| 11 | 1 | Accumulated amortization: Vehicle | -18000.00 | 173 |
| 12 | 1 | Computer | 5400.00 | 174 |
| 13 | 1 | Accumulated amortization: Computer | -3375.00 | 175 |
| **14** | **2** | **(Current liabilities)** | - | **203** |
| 15 | 2 | Account payable | 1700.00 | 204 |
| 16 | 2 | Accrued interest payable | 0 | 206 |
| 17 | 2 | Tax payable | 0 | 208 |
| **18** | **2** | **(Long term liabilities)** | - | **251** |
| 19 | 2 | Bonds payable | 50000.00 | 252 |
| 20 | 2 | Notes payable | 120000.00 | 254 |
| **21** | **3** | **(Owners' capital)** | - | **303** |
| 22 | 3 | Share capital | 160000.00 | 304 |
| 23 | 3 | Retained earnings (Conversion) | 12574.23 | 306 |
| **24** | **4** | **(Revenues)** | - | **403** |
| 25 | 4 | Sales | | 404 |
| **26** | **5** | **(Cost)** | - | **431** |
| 27 | 5 | Cost of goods sold | | 432 |

| 28 | 5 | (Operating and administrative expenses) | | - | 453 |
|---|---|---|---|---|---|
| 29 | 5 | Travelling expenses | | 0 | 454 |
| 30 | 5 | Other expenses | | 0 | 455 |
| 31 | 5 | Salary expenses | | 0 | 456 |
| 32 | 5 | Cost of goods sold | | 0 | 457 |
| 33 | 5 | Bond interest expenses | | 0 | 458 |
| 34 | 5 | Note interest expenses | | 0 | 460 |
| 35 | 5 | Amortization expenses | | 0 | 462 |
| 36 | 4 | (Other income) | | - | 475 |
| 37 | 4 | Investment incomes | | | 476 |
| 38 | 4 | Deposits interest incomes | | 0 | 478 |
| 39 | 5 | (Tax) | | - | 600 |
| 40 | 5 | Tax expenses | | 0 | 602 |

Figure 2.4-49   Proprietorship1 Converting Reference Table

From the Figure 2.4-49, there are total 29 accounts among which the balances of the Sales account, the Cost of goods sold account, and all expenses accounts are zero. In addition, the balance of the Retained earnings should be added to the balance of the Share capital, and its balance should be zero prior to conversion. However, for knowing the original share capital and the distinguishing the Retained earnings account after conversion, I keep the Retained earnings account prior to conversion and give it a different name of the Retained earnings (Conversion).

The Bonds account has four one-level subaccounts of the "Bond11 (issued by the Business Bank1 and purchased $5,000, beginning on February 1, 2014, five years, and annual interest rate 4%), the "Bond12 (issued by the Business Bank1 and purchased $3,000, beginning on July 1, 2014, five years, and annual interest rate 4.2%), the "Bond13 (issued by the Business Bank1 and purchased $2,000, beginning on September 1, 2015, six years, and annual interest rate 4.5%), and the "Bond22" (issued by the Business Bank2 and purchased $8,000, beginning on February 1, 2015, five years, and annual interest rate 4.4%).

The Proprietorship1 has only one truck2 (purchased it from the "Company1" in market price, five years, straight line, 27 months), so the Vehicle account has one three-level subaccount and its balance is $40,000. The Accumulated amortization: Vehicle account has one three-level subaccount of the "Truck21-accumulated amortization < Truck2-accumulated amortization < Truck-accumulated amortization" and its balances are -$18,000.

The Proprietorship1 has one computer server2 (two years, straight line, 15 months), one computer3" (two years, straight line, 15 months), and one computer4" (two years, straight line, 15 months), so the multi-subaccount names of the Computer parent account are the "Computer server21 < Computer server2 < Computer server", the "Computer31 < Computer3", and the "Computer41 < Computer4" respectively. Their balances are $2,700, $1,400, and $1,300 respectively. Accordingly, the multi-subaccount names of the Accumulated amortization: Computer account are the "Computer server21-accumulated amortization < Computer server2-accumulated amortization< Computer server-accumulated amortization", the "Computer31-accumulated amortization < Computer3-accumulated amortization", and the "Computer41-accumulated amortization < Computer4-accumulated amortization". Their balances are respectively -$1,687.50, -$875, and -$812.50.

The Proprietorship1 issued one bond and may issue more bonds later, so the Bonds payable account has one one-level subaccount of the "Bond61-payable" ($50,000, beginning on May 1, 2015, five years, and annual interest rate 5%). Of course, the Bonds payable has also many two-level subaccounts, seeing the Figure 2.4-50 on the next page, which shows the detail information of the issued bond. The Notes payable account has one one-level subaccounts of the "Note25" ($120,000 from the Business Bank2, beginning on September 1, 2015, three years, and annual interest rate 9.4%). Therefore, the Accrued interest payable account has two one-level subaccounts of the "Bonds-interest payable" and the "Notes-interest payable". Accordingly, the balances of the Accrued interest payable account are zero prior to the conversion.

| Order | Bond | Amount | Term | Purchaser Name | Identity |
|-------|------|--------|------|----------------|----------|
| 1 | Bond61 | 3000 | May 1, 2015, Five years, 5% annually | A4 | 909876504 |
| 2 | Bond61 | 4000 | May 1, 2015, Five years, 5% annually | A5 | 909876505 |
| 3 | Bond61 | 5000 | May 1, 2015, Five years, 5% annually | A6 | 909876506 |
| 4 | Bond61 | 2000 | May 1, 2015, Five years, 5% annually | A8 | 909876508 |
| 5 | Bond61 | 3000 | May 1, 2015, Five years, 5% annually | A10 | 909876510 |

| | | | | | |
|---|---|---|---|---|---|
| 6 | Bond61 | 5000 | May 1, 2015, Five years, 5% annually | A13 | 909876513 |
| 7 | Bond61 | 4000 | May 1, 2015, Five years, 5% annually | A15 | 909876515 |
| 8 | Bond61 | 2000 | May 1, 2015, Five years, 5% annually | A16 | 909876516 |
| 9 | Bond61 | 5000 | May 1, 2015, Five years, 5% annually | A17 | 909876517 |
| 10 | Bond61 | 3000 | May 1, 2015, Five years, 5% annually | A18 | 909876518 |
| 11 | Bond61 | 5000 | May 1, 2015, Five years, 5% annually | A19 | 909876519 |
| 12 | Bond61 | 3000 | May 1, 2015, Five years, 5% annually | A20 | 909876520 |
| 13 | Bond61 | 4000 | May 1, 2015, Five years, 5% annually | A21 | 909876521 |
| 14 | Bond61 | 2000 | May 1, 2015, Five years, 5% annually | A22 | 909876522 |
| **15** | **Total** | **50000** | | | |

Figure 2.4-50   Proprietorship1 Issued Bond Information Table

The Account receivable account and the Account payable account need transaction dates during the conversion, so I assume that their transaction dates are also on December 31, 2015 for simplification.

For the Proprietorship1, the balances of the "Cash receipts from customers<Operating activities" and the "Cash payments to suppliers<Operating activities" are respectively $17,000 and zero. The reason is as same as the Company1. The balance $17,000 of the "Cash receipts from customers<Operating activities" is only to receive from the Company1.

Following above information, I can build a table of the multi-subaccount names, seeing the Figure 2.4-51 on this page and the next pages.

| Order | Class | Multi-subaccount Name | Parent Name | Lowest Subaccount Balance |
|---|---|---|---|---|
| 1 | 1 | 909876522-i-owners < Cash receipts from owners < Financial activities | Cash | 160000.00 |
| 2 | 1 | 88-654305-i-note25 < Cash receipts from banks < Financial activities | Cash | 120000.00 |
| 3 | 1 | 88-654306-c-operating < Cash receipts from customers < Operating activities | Cash | 17000.00 |
| 4 | 1 | 88-654304-c-interest of investment bond11 < Cash receipts from investments < Investing activities | Cash | 383.33 |
| 5 | 1 | 88-654304-c-interest of investment bond12 < Cash receipts from investments < Investing activities | Cash | 189.00 |
| 6 | 1 | 88-654304-c-interest of investment bond13 < Cash receipts from investments < Investing activities | Cash | 30.00 |
| 7 | 1 | 88-654305-c-interest of investment bond22 < Cash receipts from investments < Investing activities | Cash | 322.67 |

| 8 | 1 | 909876504-i-bond61 < Cash receipts from issued bonds < Financial activities | Cash | 3000.00 |
|---|---|---|---|---|
| 9 | 1 | 909876505-i-bond61 < Cash receipts from issued bonds < Financial activities | Cash | 4000.00 |
| 10 | 1 | 909876506-i-bond61 < Cash receipts from issued bonds < Financial activities | Cash | 5000.00 |
| 11 | 1 | 909876508-i-bond61 < Cash receipts from issued bonds < Financial activities | Cash | 2000.00 |
| 12 | 1 | 909876510-i-bond61 < Cash receipts from issued bonds < Financial activities | Cash | 3000.00 |
| 13 | 1 | 909876513-i-bond61 < Cash receipts from issued bonds < Financial activities | Cash | 5000.00 |
| 14 | 1 | 909876515-i-bond61 < Cash receipts from issued bonds < Financial activities | Cash | 4000.00 |
| 15 | 1 | 909876516-i-bond61 < Cash receipts from issued bonds < Financial activities | Cash | 2000.00 |
| 16 | 1 | 909876517-i-bond61 < Cash receipts from issued bonds < Financial activities | Cash | 5000.00 |
| 17 | 1 | 909876518-i-bond61 < Cash receipts from issued bonds < Financial activities | Cash | 3000.00 |
| 18 | 1 | 909876519-i-bond61 < Cash receipts from issued bonds < Financial activities | Cash | 5000.00 |
| 19 | 1 | 909876520-i-bond61 < Cash receipts from issued bonds < Financial activities | Cash | 3000.00 |
| 20 | 1 | 909876521-i-bond61 < Cash receipts from issued bonds < Financial activities | Cash | 4000.00 |
| 21 | 1 | 909876522-i-bond61 < Cash receipts from issued bonds < Financial activities | Cash | 2000.00 |
| 22 | 1 | 88-654306-t-truck2 < Cash payments for machinery < Operating activities | Cash | -40000.00 |
| 23 | 1 | 88-654306-t-computer server2 < Cash payments for machinery < Operating activities | Cash | -2700.00 |
| 24 | 1 | 88-654306-t-computer3 < Cash payments for machinery < Operating activities | Cash | -1400.00 |
| 25 | 1 | 88-654306-t-computer4 < Cash payments for machinery < Operating activities | Cash | -1300.00 |
| 26 | 1 | Cash payments for operating expenses < Operating activities | Cash | -124356.77 |
| 27 | 1 | Cash payments for operating expenses < Operating activities | Cash | -120631.54 |
| 28 | 1 | 88-654303-n-tax < Cash payments for operating expenses < Operating activities | Cash | -20752.91 |
| 29 | 1 | Cash payments to suppliers<Operating activities | Cash | 0 |
| 30 | 1 | 88-654304-n-investment bond11 < Cash payments for investments < Investing activities | Cash | -5000.00 |
| 31 | 1 | 88-654304-n-investment bond12 < Cash payments for investments < Investing activities | Cash | -3000.00 |
| 32 | 1 | 88-654304-n-investment bond13 < Cash payments for investments < Investing activities | Cash | -2000.00 |
| 33 | 1 | 88-654305-n-investment bond22 < Cash payments for investments < Investing activities | Cash | -8000.00 |
| 34 | 1 | n | Supplies | 155.45 |
| 35 | 1 | 123456784 | Account receivable | 2040.00 |
| 36 | 1 | 123456783 | Account receivable | 500.00 |
| 37 | 1 | 123456782 | Account receivable | 1600.00 |
| 38 | 1 | 123456780 | Account receivable | 400.00 |
| 39 | 1 | Inven31 < Inven3 | Inventory | $6.00*1000 = 6000.00$ |
| 40 | 1 | Inven32 < Inven3 | Inventory | $30.00*1000 = 30000.00$ |
| 41 | 1 | Inven331 < Inven33 < Inven3 | Inventory | $10.00*1000 = 10000.00$ |

| 42 | 1 | Inven332 < Inven33 < Inven3 | Inventory | 27.00*1000 = 27000.00 |
|----|---|------------------------------|-----------|------------------------|
| 43 | 1 | HGFCVB parts < QASXC parts < Inven3 | Inventory | 6.00*1000 = 6000.00 |
| 44 | 1 | PPGHUP parts < ASDUP parts < Inven3 | Inventory | 12.00*1000 = 12000.00 |
| 45 | 1 | Food111 < Food11 < Food1 | Inventory | 5.00*1000 = 5000.00 |
| 46 | 1 | Food112 < Food11 < Food1 | Inventory | 5.50*1000 = 5500.00 |
| 47 | 1 | Food113 < Food11 < Food1 | Inventory | 6.00*1000 = 6000.00 |
| 48 | 1 | Food121 < Food12 < Food1 | Inventory | 6.50*1000 = 6500.00 |
| 49 | 1 | Food122 < Food12 < Food1 | Inventory | 7.00*1000 = 7000.00 |
| 50 | 1 | Food123 < Food12 < Food1 | Inventory | 7.50*1000 = 7500.00 |
| 51 | 1 | Food211 < Food21 < Food2 | Inventory | 4.00*1000 = 4000.00 |
| 52 | 1 | Food212 < Food21 < Food2 | Inventory | 4.50*1000 = 4500.00 |
| 53 | 1 | Food213 < Food21 < Food2 | Inventory | 5.00*1000 = 5000.00 |
| 54 | 1 | Food214 < Food21 < Food2 | Inventory | 5.50*1000 = 5500.00 |
| 55 | 1 | Food221 < Food22 < Food2 | Inventory | 6.00*1000 = 6000.00 |
| 56 | 1 | Food222 < Food22 < Food2 | Inventory | 6.50*1000 = 6500.00 |
| 57 | 1 | Food23 < Food2 | Inventory | 7.50*1000 = 7500.00 |
| 58 | 1 | Food311 < Food31 < Food3 | Inventory | 8.50*1000 = 8500.00 |
| 59 | 1 | Food312 < Food31 < Food3 | Inventory | 11.00*1000 = 11000.00 |
| 60 | 1 | Food321 < Food32 < Food3 | Inventory | 12.00*1000 = 12000.00 |
| 61 | 1 | Food322 < Food32 < Food3 | Inventory | 13.00*1000 = 13000.00 |
| 62 | 1 | Inven411 < Inven41 < Inven4 | Inventory | 5*100 = 500.00 |
| 63 | 1 | Inven412 < Inven41 < Inven4 | Inventory | 18.5*100 = 1850.00 |
| 64 | 1 | TTTCU parts < TTT parts < Inven4 | Inventory | 20*100 = 2000.00 |
| 65 | 1 | RRRHJK parts < Inven4 | Inventory | 20*100 = 2000.00 |
| 66 | 1 | Working-Inven31 < Working-Inven3 | Working-in-process inventory | 3.00*600 = 1800.00 |
| 67 | 1 | Working-Inven32 < Working-Inven3 | Working-in-process inventory | 14.00*600 = 8400.00 |
| 68 | 1 | Working-Inven331 < Working-Inven33 < Working-Inven3 | Working-in-process inventory | 5.00*600 = 3000.00 |
| 69 | 1 | Working-Inven332 < Working-Inven33 < Working-Inven3 | Working-in-process inventory | 13.00*600 = 7800.00 |
| 70 | 1 | Working-HGFCVB parts < Working-QASXC parts < Working-Inven3 | Working-in-process inventory | 3.00*600 = 1800.00 |
| 71 | 1 | Working-PPGHUP parts < Working-ASDUP parts < Working-Inven3 | Working-in-process inventory | 6.00*600 = 3600.00 |
| 72 | 1 | Working-Food111 < Working-Food11 < Working-Food1 | Working-in-process inventory | 2.40*600 = 1440.00 |
| 73 | 1 | Working-Food112 < Working-Food11 < Working-Food1 | Working-in-process inventory | 2.50*600 = 1500.00 |
| 74 | 1 | Working-Food113 < Working-Food11 < Working-Food1 | Working-in-process inventory | 3.00*600 = 1800.00 |
| 75 | 1 | Working-Food121 < Working-Food12 < Working-Food1 | Working-in-process inventory | 2.90*600 = 1740.00 |
| 76 | 1 | Working-Food122 < Working-Food12 < Working-Food1 | Working-in-process inventory | 3.00*600 = 1800.00 |
| 77 | 1 | Working-Food123 < Working-Food12 < Working-Food1 | Working-in-process inventory | 3.50*600 = 2100.00 |
| 78 | 1 | Working-Food211 < Working-Food21 < Working-Food2 | Working-in-process inventory | 2.00*600 = 1200.00 |
| 79 | 1 | Working-Food212 < Working-Food21 < Working-Food2 | Working-in-process inventory | 2.00*600 = 1200.00 |

| 80 | 1 | Working-Food213 < Working-Food21 < Working-Food2 | Working-in-process inventory | 2.20*600 = 1320.00 |
|---|---|---|---|---|
| 81 | 1 | Working-Food214 < Working-Food21 < Working-Food2 | Working-in-process inventory | 2.50*600 = 1500.00 |
| 82 | 1 | Working-Food221 < Working-Food22 < Working-Food2 | Working-in-process inventory | 3.00*600 = 1800.00 |
| 83 | 1 | Working-Food221 < Working-Food22 < Working-Food2 | Working-in-process inventory | 3.10*600 = 1860.00 |
| 84 | 1 | Working-Food23 < Working-Food2 | Working-in-process inventory | 3.50*600 = 2100.00 |
| 85 | 1 | Working-Food311 < Working-Food31 < Working-Food3 | Working-in-process inventory | 4.10*600 = 2460.00 |
| 86 | 1 | Working-Food312 < Working-Food31 < Working-Food3 | Working-in-process inventory | 5.00*600 = 3000.00 |
| 87 | 1 | Working-Food321 < Working-Food32 < Working-Food3 | Working-in-process inventory | 6.00*600 = 3600.00 |
| 88 | 1 | Working-Food322 < Working-Food32 < Working-Food3 | Working-in-process inventory | 6.00*600 = 3600.00 |
| 89 | 1 | Bond11 | Bonds | 5000.00 |
| 90 | 1 | Bond12 | Bonds | 3000.00 |
| 91 | 1 | Bond13 | Bonds | 2000.00 |
| 92 | 1 | Bond22 | Bonds | 8000.00 |
| 93 | 1 | Truck21 < Truck2 < Truck | Vehicle | 40000.00 |
| 94 | 1 | Truck21-accumulated amortization < Truck2-accumulated amortization < Truck-accumulated amortization | Accumulated amortization: Vehicle | -18000.00 |
| 95 | 1 | Computer server21 < Computer server2 < Computer server | Computer | 2700.00 |
| 96 | 1 | Computer31 < Computer3 | Computer | 1400.00 |
| 97 | 1 | Computer41 < Computer4 | Computer | 1300.00 |
| 98 | 1 | Computer server21-accumulated amortization < Computer server2-accumulated amortization < Computer server-accumulated amortization | Accumulated amortization: Computer | -1687.50 |
| 99 | 1 | Computer31-accumulated amortization < Computer3-accumulated amortization | Accumulated amortization: Computer | -875.00 |
| 100 | 1 | Computer41-accumulated amortization < Computer4-accumulated amortization | Accumulated amortization: Computer | -812.50 |
| 101 | 2 | 123456084 | Account payable | 1000.00 |
| 102 | 2 | 123456083 | Account payable | 250.00 |
| 103 | 2 | 123456082 | Account payable | 150.00 |
| 104 | 2 | 123456080 | Account payable | 300.00 |
| 105 | 2 | Bond61-interest payable < Bonds-interest payable | Accrued interest payable | 0 |
| 106 | 2 | Note25-interest payable < Notes-interest payable | Accrued interest payable | 0 |
| 107 | 2 | Bond61-909876504 < Bond61 | Bonds payable | 3000.00 |
| 108 | 2 | Bond61-909876505 < Bond61 | Bonds payable | 4000.00 |
| 109 | 2 | Bond61-909876506 < Bond61 | Bonds payable | 5000.00 |
| 110 | 2 | Bond61-909876508 < Bond61 | Bonds payable | 2000.00 |
| 111 | 2 | Bond61-88-654310 < Bond61 | Bonds payable | 3000.00 |
| 112 | 2 | Bond61-88-654313 < Bond61 | Bonds payable | 5000.00 |
| 113 | 2 | Bond61-909876515 < Bond61 | Bonds payable | 4000.00 |
| 114 | 2 | Bond61-909876516 < Bond61 | Bonds payable | 2000.00 |

| 115 | 2 | Bond61-909876517 < Bond61 | Bonds payable | 5000.00 |
|---|---|---|---|---|
| 116 | 2 | Bond61-909876518 < Bond61 | Bonds payable | 3000.00 |
| 117 | 2 | Bond61-909876519 < Bond61 | Bonds payable | 5000.00 |
| 118 | 2 | Bond61-909876520 < Bond61 | Bonds payable | 3000.00 |
| 119 | 2 | Bond61-909876521 < Bond61 | Bonds payable | 4000.00 |
| 120 | 2 | Bond61-909876522 < Bond61 | Bonds payable | 2000.00 |
| 121 | 2 | Note25-88-654305 | Notes payable | 120000.00 |
| 122 | 3 | Capital-909876522 | Share capital | 160000.00 |
| 123 | 3 | n | Retained earnings (Conversion) | 12574.23 |
| 124 | 4 | Sales-909876522 | Sales | 0 |
| 125 | 5 | 909876522-travelling < Sales department-travelling | Travelling expenses | 0 |
| 126 | 5 | 909876523-travelling < Product department-travelling | Travelling expenses | 0 |
| 127 | 5 | 909876522-other < Sales department-other | Other expenses | 0 |
| 128 | 5 | 909876523-other < Product department-other | Other expenses | 0 |
| 129 | 5 | 909876522-salary < Sales department-salary | Salary expenses | 0 |
| 130 | 5 | Supplies expenses | Cost of goods mined | 0 |
| 131 | 5 | 909876523-salary < Product department-salary < Salary expenses | Cost of goods mined | 0 |
| 132 | 5 | General parts expenses | Cost of goods mined | 0 |
| 133 | 5 | Bond61-interest | Bond interest expenses | 0 |
| 134 | 5 | Note25-interest | Note interest expenses | 0 |
| 135 | 5 | Truck21-amortization < Truck2-amortization < Vehicle-truck-amortization | Amortization expenses | 0 |
| 136 | 5 | Computer server21-amortization < Computer server2-amortization < Computer-amortization | Amortization expenses | 0 |
| 137 | 5 | Computer31-amortization < Computer3-amortization < Computer-amortization | Amortization expenses | 0 |
| 138 | 5 | Computer41-amortization < Computer4-amortization < Computer-amortization | Amortization expenses | 0 |
| 139 | 4 | Accrued interest income-bond11 < Bonds | Investment incomes | 0 |
| 140 | 4 | Accrued interest income-bond12 < Bonds | Investment incomes | 0 |
| 141 | 4 | Accrued interest income-bond13 < Bonds | Investment incomes | 0 |
| 142 | 4 | Accrued interest income-bond22 < Bonds | Investment incomes | 0 |
| 143 | 4 | n | Deposits interest income | 0 |

Figure 2.4-51   Proprietorship1 Converting Multi-Subaccount Names Table

Before entering the dynamic accounting equation on January 1, 2016 into the database dcj10, I first enter two initialization sub-equations.

Cash (1): 0 = Share capital (3): 0

0 = Sales (4): 0 - Cost of goods sold (5):0

From the Figure 2.4-49 and the Figure 2.4-51, the dynamic accounting equation on J December 31, 2015 must be divided to the N transaction sub-equations because of the restriction of the MathAccounting software. Every sub-equation has maximum twelve items. All converting transaction sub-equations can be designed and written as following.

- I build a transaction sub-equation for the Account receivable account and the Account payable account. The transaction sub-equation includes the Account receivable account with the Order 35 to the Order 38, the Account payable account with the Order 101 to the Order 104, and the part of the Share capital account with the Order 122, The first transaction sub-equation is:

  Account receivable (1): 2040 + Account receivable (1): 500 + Account receivable (1): 1600 + Account receivable (1): 400 = Account payable (2): 1000 + Account payable (2): 250 + Account payable (2): 150 + Account (2): 300 + Share capital (3): 2840

  After entering this transaction, the new balance of the Share capital account with the Order 122 is $157,160 (= $160,000 - $2,840).

- The transaction sub-equation includes the Cash account with the Order 1 to the Order 7, the part of the Cash account with the Order 26, the rest ($157,160) the Share capital account with the Order 122, and the Notes payable account with the Order 121. The second transaction sub-equation is:

  Cash (1): 160000 + Cash (1): 120000 + Cash (1): 17000 + Cash (1): 383.33 + Cash (1): 189 + Cash (1): 30 + Cash (1): 322.67 + Cash (1): -20765 = Share capital (3): 157160 + Notes payable (2): 120000

  After entering this transaction, the new balance of the Cash account with the Order 26 is -$103,591.77 (= -$124,356.77 + $20,765).

- The transaction sub-equation includes the Cash account with the Order 8 to the Order 13 and the Bonds payable account with the Order 107 to the Order 112. The third transaction sub-equation is:

  Cash (1): 3000 + Cash (1): 4000 + Cash (1): 5000 + Cash (1): 2000 + Cash (1): 3000 + Cash (1): 5000 = Bonds payable (2): 3000 + Bonds payable (2): 4000 + Bonds payable (2): 5000 + Bonds payable (2): 2000 + Bonds payable (2): 3000 + Bonds payable (2): 5000

- The transaction sub-equation includes the Cash account with the Order 14 to the Order 19 and the Bonds payable account with the Order 113 to the Order 118. The fourth transaction sub-equation is:

  Cash (1): 4000 + Cash (1): 2000 + Cash (1): 5000 + Cash (1): 3000 + Cash (1): 5000 + Cash (1): 3000 = Bonds payable (2): 4000 + Bonds payable (2): 2000 + Bonds payable (2): 5000 + Bonds payable (2): 3000 + Bonds payable (2): 5000 + Bonds payable (2): 3000

- The transaction sub-equation includes the Cash account with the Order 20 to the Order 25, the Vehicle account with the Order 93, the Computer account with the Order 95 to the Order 97, and the Bonds payable account with the Order 119 and the Order 120. The fifth transaction sub-equation is:

  Cash (1): 4000 + Cash (1): 2000 + Cash (1): -40000 + Cash (1): -2700 + Cash (1): -1400 + Cash (1): -1300 + Vehicle (1): 40000 + Computer (1): 2700 + Computer (1): 1400 + Computer (1): 1300 = Bonds payable (2): 4000 + Bonds payable (2): 2000

- The transaction sub-equation includes the Cash account with the Order 30 to the Order 33 and the Bonds account with the Order 89 to the Order 92. The sixth transaction sub-equation is:

Cash (1): -5000 + Cash (1): -3000 + Cash (1): -2000 + Cash (1): -8000 + Bonds (1): 5000 + Bonds (1): 3000 + Bonds (1): 2000 + Bonds (1): 8000 = 0

- The transaction sub-equation includes the part of the Cash account with the Order 26, the Supplies account with the Order 34, and the Inventory account with the Order 39 to the Order 46. The seventh transaction sub-equation is:

Cash (1): -101655.45 + Supplies (1): 155.45 + Inventory (1): 6000 + Inventory (1): 30000 + Inventory (1): 10000 + Inventory (1): 27000 + Inventory (1): 6000 + Inventory (1): 12000 + Inventory (1): 5000+ Inventory (1): 5500 = 0

After entering this transaction, the new balance of the Cash account with the Order 26 is -$1,936.32 (= -$103,591.77 + $101,655.45).

- The transaction sub-equation includes the rest (-$1,936.32) of the Cash account with the Order 26, the part of the Cash account with the Order 27, and the Inventory account with the Order 47 to the Order 56. The eighth transaction sub-equation is:

Cash (1): -1936.32 + Cash (1): -56563.68 + Inventory (1): 6000 + Inventory (1): 6500 + Inventory (1): 7000 + Inventory (1): 7500 + Inventory (1): 4000 + Inventory (1): 4500 + Inventory (1): 5000 + Inventory (1): 5500 + Inventory (1): 6000 + Inventory (1): 6500 = 0

After entering this transaction, the new balance of the Cash account with the Order 27 is -$64,067.86 (= -$120,631.54 + $56,563.68).

- The transaction sub-equation includes the part of the Cash account with the Order 27 and the Inventory account with the Order 57 to the Order 65. The ninth transaction sub-equation is:

Cash (1): -58350 + Inventory (1): 7500 + Inventory (1): 8500 + Inventory (1): 11000 + Inventory (1): 12000 + Inventory (1): 13000 + Inventory (1): 500 +

Inventory (1): 1850 + Inventory (1): 2000 + Inventory (1): 2000 = 0

After entering this transaction, the new balance of the Cash account with the Order 27 is -$5,717.86 (= -$64,067.86 + $58,350).

- The transaction sub-equation includes the rest (-$5,717.86) of the Cash account with the Order 27, the Cash account with the Order 28, the part of the Accumulated amortization: Vehicle account with the Order 94, and the Working-in-process inventory account with the Order 66 to the Order 74. The tenth transaction sub-equation is:

Cash (1): -5717.86 + Cash (1): -20752.91 + Accumulated amortization: Vehicle (1): -4669.23 + Working-in-process inventory (1): 1800 + Working-in-process inventory (1): 8400 + Working-in-process inventory (1): 3000 + Working-in-process inventory (1): 7800 + Working-in-process inventory (1): 3600 + Working-in-process inventory (1): 1440 + Working-in-process inventory (1): 1500 + Working-in-process inventory (1): 1800 = 0

After entering this transaction, the new balance of the Accumulated amortization: Vehicle account with the Order 94 is -$13,330.77 (= -$18,000 + $4,669.23).

- The transaction sub-equation includes the part of the Accumulated amortization: Vehicle account with the Order 94 and the Working-in-process inventory account with the Order 75 to the Order 82. The eleventh transaction sub-equation is:

Accumulated amortization: Vehicle (1): -12660 + Working-in-process inventory (1): 1740 + Working-in-process inventory (1): 1800 + Working-in-process inventory (1): 2100 + Working-in-process inventory (1): 1200 + Working-in-process inventory (1): 1200 + Working-in-process inventory (1): 1320 + Working-in-process inventory (1): 1500 + Working-in-process inventory (1): 1800 = 0

After entering this transaction, the new balance of the Accumulated amortization: Vehicle account with the Order 94 is -$670.77 (= -$13,330.77 + $12,660).

- The transaction sub-equation includes the rest (-$670.77) of the Accumulated amortization: Vehicle account with the Order 94, the Accumulated amortization: Computer account with the Order 98 to the Order 100, the Working-in-process inventory account with the Order 83 to the Order 88, and the Retained earnings (Conversion) account with the balance $12,574.23. The twelfth transaction sub-equation is:

Accumulated amortization: Vehicle (1): -670.77 + Accumulated amortization: Computer (1): -1687.5 + Accumulated amortization: Computer (1): -875 + Accumulated amortization: Computer (1): -812.5 + Working-in-process inventory (1): 1860 + Working-in-process inventory (1): 2100 + Working-in-process inventory (1): 2460 + Working-in-process inventory (1): 3000 + Working-in-process inventory (1): 3600 + Working-in-process inventory (1): 3600 = Retained earnings (Conversion) (3): 12574.23

After completing this transaction, the dynamic accounting equation of the Proprietorship1 December 31, 2015 has entered into the database dcj10.

## 2.4.6.2 Brief Summary of the Proprietorship1

The Figure 2.4-52 on the next page shows cash received or paid by other members table which is in the public database dcj100.

```
use dcj100
select sum(amount) as sum0 from CashByMembers where Recorder = '88-654309'
select * from CashByMembers where Recorder = '88-654309'
```

100 % ▾

Results  Messages

| | sum0 |
|---|---|
| 1 | -18783.78 |

| | IDM | Amount | Symbol | MultiSubaccount | Recorder | TransDate |
|---|---|---|---|---|---|---|
| 1 | 909876522 | -160000.00 | i | 909876522-i-owners < Cash receipts from owners < Financial activities | 88-654309 | 2015-12-31 |
| 2 | 88-654305 | -120000.00 | i | 88-654305-i-note25 < Cash receipts from banks < Financial activities | 88-654309 | 2015-12-31 |
| 3 | 88-654306 | -17000.00 | c | 88-654306-c-operating < Cash receipts from customers < Operating activities | 88-654309 | 2015-12-31 |
| 4 | 88-654304 | -383.33 | c | 88-654304-c-interest of investment bond11 < Cash receipts from investments < Investing activities | 88-654309 | 2015-12-31 |
| 5 | 88-654304 | -189.00 | c | 88-654304-c-interest of investment bond12 < Cash receipts from investments < Investing activities | 88-654309 | 2015-12-31 |
| 6 | | 0.00 | | Cash payments for operating expenses < Operating activities | 88-654309 | 2015-12-31 |
| 7 | 88-654304 | -30.00 | c | 88-654304-c-interest of investment bond13 < Cash receipts from investments < Investing activities | 88-654309 | 2015-12-31 |
| 8 | 88-654305 | -322.67 | c | 88-654305-c-interest of investment bond22 < Cash receipts from investments < Investing activities | 88-654309 | 2015-12-31 |
| 9 | | 20765.00 | | Cash payments for operating expenses < Operating activities | 88-654309 | 2015-12-31 |
| 10 | 909876504 | -3000.00 | i | 909876504-i-bond61 < Cash receipts from issued bonds < Financial activities | 88-654309 | 2015-12-31 |
| 11 | 909876505 | -4000.00 | i | 909876505-i-bond61 < Cash receipts from issued bonds < Financial activities | 88-654309 | 2015-12-31 |
| 12 | 909876506 | -5000.00 | i | 909876506-i-bond61 < Cash receipts from issued bonds < Financial activities | 88-654309 | 2015-12-31 |
| 13 | 909876508 | -2000.00 | i | 909876508-i-bond61 < Cash receipts from issued bonds < Financial activities | 88-654309 | 2015-12-31 |
| 14 | 909876510 | -3000.00 | i | 909876510-i-bond61 < Cash receipts from issued bonds < Financial activities | 88-654309 | 2015-12-31 |
| 15 | 909876513 | -5000.00 | i | 909876513-i-bond61 < Cash receipts from issued bonds < Financial activities | 88-654309 | 2015-12-31 |
| 16 | 909876515 | -4000.00 | i | 909876515-i-bond61 < Cash receipts from issued bonds < Financial activities | 88-654309 | 2015-12-31 |
| 17 | 909876516 | -2000.00 | i | 909876516-i-bond61 < Cash receipts from issued bonds < Financial activities | 88-654309 | 2015-12-31 |
| 18 | 909876517 | -5000.00 | i | 909876517-i-bond61 < Cash receipts from issued bonds < Financial activities | 88-654309 | 2015-12-31 |
| 19 | 909876518 | -3000.00 | i | 909876518-i-bond61 < Cash receipts from issued bonds < Financial activities | 88-654309 | 2015-12-31 |
| 20 | 909876519 | -5000.00 | i | 909876519-i-bond61 < Cash receipts from issued bonds < Financial activities | 88-654309 | 2015-12-31 |
| 21 | 909876520 | -3000.00 | i | 909876520-i-bond61 < Cash receipts from issued bonds < Financial activities | 88-654309 | 2015-12-31 |
| 22 | 909876521 | -4000.00 | i | 909876521-i-bond61 < Cash receipts from issued bonds < Financial activities | 88-654309 | 2015-12-31 |
| 23 | 909876522 | -2000.00 | i | 909876522-i-bond61 < Cash receipts from issued bonds < Financial activities | 88-654309 | 2015-12-31 |
| 24 | 88-654306 | 40000.00 | t | 88-654306-t-truck2 < Cash payments for machinery < Operating activities | 88-654309 | 2015-12-31 |
| 25 | 88-654306 | 2700.00 | t | 88-654306-t-computer server2 < Cash payments for machinery < Operating activities | 88-654309 | 2015-12-31 |
| 26 | 88-654306 | 1400.00 | t | 88-654306-t-computer3 < Cash payments for machinery < Operating activities | 88-654309 | 2015-12-31 |
| 27 | 88-654306 | 1300.00 | t | 88-654306-t-computer4 < Cash payments for machinery < Operating activities | 88-654309 | 2015-12-31 |
| 28 | 88-654304 | 5000.00 | n | 88-654304-n-investment bond11 < Cash payments for investments < Investing activities | 88-654309 | 2017-12-31 |
| 29 | 88-654304 | 3000.00 | n | 88-654304-n-investment bond12 < Cash payments for investments < Investing activities | 88-654309 | 2017-12-31 |
| 30 | 88-654304 | 2000.00 | n | 88-654304-n-investment bond13 < Cash payments for investments < Investing activities | 88-654309 | 2017-12-31 |
| 31 | 88-654305 | 8000.00 | n | 88-654305-n-investment bond22 < Cash payments for investments < Investing activities | 88-654309 | 2017-12-31 |
| 32 | | 101655.45 | | Cash payments for operating expenses < Operating activities | 88-654309 | 2015-12-31 |
| 33 | | 1936.32 | | Cash payments for operating expenses < Operating activities | 88-654309 | 2015-12-31 |
| 34 | | 56563.68 | | Cash payments for operating expenses < Operating activities | 88-654309 | 2015-12-31 |
| 35 | | 58350.00 | | Cash payments for operating expenses < Operating activities | 88-654309 | 2015-12-31 |
| 36 | | 5717.86 | | Cash payments for operating expenses < Operating activities | 88-654309 | 2015-12-31 |
| 37 | 88-654303 | 20752.91 | n | 88-654303-n-tax < Cash payments for operating expenses < Operating activities | 88-654309 | 2015-12-31 |

 Query executed successfully.    LIU\SQLEXPR

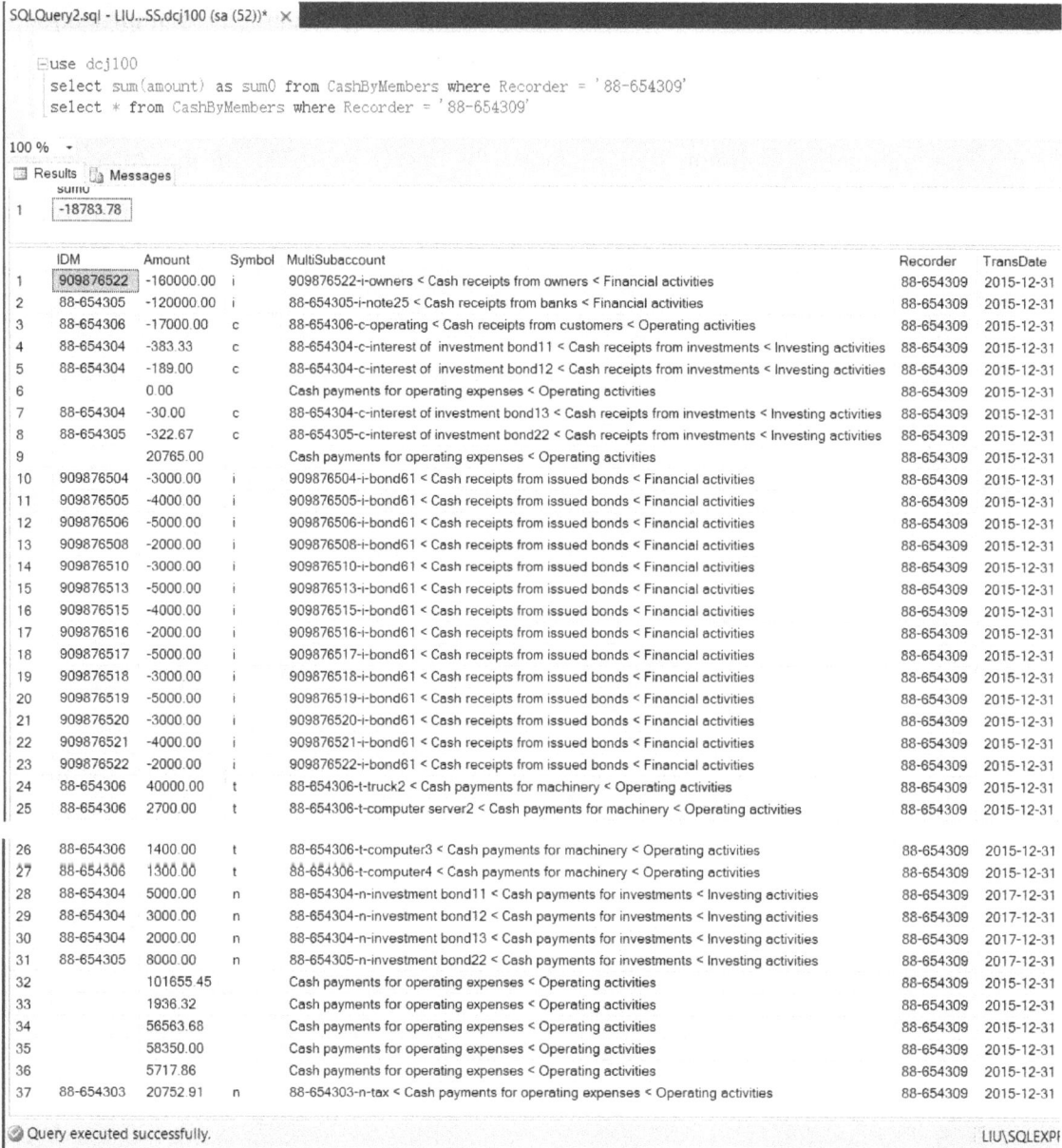

Figure 2.4-52   Proprietorship1 Cash Received or Paid by Other Members

The Figure 2.4-53 on the next page shows cash flows statement of the Proprietorship1 on December 31, 2015.

| Cash Flows Statement Year Ended 2015-12-31 | |
|---|---|
| **Operating activities** | |
| Cash payments for machinery | -$45,400.00 |
| Cash payments for operating expenses | -$265,741.22 |
| Cash receipts from customers | $17,000.00 |
| Net cash provided by Operating activities | -$294,141.22 |
| | |
| Investing activities | |
| Cash payments for investments | -$18,000.00 |
| Cash receipts from investments | $925.00 |
| Net cash provided by Investing activities | -$17,075.00 |
| | |
| Financial activities | |
| Cash receipts from banks | $120,000.00 |
| Cash receipts from issued bonds | $50,000.00 |
| Cash receipts from owners | $160,000.00 |
| Net cash provided by Financial activities | $330,000.00 |
| | |
| Net change in cash | $18,783.78 |
| Cash, Beginning | $0.00 |
| Cash, Ending | $18,783.78 |

Figure 2.4-53   Proprietorship1 Cash Flows Statement

The Figure 2.4-54 on the next page shows cash account table of the Proprietorship1 on December 31, 2015.

Cash

| ID | Multi-Name | Amount | Balance | General ID | Transaction Date |
|---|---|---|---|---|---|
| 1 | Cash payments for operating expenses < Operating activities | $0.00 | $0.00 | 1 | 2015-12-31 |
| 2 | 909876522-i-owners < Cash receipts from owners < Financial activities | $160,000.00 | $160,000.00 | 4 | 2015-12-31 |
| 3 | 88-654305-i-note25 < Cash receipts from banks < Financial activities | $120,000.00 | $280,000.00 | 4 | 2015-12-31 |
| 4 | 88-654306-c-operating < Cash receipts from customers < Operating activities | $17,000.00 | $297,000.00 | 4 | 2015-12-31 |
| 5 | 88-654304-c-interest of investment bond11 < Cash receipts from investment... | $383.33 | $297,383.33 | 4 | 2015-12-31 |
| 6 | 88-654304-c-interest of investment bond12 < Cash receipts from investment... | $189.00 | $297,572.33 | 4 | 2015-12-31 |
| 7 | 88-654304-c-interest of investment bond13 < Cash receipts from investment... | $30.00 | $297,602.33 | 4 | 2015-12-31 |
| 8 | 88-654305-c-interest of investment bond22 < Cash receipts from investment... | $322.67 | $297,925.00 | 4 | 2015-12-31 |
| 9 | Cash payments for operating expenses < Operating activities | -$20,765.00 | $277,160.00 | 4 | 2015-12-31 |
| 10 | 909876504-i-bond61 < Cash receipts from issued bonds < Financial activities | $3,000.00 | $280,160.00 | 5 | 2015-12-31 |
| 11 | 909876505-i-bond61 < Cash receipts from issued bonds < Financial activities | $4,000.00 | $284,160.00 | 5 | 2015-12-31 |
| 12 | 909876506-i-bond61 < Cash receipts from issued bonds < Financial activities | $5,000.00 | $289,160.00 | 5 | 2015-12-31 |
| 13 | 909876508-i-bond61 < Cash receipts from issued bonds < Financial activities | $2,000.00 | $291,160.00 | 5 | 2015-12-31 |
| 14 | 909876510-i-bond61 < Cash receipts from issued bonds < Financial activities | $3,000.00 | $294,160.00 | 5 | 2015-12-31 |
| 15 | 909876513-i-bond61 < Cash receipts from issued bonds < Financial activities | $5,000.00 | $299,160.00 | 5 | 2015-12-31 |
| 16 | 909876515-i-bond61 < Cash receipts from issued bonds < Financial activities | $4,000.00 | $303,160.00 | 6 | 2015-12-31 |
| 17 | 909876516-i-bond61 < Cash receipts from issued bonds < Financial activities | $2,000.00 | $305,160.00 | 6 | 2015-12-31 |
| 18 | 909876517-i-bond61 < Cash receipts from issued bonds < Financial activities | $5,000.00 | $310,160.00 | 6 | 2015-12-31 |
| 19 | 909876518-i-bond61 < Cash receipts from issued bonds < Financial activities | $3,000.00 | $313,160.00 | 6 | 2015-12-31 |
| 20 | 909876519-i-bond61 < Cash receipts from issued bonds < Financial activities | $5,000.00 | $318,160.00 | 6 | 2015-12-31 |
| 21 | 909876520-i-bond61 < Cash receipts from issued bonds < Financial activities | $3,000.00 | $321,160.00 | 6 | 2015-12-31 |
| 22 | 909876521-i-bond61 < Cash receipts from issued bonds < Financial activities | $4,000.00 | $325,160.00 | 7 | 2015-12-31 |
| 23 | 909876522-i-bond61 < Cash receipts from issued bonds < Financial activities | $2,000.00 | $327,160.00 | 7 | 2015-12-31 |
| 24 | 88-654306-t-truck2 < Cash payments for machinery < Operating activities | -$40,000.00 | $287,160.00 | 7 | 2015-12-31 |
| 25 | 88-654306-t-computer server2 < Cash payments for machinery < Operating ... | -$2,700.00 | $284,460.00 | 7 | 2015-12-31 |
| 26 | 88-654306-t-computer3 < Cash payments for machinery < Operating activities | -$1,400.00 | $283,060.00 | 7 | 2015-12-31 |
| 27 | 88-654306-t-computer4 < Cash payments for machinery < Operating activities | -$1,300.00 | $281,760.00 | 7 | 2015-12-31 |
| 28 | 88-654304-n-investment bond11 < Cash payments for investments < Investin... | -$5,000.00 | $276,760.00 | 8 | 2017-12-31 |
| 29 | 88-654304-n-investment bond12 < Cash payments for investments < Investin... | -$3,000.00 | $273,760.00 | 8 | 2017-12-31 |
| 30 | 88-654304-n-investment bond13 < Cash payments for investments < Investin... | -$2,000.00 | $271,760.00 | 8 | 2017-12-31 |
| 31 | 88-654305-n-investment bond22 < Cash payments for investments < Investin... | -$8,000.00 | $263,760.00 | 8 | 2017-12-31 |
| 32 | Cash payments for operating expenses < Operating activities | -$101,655.45 | $162,104.55 | 9 | 2015-12-31 |
| 33 | Cash payments for operating expenses < Operating activities | -$1,936.32 | $160,168.23 | 10 | 2015-12-31 |
| 34 | Cash payments for operating expenses < Operating activities | -$56,563.68 | $103,604.55 | 10 | 2015-12-31 |
| 35 | Cash payments for operating expenses < Operating activities | -$58,350.00 | $45,254.55 | 11 | 2015-12-31 |
| 36 | Cash payments for operating expenses < Operating activities | -$5,717.86 | $39,536.69 | 12 | 2015-12-31 |
| 37 | 88-654303-n-tax < Cash payments for operating expenses < Operating activit... | -$20,752.91 | $18,783.78 | 12 | 2015-12-31 |

Figure 2.4-54   Proprietorship1 Cash Account Table

The Figure 2.4-55 on the next page shows balance sheet table of the Proprietorship1 on December 31, 2015.

| | As at 12/31/2015 |
|---|---|
| **ASSETS** | |
| Current assets | |
| Cash | $18,783.78 |
| Supplies | $155.45 |
| Account receivable | $4,540.00 |
| Inventory | $218,350.00 |
| Working-in-process inventory | $60,420.00 |
| | $302,249.23 |
| Long term investments | |
| Bonds | $18,000.00 |
| Equipment | |
| Vehicle | $40,000.00 |
| Accumulated amortization: Vehicle | -$18,000.00 |
| Computer | $5,400.00 |
| Accumulated amortization: Computer | -$3,375.00 |
| | $24,025.00 |
| Total Assets | $344,274.23 |
| | |
| | |
| LIABILITIES | |
| Current liabilities | |
| Account payable | $1,700.00 |
| Long term liabilities | |
| Bonds payable | $50,000.00 |
| Notes payable | $120,000.00 |
| | $170,000.00 |
| Total Liability | $171,700.00 |
| | |
| SHAREHOLDERS' EQUITY | |
| Owners capital | |
| Share capital | $160,000.00 |
| Retained earnings (Conversion) | $12,574.23 |
| | $172,574.23 |
| Retined earnings | $0.00 |
| Accumulated other comprehensive income | $0.00 |
| Total Shareholders' Equity | $172,574.23 |
| | |
| Total Liabilities and Shareholders' Equity | $344,274.23 |

Figure 2.4-55   Proprietorship1 Balance Sheet

## 2.4.7 Sample of the Proprietorship2

The Proprietorship2 is owned by the individual A24 completely and has total share capital $150,000. The Proprietorship1 produces the general parts and the foods. The Figure 2.4-56 shows its product names, costs, and sale prices.

| Order | Product (the Lowest-level Subaccount) Names | Multi-subaccount Names | Costs | Sale Prices |
|-------|---------------------------------------------|------------------------|-------|-------------|
| 1 | Inven411 | Inven411 < Inven41 < Inven4 | 3.00 | 5.00 |
| 2 | Inven412 | Inven412 < Inven41 < Inven4 | 11.10 | 18.50 |
| 3 | TTTCU parts | TTTCU parts < TTT parts < Inven4 | 12.00 | 20.00 |
| 4 | RRRHJK parts | RRRHJK parts < Inven4 | 12.00 | 20.00 |
| 5 | Food411 | Food411 < Food41 < Food4 | 5.00 | 10.00 |
| 6 | Food412 | Food412 < Food41 < Food4 | 5.50 | 11.00 |
| 7 | Food421 | Food421 < Food42 < Food4 | 6.00 | 12.00 |
| 8 | Food422 | Food422 < Food42 < Food4 | 6.50 | 13.00 |
| 9 | Food43 | Food43 < Food4 | 7.00 | 14.00 |
| 10 | Food44 | Food44 < Food4 | 7.50 | 15.00 |
| 11 | Food511 | Food511 < Food51 < Food5 | 4.00 | 8.00 |
| 12 | Food512 | Food512 < Food51 < Food5 | 4.50 | 9.00 |
| 13 | Food513 | Food513 < Food51 < Food5 | 5.00 | 10.00 |
| 14 | Food514 | Food514 < Food51 < Food5 | 5.50 | 11.00 |
| 15 | Food521 | Food521 < Food52 < Food5 | 6.00 | 12.00 |
| 16 | Food522 | Food522 < Food52 < Food5 | 6.50 | 13.00 |
| 17 | Food53 | Food53 < Food5 | 8.00 | 16.00 |
| 18 | Food611 | Food611 < Food61 < Food6 | 10.00 | 20.00 |
| 19 | Food612 | Food612 < Food61 < Food6 | 12.00 | 24.00 |
| 20 | Food613 | Food613 < Food61 < Food6 | 13.00 | 26.00 |
| 21 | Food614 | Food614 < Food61 < Food6 | 15.00 | 30.00 |
| 22 | Food621 | Food621 < Food62 < Food6 | 13.00 | 26.00 |
| 23 | Food622 | Food622 < Food62 < Food6 | 14.00 | 28.00 |
| 24 | Supplies1 | Supplies1 | 7.00 | 14.00 |
| 25 | Supplies2 | Supplies2 | 8.00 | 16.00 |

Figure 2.4-56   Proprietorship2 Products and Sale Prices Table

For a producing foods company of the Proprietorship2, the costs of its food products are most the labor and inventory costs. When the Proprietorship2 uses the MathAccounting software, the Working-in-process inventory account is treated as a parent account of the class 1 and the Cost of goods sold account is treated as the parent accounts of the class 5. For simplification, the Cost of goods sold account has only three one-level subaccounts of the "Supplies expenses", the "Salary expenses" for employee A25, and the "Other general parts" in this book.

## 2.4.7.1 Conversion of the Proprietorship2

The Proprietorship2 will convert to the MathAccounting software on January 1, 2016, so I design a converting reference table, seeing the Figure 2.4-57 on this page and the next page, in order to enter its dynamic accounting equation on December 31, 2015 into the database dcj11.

| Order | Class | Account Name (**Subtotal Name**) | Balance | Row |
|---|---|---|---|---|
| **1** | **1** | **(Current assets)** | - | **103** |
| 2 | 1 | Cash | 8768.69 | 104 |
| 3 | 1 | Supplies | 167.85 | 106 |
| 4 | 1 | Account receivable | 2400.00 | 108 |
| 5 | 1 | Inventory | 149000.00 | 110 |
| 6 | 1 | Working-in-process inventory | 72350.00 | 112 |
| **7** | **1** | **(Long term investments)** | - | **141** |
| 8 | 1 | Bonds | 17000.00 | 142 |
| **9** | **1** | **(Equipment)** | - | **171** |
| 10 | 1 | Vehicle | 40000.00 | 172 |
| 11 | 1 | Accumulated amortization: Vehicle | -13333.33 | 173 |
| 12 | 1 | Computer | 5400.00 | 174 |
| 13 | 1 | Accumulated amortization: Computer | -2925.00 | 175 |
| **14** | **2** | **(Current liabilities)** | - | **203** |
| 15 | 2 | Account payable | 2600.00 | 204 |
| 16 | 2 | Accrued interest payable | 0 | 206 |
| 17 | 2 | Tax payable | 0 | 208 |
| **18** | **2** | **(Long term liabilities)** | - | **251** |
| 19 | 2 | Bonds payable | 120000.00 | 252 |
| 20 | 2 | Notes payable | 0 | 254 |
| **21** | **3** | **(Owners' capital)** | - | **303** |
| 22 | 3 | Share capital | 150000.00 | 304 |
| 23 | 3 | Retained earnings (conversion) | 6228.21 | 306 |

| 24 | 4 | (Revenues) | - | 403 |
|---|---|---|---|---|
| 25 | 4 | Sales | | 404 |
| 26 | 5 | (Cost) | - | 431 |
| 27 | 5 | Cost of goods sold | | 432 |
| 28 | 5 | (Operating and administrative expenses) | - | 453 |
| 29 | 5 | Travelling expenses | 0 | 454 |
| 30 | 5 | Other expenses | 0 | 455 |
| 31 | 5 | Salary expenses | 0 | 456 |
| 32 | 5 | Cost of goods sold | 0 | 457 |
| 33 | 5 | Bond interest expenses | 0 | 458 |
| 34 | 5 | Note interest expenses | 0 | 460 |
| 35 | 5 | Amortization expenses | 0 | 462 |
| 36 | 4 | (Other income) | - | 475 |
| 37 | 4 | Investment incomes | | 476 |
| 38 | 4 | Deposits interest incomes | 0 | 478 |
| 39 | 5 | (Tax) | - | 600 |
| 40 | 5 | Tax expenses | 0 | 602 |

Figure 2.4-57   Proprietorship2 Converting Reference Table

From the Figure 2.4-57, there are total 28 accounts among which the balances of the Sales account, the Cost of goods sold account, and all expenses accounts are zero. In addition, the balance of the Retained earnings should be added to the balance of the Share capital, and its balance should be zero prior to conversion. However, for knowing the original share capital and the distinguishing the Retained earnings account after conversion, I keep the Retained earnings account prior to conversion and give it a different name of the Retained earnings (Conversion).

The Bonds account has three one-level subaccounts of the "Bond12 (issued by the Business Bank1 and purchased $6,000, beginning on July 1, 2014, five years, and annual interest rate 4.2%), the "Bond21 (issued by the Business Bank2 and purchased $7,000, beginning on May 1, 2014, five years, and annual interest rate 4.1%), and the "Bond22" (issued by the Business Bank2 and purchased $4,000, beginning on February 1, 2015, five years, and annual interest rate 4.4%).

The Proprietorship2 has only one truck2 (purchased it from the "Company1" in market price, five years, straight line, 20 months), so the Vehicle account has one three-level subaccount and its balance is $40,000. The Accumulated amortization: Vehicle account has one three-level subaccount of the "Truck21-accumulated amortization<Truck2-accumulated amortization < Truck-accumulated amortization" and its balances are -$13,333.33.

The Proprietorship2 has one computer server2 (two years, straight line, 13 months), one computer3" (two years, straight line, 13 months), and one computer4" (two years, straight line, 13 months), so the multi-subaccount names of the Computer parent account are the "Computer server21<Computer server2< Computer server", the "Computer31< Computer3", and the "Computer41 < Computer4" respectively. Their balances are $2,700, $1,400, and $1,300 respectively. Accordingly, the multi-subaccount names of the Accumulated amortization: Computer account are the "Computer server21-accumulated amortization < Computer server2-accumulated amortization< Computer server-accumulated amortization", the "Computer31-accumulated amortization < Computer3-accumulated amortization", and the "Computer41-accumulated amortization < Computer4-accumulated amortization". Their balances are respectively -$1,462.50, -$758.33, and -$704.17.

The Proprietorship2 issued two bonds, seeing the Figure 2.4-58 on this page and the next page, which shows the detail information of the issued bonds, so the Bonds payable account has two one-level subaccount of the "Bond71-payable" ($70,000, beginning on June 1, 2014, five years, and annual interest rate 5%) and the "Bond72-payable" ($50,000, beginning on July 1, 2015, five years, and annual interest rate 5.2%). Of course, the Bonds payable account has also many two-level subaccounts.

| Order | Bond | Amount | Term | Purchaser Name | Identity |
|---|---|---|---|---|---|
| 1 | Bond71 | 7000 | June 1, 2014, Five years, 5.2% annually | A1 | 909876501 |
| 2 | Bond71 | 6000 | June 1, 2014, Five years, 5.2% annually | A2 | 909876502 |
| 3 | Bond71 | 5000 | June 1, 2014, Five years, 5.2% annually | A4 | 909876504 |
| 4 | Bond71 | 6000 | June 1, 2014, Five years, 5.2% annually | A7 | 909876507 |
| 5 | Bond71 | 6000 | June 1, 2014, Five years, 5.2% annually | A9 | 909876509 |
| 6 | Bond71 | 5000 | June 1, 2014, Five years, 5.2% annually | A11 | 909876511 |
| 7 | Bond71 | 4000 | June 1, 2014, Five years, 5.2% annually | A12 | 909876512 |
| 8 | Bond71 | 7000 | June 1, 2014, Five years, 5.2% annually | A16 | 909876516 |

| 9 | Bond71 | 5000 | June 1, 2014, Five years, 5.2% annually | A17 | 909876517 |
|---|---|---|---|---|---|
| 10 | Bond71 | 6000 | June 1, 2014, Five years, 5.2% annually | A18 | 909876518 |
| 11 | Bond71 | 5000 | June 1, 2014, Five years, 5.2% annually | A19 | 909876519 |
| 12 | Bond71 | 8000 | June 1, 2014, Five years, 5.2% annually | A20 | 909876520 |
| 13 | Bond72 | 4000 | July 1, 2015, Five years, 5.5% annually | A4 | 909876504 |
| 14 | Bond72 | 5000 | July 1, 2015, Five years, 5.5% annually | A5 | 909876505 |
| 15 | Bond72 | 6000 | July 1, 2015, Five years, 5.5% annually | A6 | 909876506 |
| 16 | Bond72 | 5000 | July 1, 2015, Five years, 5.5% annually | A8 | 909876508 |
| 17 | Bond72 | 6000 | July 1, 2015, Five years, 5.5% annually | A10 | 909876510 |
| 18 | Bond72 | 4000 | July 1, 2015, Five years, 5.5% annually | A13 | 909876513 |
| 19 | Bond72 | 5000 | July 1, 2015, Five years, 5.5% annually | A15 | 909876515 |
| 20 | Bond72 | 6000 | July 1, 2015, Five years, 5.5% annually | A16 | 909876516 |
| 21 | Bond72 | 5000 | July 1, 2015, Five years, 5.5% annually | A17 | 909876517 |
| 22 | Bond72 | 4000 | July 1, 2015, Five years, 5.5% annually | A18 | 909876518 |
| **15** | **Total** | **120000** | | | |

Figure 2.4-58   Proprietorship2 Issued Bonds Information Table

The balance of the Notes payable account is zero on December 31, 2016, but the Accrued interest payable account has two one-level subaccounts of the "Bonds-interest payable" and the "Notes-interest payable". Accordingly, the balances of the Accrued interest payable account are zero prior to the conversion.

The Account receivable account and the Account payable account need transaction dates during the conversion, so I assume that their transaction dates are also on November 1, 2015 for simplification.

For the Proprietorship2, the balances of the "Cash receipts from customers<Operating activities" and the "Cash payments to suppliers<Operating activities" are respectively $12,000 and zero. The reason is as same as the Company1. The balance $12,000 of the "Cash receipts from customers<Operating activities" is only to receive from the Company1.

Following above information, I can build a table of the multi-subaccount names, seeing the Figure 2.4-59 on the next pages.

| Order | Class | Multi-subaccount Name | Parent Name | Lowest Subaccount Balance |
|---|---|---|---|---|
| 1 | 1 | 909876524-i-owners < Cash receipts from owners < Financial activities | Cash | 150000.00 |
| 2 | 1 | 88-654305-i-note25 < Cash receipts from banks < Financial activities | Cash | 0 |
| 3 | 1 | 88-654306-c-operating < Cash receipts from customers < Operating activities | Cash | 12000.00 |
| 4 | 1 | 88-654304-c-interest of investment bond12 < Cash receipts from investments < Investing activities | Cash | 378.00 |
| 5 | 1 | 88-654305-c-interest of investment bond21 < Cash receipts from investments < Investing activities | Cash | 478.33 |
| 6 | 1 | 88-654305-c-interest of investment bond22 < Cash receipts from investments < Investing activities | Cash | 161.33 |
| 7 | 1 | 909876501-i-bond71 < Cash receipts from issued bonds < Financial activities | Cash | 7000.00 |
| 8 | 1 | 909876502-i-bond71 < Cash receipts from issued bonds < Financial activities | Cash | 6000.00 |
| 9 | 1 | 909876504-i-bond71 < Cash receipts from issued bonds < Financial activities | Cash | 5000.00 |
| 10 | 1 | 909876507-i-bond71 < Cash receipts from issued bonds < Financial activities | Cash | 6000.00 |
| 11 | 1 | 909876509-i-bond71 < Cash receipts from issued bonds < Financial activities | Cash | 6000.00 |
| 12 | 1 | 909876511-i-bond71 < Cash receipts from issued bonds < Financial activities | Cash | 5000.00 |
| 13 | 1 | 909876512-i-bond71 < Cash receipts from issued bonds < Financial activities | Cash | 4000.00 |
| 14 | 1 | 909876516-i-bond71 < Cash receipts from issued bonds < Financial activities | Cash | 7000.00 |
| 15 | 1 | 909876517-i-bond71 < Cash receipts from issued bonds < Financial activities | Cash | 5000.00 |
| 16 | 1 | 909876518-i-bond71 < Cash receipts from issued bonds < Financial activities | Cash | 6000.00 |
| 17 | 1 | 909876519-i-bond71 < Cash receipts from issued bonds < Financial activities | Cash | 5000.00 |
| 18 | 1 | 909876520-i-bond71 < Cash receipts from issued bonds < Financial activities | Cash | 8000.00 |
| 19 | 1 | 909876504-i-bond72 < Cash receipts from issued bonds < Financial activities | Cash | 4000.00 |
| 20 | 1 | 909876505-i-bond72 < Cash receipts from issued bonds < Financial activities | Cash | 5000.00 |
| 21 | 1 | 909876506-i-bond72 < Cash receipts from issued bonds < Financial activities | Cash | 6000.00 |
| 22 | 1 | 909876508-i-bond72 < Cash receipts from issued bonds < Financial activities | Cash | 5000.00 |
| 23 | 1 | 909876510-i-bond72 < Cash receipts from issued bonds < Financial activities | Cash | 6000.00 |
| 24 | 1 | 909876513-i-bond72 < Cash receipts from issued bonds < Financial activities | Cash | 4000.00 |
| 25 | 1 | 909876515-i-bond72 < Cash receipts from issued bonds < Financial activities | Cash | 5000.00 |
| 26 | 1 | 909876516-i-bond72 < Cash receipts from issued bonds < Financial activities | Cash | 6000.00 |
| 27 | 1 | 909876517-i-bond72 < Cash receipts from issued bonds < Financial activities | Cash | 5000.00 |
| 28 | 1 | 909876518-i-bond72 < Cash receipts from issued bonds < Financial activities | Cash | 4000.00 |
| 29 | 1 | 88-654306-t-truck2 < Cash payments for machinery < Operating activities | Cash | -40000.00 |
| 30 | 1 | 88-654306-t-computer server2 < Cash payments for machinery < Operating activities | Cash | -2700.00 |
| 31 | 1 | 88-654306-t-computer3 < Cash payments for machinery < Operating activities | Cash | -1400.00 |

| 32 | 1 | 88-654306-t-computer4 < Cash payments for machinery < Operating activities | Cash | -1300.00 |
|---|---|---|---|---|
| 33 | 1 | Cash payments for operating expenses < Operating activities | Cash | -101132.56 |
| 34 | 1 | Cash payments for operating expenses < Operating activities | Cash | -100637.18 |
| 35 | 1 | 88-654303-n-tax < Cash payments for operating expenses < Operating activities | Cash | -10079.23 |
| 36 | 1 | Cash payments to suppliers<Operating activities | Cash | 0 |
| 37 | 1 | 88-654304-n-investment bond12 < Cash payments for investments < Investing activities | Cash | -6000.00 |
| 38 | 1 | 88-654305-n-investment bond21 < Cash payments for investments < Investing activities | Cash | -7000.00 |
| 39 | 1 | 88-654305-n-investment bond22 < Cash payments for investments < Investing activities | Cash | -4000.00 |
| 40 | 1 | n | Supplies | 167.85 |
| 41 | 1 | 123456784 | Account receivable | 1000.00 |
| 42 | 1 | 123456783 | Account receivable | 300.00 |
| 43 | 1 | 123456782 | Account receivable | 800.00 |
| 44 | 1 | 123456781 | Account receivable | 300.00 |
| 45 | 1 | Inven411 < Inven41 < Inven4 | Inventory | $3.00*1000 = 3000.00$ |
| 46 | 1 | Inven412 < Inven41 < Inven4 | Inventory | $11.10*1000 = 11100.00$ |
| 47 | 1 | TTTCU parts < TTT parts < Inven4 | Inventory | $12.00*1000 = 12000.00$ |
| 48 | 1 | RRRHJK parts < Inven4 | Inventory | $12.00*1000 = 12000.00$ |
| 49 | 1 | Food411 < Food41 < Food4 | Inventory | $5.00*1000 = 5000.00$ |
| 50 | 1 | Food412 < Food41 < Food4 | Inventory | $5.50*1000 = 5500.00$ |
| 51 | 1 | Food421 < Food42 < Food4 | Inventory | $6.00*1000 = 6000.00$ |
| 52 | 1 | Food422 < Food42 < Food4 | Inventory | $6.50*1000 = 6500.00$ |
| 53 | 1 | Food43 < Food4 | Inventory | $7.00*1000 = 7000.00$ |
| 54 | 1 | Food44 < Food4 | Inventory | $7.50*1000 = 7500.00$ |
| 55 | 1 | Food511 < Food51 < Food5 | Inventory | $4.00*1000 = 4000.00$ |
| 56 | 1 | Food512 < Food51 < Food5 | Inventory | $4.50*1000 = 4500.00$ |
| 57 | 1 | Food513 < Food51 < Food5 | Inventory | $5.00*1000 = 5000.00$ |
| 58 | 1 | Food514 < Food51 < Food5 | Inventory | $5.50*1000 = 5500.00$ |
| 59 | 1 | Food521 < Food52 < Food5 | Inventory | $6.00*1000 = 6000.00$ |
| 60 | 1 | Food522 < Food52 < Food5 | Inventory | $6.50*1000 = 6500.00$ |
| 61 | 1 | Food53 < Food5 | Inventory | $8.00*1000 = 8000.00$ |
| 62 | 1 | Food611 < Food61 < Food6 | Inventory | $10.00*200 = 2000.00$ |
| 63 | 1 | Food612 < Food61 < Food6 | Inventory | $12.00*200 = 2400.00$ |
| 64 | 1 | Food613 < Food61 < Food6 | Inventory | $13.00*200 = 2600.00$ |
| 65 | 1 | Food614 < Food61 < Food6 | Inventory | $15.00*200 = 3000.00$ |
| 66 | 1 | Food621 < Food62 < Food6 | Inventory | $13.00*200 = 2600.00$ |
| 67 | 1 | Food622 < Food62 < Food6 | Inventory | $14.00*200 = 2800.00$ |
| 68 | 1 | Supplies1 | Inventory | $7.00*200 = 1400.00$ |
| 69 | 1 | Supplies2 | Inventory | $8.00*200 = 1600.00$ |
| 70 | 1 | Inven31 < Inven3 | Inventory | $10.00*100 = 1000.00$ |
| 71 | 1 | Inven32 < Inven3 | Inventory | $50.00*100 = 5000.00$ |

| 72 | 1 | Inven331 < Inven33 < Inven3 | Inventory | 20.00*100 = 2000.00 |
|---|---|---|---|---|
| 73 | 1 | Inven332 < Inven33 < Inven3 | Inventory | 45.00*100 = 4500.00 |
| 74 | 1 | HGFCVB parts < QASXC parts < Inven3 | Inventory | 10.00*100 = 1000.00 |
| 75 | 1 | PPGHUP parts < ASDUP parts < Inven3 | Inventory | 20.00*100 = 2000.00 |
| 76 | 1 | Working-Inven411 < Working-Inven41 < Working-Inven4 | Working-in-process inventory | 2.00*1000 = 2000.00 |
| 77 | 1 | Working-Inven412 < Working-Inven41 < Working-Inven4 | Working-in-process inventory | 6.10*1000 = 6100.00 |
| 78 | 1 | Working-TTTCU parts < Working-TTT parts < Working-Inven4 | Working-in-process inventory | 6.50*1000 = 6500.00 |
| 79 | 1 | Working-RRRHJK parts < Working-Inven4 | Working-in-process inventory | 7.00*1000 = 7000.00 |
| 80 | 1 | Working-Food411 < Working-Food41 < Working-Food4 | Working-in-process inventory | 3.00*1000 = 3000.00 |
| 81 | 1 | Working-Food412 < Working-Food41 < Working-Food4 | Working-in-process inventory | 3.25*1000 = 3250.00 |
| 82 | 1 | Working-Food421 < Working-Food42 < Working-Food4 | Working-in-process inventory | 3.00*1000 = 3000.00 |
| 83 | 1 | Working-Food422 < Working-Food42 < Working-Food4 | Working-in-process inventory | 3.50*1000 = 3500.00 |
| 84 | 1 | Working-Food43 < Working-Food4 | Working-in-process inventory | 4.00*1000 = 4000.00 |
| 85 | 1 | Working-Food44 < Working-Food4 | Working-in-process inventory | 3.50*1000 = 3500.00 |
| 86 | 1 | Working-Food511 < Working-Food51 < Working-Food5 | Working-in-process inventory | 2.00*1000 = 2000.00 |
| 87 | 1 | Working-Food512 < Working-Food51 < Working-Food5 | Working-in-process inventory | 2.50*1000 = 2500.00 |
| 88 | 1 | Working-Food513 < Working-Food51 < Working-Food5 | Working-in-process inventory | 3.00*1000 = 3000.00 |
| 89 | 1 | Working-Food514 < Working-Food51 < Working-Food5 | Working-in-process inventory | 3.50*1000 = 3500.00 |
| 90 | 1 | Working-Food521 < Working-Food52 < Working-Food5 | Working-in-process inventory | 3.00*1000 = 3000.00 |
| 91 | 1 | Working-Food522 < Working-Food52 < Working-Food5 | Working-in-process inventory | 3.50*1000 = 3500.00 |
| 92 | 1 | Working-Food53 < Working-Food5 | Working-in-process inventory | 4.00*1000 = 4000.00 |
| 93 | 1 | Working-Food611 < Working-Food61 < Working-Food6 | Working-in-process inventory | 5.00*200 = 1000.00 |
| 94 | 1 | Working-Food612 < Working-Food61 < Working-Food6 | Working-in-process inventory | 6.00*200 = 1200.00 |
| 95 | 1 | Working-Food613 < Working-Food61 < Working-Food6 | Working-in-process inventory | 6.50*200 = 1300.00 |
| 96 | 1 | Working-Food614 < Working-Food61 < Working-Food6 | Working-in-process inventory | 7.50*200 = 1500.00 |
| 97 | 1 | Working-Food621 < Working-Food62 < Working-Food6 | Working-in-process inventory | 6.00*200 = 1200.00 |
| 98 | 1 | Working-Food622 < Working-Food62 < Working-Food6 | Working-in-process inventory | 7.00*200 = 1400.00 |
| 99 | 1 | Working-Supplies1 | Working-in-process inventory | 3.00*200 = 600.00 |
| 100 | 1 | Working-Supplies2 | Working-in-process inventory | 4.00*200 = 800.00 |
| 101 | 1 | Bond11 | Bonds | 0 |
| 102 | 1 | Bond12 | Bonds | 6000.00 |
| 103 | 1 | Bond21 | Bonds | 7000.00 |
| 104 | 1 | Bond22 | Bonds | 4000.00 |
| 105 | 1 | Truck21 < Truck2 < Truck | Vehicle | 40000.00 |

| | | | | |
|---|---|---|---|---|
| 106 | 1 | Truck21-accumulated amortization < Truck2-accumulated amortization < Truck-accumulated amortization | Accumulated amortization: Vehicle | -13333.33 |
| 107 | 1 | Computer server21 < Computer server2 < Computer server | Computer | 2700.00 |
| 108 | 1 | Computer31 < Computer3 | Computer | 1400.00 |
| 109 | 1 | Computer41 < Computer4 | Computer | 1300.00 |
| 110 | 1 | Computer server21-accumulated amortization < Computer server2-accumulated amortization < Computer server-accumulated amortization | Accumulated amortization: Computer | -1462.50 |
| 111 | 1 | Computer31-accumulated amortization < Computer3-accumulated amortization | Accumulated amortization: Computer | -758.33 |
| 112 | 1 | Computer41-accumulated amortization < Computer4-accumulated amortization | Accumulated amortization: Computer | -704.17 |
| 113 | 2 | 123456084 | Account payable | 2000.00 |
| 114 | 2 | 123456083 | Account payable | 0 |
| 115 | 2 | 123456082 | Account payable | 200.00 |
| 116 | 2 | 123456081 | Account payable | 400.00 |
| 117 | 2 | Bond71-interest payable < Bonds-interest payable | Accrued interest payable | 0 |
| 118 | 2 | Bond72-interest payable < Bonds-interest payable | Accrued interest payable | 0 |
| 119 | 2 | Notes-interest payable | Accrued interest payable | 0 |
| 120 | 2 | Bond71-909876501 < Bond71 | Bonds payable | 7000.00 |
| 121 | 2 | Bond71-909876502 < Bond71 | Bonds payable | 6000.00 |
| 122 | 2 | Bond71-909876504 < Bond71 | Bonds payable | 5000.00 |
| 123 | 2 | Bond71-909876507 < Bond71 | Bonds payable | 6000.00 |
| 124 | 2 | Bond71-909876509 < Bond71 | Bonds payable | 6000.00 |
| 125 | 2 | Bond71-909876511 < Bond71 | Bonds payable | 5000.00 |
| 126 | 2 | Bond71-909876512 < Bond71 | Bonds payable | 4000.00 |
| 127 | 2 | Bond71-909876516 < Bond71 | Bonds payable | 7000.00 |
| 128 | 2 | Bond71-909876517 < Bond71 | Bonds payable | 5000.00 |
| 129 | 2 | Bond71-909876518 < Bond71 | Bonds payable | 6000.00 |
| 130 | 2 | Bond71-909876519 < Bond71 | Bonds payable | 5000.00 |
| 131 | 2 | Bond71-909876520 < Bond71 | Bonds payable | 8000.00 |
| 132 | 2 | Bond72-909876504 < Bond72 | Bonds payable | 4000.00 |
| 133 | 2 | Bond72-909876505 < Bond72 | Bonds payable | 5000.00 |
| 134 | 2 | Bond72-909876506 < Bond72 | Bonds payable | 6000.00 |
| 135 | 2 | Bond72-909876508 < Bond72 | Bonds payable | 5000.00 |
| 136 | 2 | Bond72-909876510 < Bond72 | Bonds payable | 6000.00 |
| 137 | 2 | Bond72-909876513 < Bond72 | Bonds payable | 4000.00 |
| 138 | 2 | Bond72-909876515 < Bond72 | Bonds payable | 5000.00 |
| 139 | 2 | Bond72-909876516 < Bond72 | Bonds payable | 6000.00 |
| 140 | 2 | Bond72-909876517 < Bond72 | Bonds payable | 5000.00 |
| 141 | 2 | Bond72-909876518 < Bond72 | Bonds payable | 4000.00 |
| 142 | 3 | Capital-909876524 | Share capital | 150000.00 |

| 143 | 3 | n | Retained earnings (Conversion) | 6228.21 |
|-----|---|---|---|---|
| 144 | 4 | Sales-909876525 | Sales | 0 |
| 145 | 5 | 909876524-travelling < Sales department-travelling | Travelling expenses | 0 |
| 146 | 5 | 909876525-travelling < Product department-travelling | Travelling expenses | 0 |
| 147 | 5 | 909876524-other < Sales department-other | Other expenses | 0 |
| 148 | 5 | 909876525-other < Product department-other | Other expenses | 0 |
| 149 | 5 | 909876524-salary < Sales department-salary | Salary expenses | 0 |
| 150 | 5 | Supplies expenses | Cost of goods mined | 0 |
| 151 | 5 | 909876525-salary < Product department-salary < Salary expenses | Cost of goods mined | 0 |
| 152 | 5 | General parts expenses | Cost of goods mined | 0 |
| 153 | 5 | Bond71-interest | Bond interest expenses | 0 |
| 154 | 5 | Bond72-interest | Bond interest expenses | 0 |
| 155 | 5 | Note25-interest | Note interest expenses | 0 |
| 156 | 5 | Truck21-amortization < Truck2-amortization < Vehicle-truck-amortization | Amortization expenses | 0 |
| 157 | 5 | Computer server21-amortization < Computer server2-amortization < Computer-amortization | Amortization expenses | 0 |
| 158 | 5 | Computer31-amortization < Computer3-amortization < Computer-amortization | Amortization expenses | 0 |
| 159 | 5 | Computer41-amortization < Computer4-amortization < Computer-amortization | Amortization expenses | 0 |
| 160 | 4 | Accrued interest income-bond12 < Bonds | Investment incomes | 0 |
| 161 | 4 | Accrued interest income-bond21 < Bonds | Investment incomes | 0 |
| 162 | 4 | Accrued interest income-bond22 < Bonds | Investment incomes | 0 |
| 163 | 4 | n | Deposits interest income | 0 |

Figure 2.4-59   Proprietorship2 Converting Multi-Subaccount Names Table

Before entering the dynamic accounting equation on December 31, 2015 into the database dcj11, I first enter two initialization sub-equations.

Cash (1): 0 = Share capital (3): 0

0 = Sales (4): 0 – Cost of goods sold (5):0

From the Figure 2.4-57 and the Figure 2.4-59, the dynamic accounting equation on December 31, 2015 must be divided to the N transaction sub-equations because of the restriction of the MathAccounting software. Every sub-equation has maximum twelve items. All converting transaction sub-equations can be designed and written as following.

- I build a transaction sub-equation for the Account receivable and the Account payable accounts. The transaction sub-equation includes the Account receivable account with the Order 41 to the Order 44, the Account payable account with the Order 113 to the Order 116, and the part of the Cash account with the Order 3, The first transaction sub-equation is:

Cash (1): 200 + Account receivable (1): 1000 + Account receivable (1): 300 + Account receivable (1): 800 + Account receivable (1): 300 = Account payable (2): 2000 + Account payable (2): 200 + Account payable (2): 400

After entering this transaction, the new balance of the Cash account with the Order 3 is $11,800 (= $120,000 - $200).

- The transaction sub-equation includes the Cash account with the Order 1 and the Order 2, the rest ($11,800) of the Cash account with the Order 3, the part the Cash account with the Order 33, the Cash account with the Order 4 to the Order 6, and the Share capital account with the Order 142. Because the balance of the Cash account with the Order 2 is zero, the second transaction sub-equation is:

Cash (1): 150000 + Cash (1): 11800 + Cash (1): -12817.66 + Cash (1): 378 + Cash (1): 478.33 + Cash (1): 161.33 = Share capital (3): 150000

After entering this transaction, the new balance of the Cash account with the Order 33 is -$88,314.90 (= -$101,132.56 + $12,817.66).

- The transaction sub-equation includes the Cash account with the Order 7 to the Order 12 and the Bonds payable account with the Order 120 to the Order 125. The third transaction sub-equation is:

Cash (1): 7000 + Cash (1): 6000 + Cash (1): 5000 + Cash (1): 6000 + Cash (1): 6000 + Cash (1): 5000 = Bonds payable (2): 7000 + Bonds payable (2): 6000 +

Bonds payable (2): 5000 + Bonds payable (2): 6000 + Bonds payable (2): 6000 + Bonds payable (2): 5000

- The transaction sub-equation includes the Cash account with the Order 13 to the Order 18 and the Bonds payable account with the Order 126 to the Order 131. The fourth transaction sub-equation is:

  Cash (1): 4000 + Cash (1):7000 + Cash (1): 5000 + Cash (1): 6000 + Cash (1): 5000 + Cash (1): 8000 = Bonds payable (2): 4000 + Bonds payable (2): 7000 + Bonds payable (2): 5000 + Bonds payable (2): 6000 + Bonds payable (2): 5000 + Bonds payable (2): 8000

- The transaction sub-equation includes the Cash account with the Order 19 to the Order 24 and the Bonds payable account with the Order 132 and the Order 137. The fifth transaction sub-equation is:

  Cash (1): 4000 + Cash (1):5000 + Cash (1): 6000 + Cash (1): 5000 + Cash (1): 6000 + Cash (1): 4000 = Bonds payable (2): 4000 + Bonds payable (2): 5000 + Bonds payable (2): 6000 + Bonds payable (2): 5000 + Bonds payable (2): 6000 + Bonds payable (2): 4000

- The transaction sub-equation includes the Cash account with the Order 25 to the Order 28 and the Bonds account with the Order 138 to the Order 141. The sixth transaction sub-equation is:

  Cash (1): 5000 + Cash (1): 6000 + Cash (1): 5000 + Cash (1): 4000 = Bonds payable (2): 5000 + Bonds payable (2): 6000 + Bonds payable (2): 5000 + Bonds payable (2): 4000

- The transaction sub-equation includes the Cash account with the Order 29 to the Order 32, the Vehicle account with the Order 105, and the Computer account with the Order 107 to the Order 109. The seventh transaction sub-equation is:

Cash (1): -40000 + Cash (1): -2700 + Cash (1): -1400 + Cash (1): -1300 + Vehicle (1): 40000 + Computer (1): 2700 + Computer (1): 1400 + Computer (1): 1300 = 0

- The transaction sub-equation includes the Cash account with the Order 37 to the Order 39 and the Bonds account with the Order 102 to the Order 104. The eighth transaction sub-equation is:

Cash (1): -6000 + Cash (1): -7000 + Cash (1): -4000 + Bonds (1): 6000 + Bonds (1): 7000 + Bonds (1): 4000 = 0

- The transaction sub-equation includes the part of the Cash account with the Order 33, the Supplies account with the Order 40, and the Inventory account with the Order 45 to the Order 54. The ninth transaction sub-equation is:

Cash (1): -75767.85 + Supplies (1): 167.85 + Inventory (1): 3000 + Inventory (1): 11100 + Inventory (1): 12000 + Inventory (1): 12000 + Inventory (1): 5000 + Inventory (1): 5500 + Inventory (1): 6000 + Inventory (1): 6500 + Inventory (1): 7000 + Inventory (1): 7500 = 0

After entering this transaction, the new balance of the Cash account with the Order 33 is -$12,547.05 (= -$88,314.90 + $75,767.85).

- The transaction sub-equation includes the rest (-$12,547.05) of the Cash account with the Order 33, the part of the Cash account with the Order 34, and the Inventory account with the Order 55 to the Order 64. The tenth transaction sub-equation is:

Cash (1): -12547.05 + Cash (1): -33,952.95 + Inventory (1): 4000 + Inventory (1): 4500 + Inventory (1): 5000 + Inventory (1): 5500 + Inventory (1): 6000 + Inventory (1): 6500 + Inventory (1): 8000 + Inventory (1): 2000 + Inventory (1): 2400 + Inventory (1): 2600 = 0

After entering this transaction, the new balance of the Cash account with the Order 34 is -$66,684.23 (= -$100637.18 + $33,952.95).

- The transaction sub-equation includes the part of the Cash account with the Order 34 and the Inventory account with the Order 65 to the Order 75. The eleventh transaction sub-equation is:

Cash (1): -26900 + Inventory (1): 3000 + Inventory (1): 2600 + Inventory (1): 2800 + Inventory (1): 1400 + Inventory (1): 1600 + Inventory (1): 1000 + Inventory (1): 5000 + Inventory (1): 2000 + Inventory (1): 4500 + Inventory (1): 1000 + Inventory (1): 2000 = 0

After entering this transaction, the new balance of the Cash account with the Order 34 is -$39,784.23 (= -$66,684.23 + $26,900).

- The transaction sub-equation includes the rest (-$39,784.23) of the Cash account with the Order 34, the part of the Accumulated amortization: Vehicle account with the Order 106, and the Working-in-process inventory account with the Order 76 to the Order 85. The twelfth transaction sub-equation is:

Cash (1): -39784.23 + Accumulated amortization: Vehicle (1): -2065.77 + Working-in-process inventory (1): 2000 + Working-in-process inventory (1): 6100 + Working-in-process inventory (1): 6500 + Working-in-process inventory (1): 7000 + Working-in-process inventory (1): 3000 + Working-in-process inventory (1): 3250 + Working-in-process inventory (1): 3000 + Working-in-process inventory (1): 3500 + Working-in-process inventory (1): 4000 + Working-in-process inventory (1): 3500 = 0

After entering this transaction, the new balance of the Accumulated amortization: Vehicle account with the Order 106 is -$11,267.56 (= -$13,333.33 + $2,065.77).

- The transaction sub-equation includes the Cash account with the Order 35, the part of the Accumulated amortization: Vehicle account with the Order 106, the Accumulated amortization: Computer account with the Order 110 to the Order 112, and the Working-in-process inventory account with the Order 86 to the Order 91. The thirteenth transaction sub-equation is:

   Cash (1): -10079.23 + Accumulated amortization: Vehicle (1): -4495.77 + Accumulated amortization: Computer (1): -1462.50 + Accumulated amortization: Computer (1): -758.33 + Accumulated amortization: Computer (1): -704.17 + Working-in-process inventory (1): 2000 + Working-in-process inventory (1): 2500 + Working-in-process inventory (1): 3000 + Working-in-process inventory (1): 3500 + Working-in-process inventory (1): 3000 + Working-in-process inventory (1): 3500 = 0

   After entering this transaction, the new balance of the Accumulated amortization: Vehicle account with the Order 106 is -\$6,771.79 (= -\$11,267.56 + \$4,495.77).

- The transaction sub-equation includes the rest (-\$6,771.79) of the Accumulated amortization: Vehicle account with the Order 106, the Working-in-process inventory account with the Order 92 to the Order 100, and the Retained earnings (Conversion) account with the balance \$12,574.23. The fourteenth transaction sub-equation is:

   Accumulated amortization: Vehicle (1): -6771.79 + Working-in-process inventory (1): 4000 + Working-in-process inventory (1): 1000 + Working-in-process inventory (1): 1200 + Working-in-process inventory (1): 1300 Working-in-process inventory (1): 1500 + Working-in-process inventory (1): 1200 + Working-in-process inventory (1): 1400 + Working-in-process inventory (1): 600 + Working-in-process inventory (1): 800 = Retained earnings (Conversion) (3): 6228.21

After completing this transaction, the dynamic accounting equation of the Proprietorship2 December 31, 2015 has entered into the database dcj11.

## 2.4.7.2 Brief Summary of the Proprietorship2

The following Figure 2.4-60 shows cash received or paid by other members table which is in the public database dcj100.

Figure 2.4-60   Proprietorship2 Cash Received or Paid by Other Members (Continue)

Figure 2.4-60   Proprietorship2 Cash Received or Paid by Other Members

The Figure 2.4-61 on the next page shows cash flows statement of the Proprietorship2 on December 31, 2015.

| Cash Flows Statement Year Ended 2015-12-31 | |
|---|---:|
| **Operating activities** | |
| Cash payments for machinery | -$45,400.00 |
| Cash payments for operating expenses | -$211,848.97 |
| Cash receipts from customers | $12,000.00 |
| Net cash provided by Operating activities | -$245,248.97 |
| | |
| Investing activities | |
| Cash payments for investments | -$17,000.00 |
| Cash receipts from investments | $1,017.66 |
| Net cash provided by Investing activities | -$15,982.34 |
| | |
| Financial activities | |
| Cash receipts from issued bonds | $120,000.00 |
| Cash receipts from owners | $150,000.00 |
| Net cash provided by Financial activities | $270,000.00 |
| | |
| Net change in cash | $8,768.69 |
| Cash, Begining | $0.00 |
| Cash, Ending | $8,768.69 |

Figure 2.4-61   Proprietorship2 Cash Flows Statement

The Figure 2.4-62 on the next page shows cash account table of the Proprietorship2 on December 31, 2015.

The Figure 2.4-63 on the page 213 shows balance sheet table of the Proprietorship2 on December 31, 2015.

Cash

| ID | Multi-Name | Amount | Balance | General ID | Transaction Date |
|---|---|---|---|---|---|
| 1 | Cash payments for operating expenses < Operating activities | $0.00 | $0.00 | 1 | 2015-12-31 |
| 2 | 88-654306-c-operating < Cash receipts from customers < Operating activities | $200.00 | $200.00 | 3 | 2015-12-31 |
| 3 | 909876524-i-owners < Cash receipts from owners < Financial activities | $150,000.00 | $150,200.00 | 4 | 2015-12-31 |
| 4 | 88-654306-c-operating < Cash receipts from customers < Operating activities | $11,800.00 | $162,000.00 | 4 | 2015-12-31 |
| 5 | Cash payments for operating expenses < Operating activities | -$12,817.66 | $149,182.34 | 4 | 2015-12-31 |
| 6 | 88-654304-c-interest of investment bond12 < Cash receipts from investments < Inv… | $378.00 | $149,560.34 | 4 | 2015-12-31 |
| 7 | 88-654305-c-interest of investment bond21 < Cash receipts from investments < Inv… | $478.33 | $150,038.67 | 4 | 2015-12-31 |
| 8 | 88-654305-c-interest of investment bond22 < Cash receipts from investments < Inv… | $161.33 | $150,200.00 | 4 | 2015-12-31 |
| 9 | 909876501-i-bond71 < Cash receipts from issued bonds < Financial activities | $7,000.00 | $157,200.00 | 5 | 2015-12-31 |
| 10 | 909876502-i-bond71 < Cash receipts from issued bonds < Financial activities | $6,000.00 | $163,200.00 | 5 | 2015-12-31 |
| 11 | 909876504-i-bond71 < Cash receipts from issued bonds < Financial activities | $5,000.00 | $168,200.00 | 5 | 2015-12-31 |
| 12 | 909876507-i-bond71 < Cash receipts from issued bonds < Financial activities | $6,000.00 | $174,200.00 | 5 | 2015-12-31 |
| 13 | 909876509-i-bond71 < Cash receipts from issued bonds < Financial activities | $6,000.00 | $180,200.00 | 5 | 2015-12-31 |
| 14 | 909876511-i-bond71 < Cash receipts from issued bonds < Financial activities | $5,000.00 | $185,200.00 | 5 | 2015-12-31 |
| 15 | 909876512-i-bond71 < Cash receipts from issued bonds < Financial activities | $4,000.00 | $189,200.00 | 6 | 2015-12-31 |
| 16 | 909876516-i-bond71 < Cash receipts from issued bonds < Financial activities | $7,000.00 | $196,200.00 | 6 | 2015-12-31 |
| 17 | 909876517-i-bond71 < Cash receipts from issued bonds < Financial activities | $5,000.00 | $201,200.00 | 6 | 2015-12-31 |
| 18 | 909876518-i-bond71 < Cash receipts from issued bonds < Financial activities | $6,000.00 | $207,200.00 | 6 | 2015-12-31 |
| 19 | 909876519-i-bond71 < Cash receipts from issued bonds < Financial activities | $5,000.00 | $212,200.00 | 6 | 2015-12-31 |
| 20 | 909876520-i-bond71 < Cash receipts from issued bonds < Financial activities | $8,000.00 | $220,200.00 | 6 | 2015-12-31 |
| 21 | 909876504-i-bond72 < Cash receipts from issued bonds < Financial activities | $4,000.00 | $224,200.00 | 7 | 2015-12-31 |
| 22 | 909876505-i-bond72 < Cash receipts from issued bonds < Financial activities | $5,000.00 | $229,200.00 | 7 | 2015-12-31 |
| 23 | 909876506-i-bond72 < Cash receipts from issued bonds < Financial activities | $6,000.00 | $235,200.00 | 7 | 2015-12-31 |
| 24 | 909876508-i-bond72 < Cash receipts from issued bonds < Financial activities | $5,000.00 | $240,200.00 | 7 | 2015-12-31 |
| 25 | 909876510-i-bond72 < Cash receipts from issued bonds < Financial activities | $6,000.00 | $246,200.00 | 7 | 2015-12-31 |
| 26 | 909876513-i-bond72 < Cash receipts from issued bonds < Financial activities | $4,000.00 | $250,200.00 | 7 | 2015-12-31 |
| 27 | 909876515-i-bond72 < Cash receipts from issued bonds < Financial activities | $5,000.00 | $255,200.00 | 8 | 2015-12-31 |
| 28 | 909876516-i-bond72 < Cash receipts from issued bonds < Financial activities | $6,000.00 | $261,200.00 | 8 | 2015-12-31 |
| 29 | 909876517-i-bond72 < Cash receipts from issued bonds < Financial activities | $5,000.00 | $266,200.00 | 8 | 2015-12-31 |
| 30 | 909876518-i-bond72 < Cash receipts from issued bonds < Financial activities | $4,000.00 | $270,200.00 | 8 | 2015-12-31 |
| 31 | 88-654306-t-truck2 < Cash payments for machinery < Operating activities | -$40,000.00 | $230,200.00 | 9 | 2015-12-31 |
| 32 | 88-654306-t-computer server2 < Cash payments for machinery < Operating activities | -$2,700.00 | $227,500.00 | 9 | 2015-12-31 |
| 33 | 88-654306-t-computer3 < Cash payments for machinery < Operating activities | -$1,400.00 | $226,100.00 | 9 | 2015-12-31 |
| 34 | 88-654306-t-computer4 < Cash payments for machinery < Operating activities | -$1,300.00 | $224,800.00 | 9 | 2015-12-31 |
| 35 | 88-654304-n-investment bond12 < Cash payments for investments < Investing acti… | -$6,000.00 | $218,800.00 | 10 | 2015-12-31 |
| 36 | 88-654305-n-investment bond21 < Cash payments for investments < Investing acti… | -$7,000.00 | $211,800.00 | 10 | 2015-12-31 |
| 37 | 88-654305-n-investment bond22 < Cash payments for investments < Investing acti… | -$4,000.00 | $207,800.00 | 10 | 2015-12-31 |
| 38 | Cash payments for operating expenses < Operating activities | -$75,767.85 | $132,032.15 | 11 | 2015-12-31 |
| 39 | Cash payments for operating expenses < Operating activities | -$12,547.05 | $119,485.10 | 12 | 2015-12-31 |
| 40 | Cash payments for operating expenses < Operating activities | -$33,952.95 | $85,532.15 | 12 | 2015-12-31 |
| 41 | Cash payments for operating expenses < Operating activities | -$26,900.00 | $58,632.15 | 13 | 2015-12-31 |
| 42 | Cash payments for operating expenses < Operating activities | -$39,784.23 | $18,847.92 | 14 | 2015-12-31 |
| 43 | 88-654303-n-tax < Cash payments for operating expenses < Operating activities | -$10,079.23 | $8,768.69 | 15 | 2015-12-31 |

Figure 2.4-62   Proprietorship2 Cash Account Table

Balance Sheet

| | As at 12/31/2015 |
|---|---|
| **ASSETS** | |
| Current assets | |
| Cash | $8,768.69 |
| Supplies | $167.85 |
| Account receivable | $2,400.00 |
| Inventory | $149,000.00 |
| Working-in-process inventory | $72,350.00 |
| | $232,686.54 |
| Long term investments | |
| Bonds | $17,000.00 |
| Equipment | |
| Vehicle | $40,000.00 |
| Accumulated amortization: Vehicle | -$13,333.33 |
| Computer | $5,400.00 |
| Accumulated amortization: Computer | -$2,925.00 |
| | $29,141.67 |
| Total Assets | $278,828.21 |
| | |
| | |
| LIABILITIES | |
| Current liabilities | |
| Account payable | $2,600.00 |
| Long term liabilities | |
| Bonds payable | $120,000.00 |
| Total Liability | $122,600.00 |
| | |
| SHAREHOLDERS' EQUITY | |
| Owners' capital | |
| Share capital | $150,000.00 |
| Retained earnings (Conversion) | $6,228.21 |
| | $156,228.21 |
| Retined earnings | $0.00 |
| Accumulated other comprehensive income | $0.00 |
| Total Shareholders' Equity | $156,228.21 |
| | |
| Total Liabilities and Shareholders' Equity | $278,828.21 |

Figure 2.4-63   Proprietorship2 Balance Sheet

## 2.5 Button Rank of Social Members

The button rank of social members is all individuals. These individuals do not do business and there is no paper money in circulating process, so there is not any transaction to be recorded in this rank. Their employers and suppliers have recorded their transaction information while they get their salary and purchase various commodities by using of the various smart cards issued by different business bank. Of course, the children can use their parents' second card.

# REFERENCES

[JIE] Guoping Jie, *A Mathematical Accounting Model and its MathAccounting Software*

First Edition. Guoping Jie Press. Ontario, 2016.

[JIE] Guoping Jie, *A Mathematical Accounting Model and its MathAccounting Software*

Second Edition. Guoping Jie Press. Ontario, 2017.

www.ingramcontent.com/pod-product-compliance
Lightning Source LLC
Chambersburg PA
CBHW061754210326
41518CB00036B/2339